Approaches to Teaching Milton's *Paradise Lost*

Second Edition

Approaches to Teaching
World Literature

For a complete listing of titles,
see the last pages of this book.

Approaches to Teaching Milton's *Paradise Lost*

Second Edition

Edited by

Peter C. Herman

The Modern Language Association of America
New York   2012

MLA and the MODERN LANGUAGE ASSOCIATION are trademarks
owned by the Modern Language Association of America.
For information about obtaining permission to reprint material from
MLA book publications, send your request by mail (see address below),
e-mail (permissions@mla.org), or fax (646 458-0030).

Library of Congress Cataloging-in-Publication Data
Approaches to teaching Milton's Paradise lost / edited by Peter C. Herman. — 2nd ed.
p. cm. — (Approaches to teaching world literature ; 122)
Includes bibliographical references and index.
ISBN 978-1-60329-116-3 (cloth : alk. paper) —
ISBN 978-1-60329-117-0 (pbk. : alk. paper)
1. Milton, John, 1608–1674. Paradise lost. 2. Milton, John, 1608–1674—
Study and teaching.   I. Herman, Peter C., 1958–
PR3562.A84 2012
821'.4—dc23   2012028528

Approaches to Teaching World Literature 122
ISSN 1059-1133

Cover illustration of the paperback edition: *The Temptation*, by William Strang. 1899.
Oil on canvas. 1,372 cm. × 122 cm.

Published by The Modern Language Association of America
26 Broadway, New York, NY 10004-1789
www.mla.org

CONTENTS

Professor John T. Shawcross passed on during the production of this book and so did not have a chance to review the final copy. That sad task belonged to Edward Jones, and I am grateful for his help in bringing one of Professor Shawcross's final essays into print. There are very few Miltonists who have not benefitted from Professor Shawcross's scholarship, and we mourn his loss. The contributors and I dedicate this book to his memory.

PREFACE

Why a second edition of *Approaches to Teaching Milton's* Paradise Lost? While the original edition, ably edited by Galbraith M. Crump, remains very helpful, it was published over twenty-five years ago, in 1986. To say the least, much has happened since then in both the academy and the world. The theory wars marking the 1980s may have faded, but the approaches that caused the uproar have left an indelible impact on how we teach and write about literature in general and Milton in particular. Equally important, Crump's volume predates the digital revolution. For Crump and his contributors, the term *web* signified Arachne. For students and teachers in the early twenty-first century, it means something very different, and that changed meaning has had an incalculable effect on how we teach. In addition, a revision of the volume on approaches to teaching *Paradise Lost* is especially timely given the ongoing interest in Milton's epic outside the academy and the recent intensification (*revival* is the wrong word) of Milton studies. In contemporary culture, one finds all sorts of uses, references, and allusions to Milton and his works. The young adult fiction writer Philip Pullman uses *Paradise Lost* as a shaping presence in the trilogy His Dark Materials (the first book, *The Golden Compass*, was made into a movie, albeit one with a mixed critical reception), as does Salman Rushdie in *The Satanic Verses*. Milton's Satan makes a significant appearance in Neil Gaiman's Sandman graphic novel *Season of Mists* (in this work, Satan invokes his right to choose by quitting his position as hell's monarch; at the book's conclusion, God reinstates hell, but without Satan, who is last seen on a beach in Australia, admiring the sunset). A quick search of *LexisNexis* turned up hundreds of references to "John Milton" in various newspapers, journals, and magazines. There is even a heavy metal band called Paradise Lost.[1]

The ongoing vitality of *Paradise Lost* outside the academy mirrors a recent efflorescence within Milton studies. After a period of relative calm, there has been an upsurge in new editions of *Paradise Lost* in a variety of formats and a broadening of critical approaches. In addition to deconstruction, feminism, and new historicism, we now have the option of reading *Paradise Lost* through the lens of ecocriticism, the critical study of masculinity, new versions of biblical studies, the Web, and the new Milton criticism, which questions the fundamental assumption of Miltonic certainty. There are new studies asking Miltonists to reconsider the fundamental issues of Milton's epic, such as the relationship between Adam and Eve, why God the Father seems to be such an unattractive character, and the manifold connections between Milton's epic and the English Revolution. Students still also need help approaching Milton's language and his learning.

To paraphrase Milton's excuse for abandoning the epic project in the 1640s, "time serves now" for a new volume of essays on how to teach Milton in the twenty-first century, and the essays in this volume collectively intend to help instructors harness new approaches to enliven the teaching of *Paradise Lost*. Today's students confront significant roadblocks to their understanding and enjoyment of Milton's epic. Milton poses special challenges in addition to the usual problems facing students (and teachers) of early modern literature — difficulties understanding early modern syntax and vocabulary, different historical circumstances, different social structures, and different cosmology. Few authors were as learned in the classics and in theology as Milton. Students also need to have some understanding of the civil wars and why Charles I was executed by Parliament, an act Milton publicly defended, as Milton wrote *Paradise Lost* in the shadow of, and as a reaction to, the collapse of nonmonarchic rule and the Restoration. Students also need to have some acquaintance with Milton's earlier poetry and prose, to understand Milton's allusions to previous positions at key moments in the epic (e.g., Beelzebub's justifications for rebellion, Adam's request to God for a companion, Eve's justifications for leaving Adam to labor alone in the garden). Finally, students often assume before reading the poem that *Paradise Lost* is, at best, a monument to dead ideas and, at worst, the epitome of misogyny. Nothing could be further from the truth, and the essays in this volume provide avenues for allowing students to discover that *Paradise Lost* remains deeply meaningful, that it asks questions instead of providing answers, and that mastering this poem can be a life-altering experience.

NOTE

[1] See Knoppers and Semenza for an excellent sense of how Milton permeates contemporary film, novels, and music.

Part One

MATERIALS

Editions and Texts

Milton oversaw the publication of two editions and numerous issues of *Paradise Lost*. The first version (1667) did not have any prefatory material and contained ten books. For the fourth issue of the poem (1668), the printer, Samuel Simmons, added a note telling the reader that while "no Argument [was] at first intended to the Book," since many desired it, he had "procur'd it," along with "a reason of that which stumbled many others, why the Poem Rimes not" (sig. A2). Simmons prints the arguments for each book seriatem, then "The Verse" (Milton's justification for not using rhyme), then the poem itself. In 1674, Milton and Simmons issued a second edition of *Paradise Lost*, "Revised and Augmented by the same Author." The poem is divided into twelve books (book 7 has been split into books 7 and 8; book 10 has become books 11 and 12), and, while there are only a few new lines, Milton has tinkered extensively with words, phrases, typography, spelling, and punctuation. The arguments now come before each of the books, and prefatory poems by "S.B." (in Latin) and Andrew Marvell (in English) have been added. Contemporary editors assume that the 1674 edition represents Milton's last word, and while there has been a recent flurry of interest in the 1667 iteration of the poem (see Shawcross and Lieb), almost all editions are based on the 1674 *Paradise Lost*.

The question of which modern edition represents the best text for teaching and research remains unresolved. The survey made available by the MLA to instructors likely to teach Milton showed that the favorite remains *Complete Poems and Major Prose*, edited by Merritt Y. Hughes, first published in 1957, and now available in a reprint edition published by Hackett. Respondents, however, recognized that the notes of this edition are "badly out of date" and "the instructor who uses this edition has to build in some exposure to a variety of recent criticism or class discussion will be awkwardly divorced from the last half-century of Milton studies." But no consensus has emerged on which edition should replace Hughes (one respondent complained, after listing the numerous versions of *Paradise Lost* he has used, "I am still in the market for a good Milton textbook") or on what kind of edition would be optimal in the classroom (original spelling? a stand-alone text or one that includes Milton's other works? electronic or print? if electronic, Web-based or e-reader?). The question of modernizing is especially vexed because of the various shades of modernizing. A text may not use "old spelling" but may retain elisions to indicate prosody or retain certain characteristically Miltonic spellings (Shawcross, "Milton in Print" 221–22). The 1674 "Say first, for Heav'n hides nothing from thy view" (1.28) becomes in Stephen Orgel and Jonathan's Goldberg edition, "Say first, for heaven hides nothing from thy view." The 1674 "Sovran" (1.274) becomes in Gordon Teskey's and the Modern Library (ed. Kerrigan, Rumrich, and Fallon) editions, "Sov'reign," and in David Hawkes's, "sovereign." Hughes and Roy Flannagan retain the 1674 edition's use of italics, but Alastair Fowler, John Leonard, David Scott Kastan, and Teskey do not. Milton's invocation, "Sing Heav'nly Muse, that on the secret top / Of *Oreb*, or of *Sinai*, didst inspire / That Shepherd" (1674; 1.6–8), appears differently in each edition, in use of italics as well as use of punctuation and capital letters:

> Sing heavenly Muse, that on the secret top
> Of Oreb, or of Sinai, didst inspire
> That shepherd   (Fowler)

> Sing Heaven'ly Muse, that on the secret top
> Of Oreb, or of Sinai, didst inpire
> That shepherd   (Leonard)

> Sing heavenly muse, that on the secret top
> Of Oreb, or of Sinai, didst inspire
> That shepherd   (Kastan)

> Sing Heav'nly Muse, that on the secret top
> Of Oreb or of Sinai didst inspire
> That shepherd   (Teskey)

There are gradations in modernizing; Barbara K. Lewalski's Blackwell edition, Hughes, and Flannagan lean toward reproducing the spelling and orthography of 1674, while Kastan, Hawkes, Fowler, and the Modern Library editors lean toward current usages. As John T. Shawcross points out, these decisions have thematic and pedagogic consequences. To alter "Heaven'ly" (1.6) to "heavenly" means "not pointing to the prosody and at the same time making a religiously reductive statement by using lowercase" ("Milton in Print" 222). Using lowercase rather than capitalizing "shepherd" also implicitly removes the stress on this figure and Milton's paralleling himself with Moses, present in the 1674 edition. On the other hand, a text that consistently employs contemporary conventions of grammar, spelling, and orthography breaks down one of the barriers separating our students from *Paradise Lost*.

The survey responses showed that the most popular teaching edition of *Paradise Lost* is the one included in the Norton anthology of English edited by Lewalski. The runners-up are, in order, Hughes; Flannagan's *Riverside Milton*; and Leonard's *Complete Poems*. Because no edition seems entirely satisfactory, many respondents indicated that they frequently make use of multiple texts in their classes. Versions of *Paradise Lost* come in all shapes, sizes, and formats (including digital), but they can be roughly divided into three categories: poetry and prose; complete poetry; and *Paradise Lost* exclusively. I outline here the various options and give some sense of their virtues and drawbacks.

Poetry and Prose

Since teaching *Paradise Lost* often requires citing Milton's earlier poetry and prose, having both immediately accessible has obvious advantages. These editions contain almost everything one needs in a Milton course.

> *Complete Poems and Major Prose*, ed. Merritt Y. Hughes. While in many ways Hughes remains the favored edition, the notes, especially the bibliography of secondary sources, are badly out of date. The print is very easy to read, however, and the line numbers easily accord with the lines. Footnotes are very helpful with classical and early modern allusions but refer often to outdated critical controversies. Modernized spelling and punctuation; available only in hardback; moderately priced.
>
> *The Riverside Milton*, ed. Roy Flannagan. Intended to replace Hughes, Flannagan's edition remains controversial. Many complain that the footnotes, while learned, are needlessly didactic, and the first printings contain many errors. Almost alone among Milton's modern editors, Flannagan believes that "Milton's texts should be distanced by time and the evolution and the fluidity of the English language" (vii) and so he retains the original spellings and punctuation. The text font is very small, and while there are large margins for notes, line numbers are hard to correlate with lines. The book itself is very large and very heavy. Available only in hardback; very expensive.
>
> *The Complete Poetry and Essential Prose of John Milton*, ed. William Kerrigan, John Rumrich, and Stephen M. Fallon. This is the most user-friendly and readable edition and the most up-to-date. The introductions to *Paradise Lost* and the other texts take into account revisionary views of Milton, and the texts "of both poetry and prose have been almost entirely modernized" (xi). The edition features very clear print on very smooth paper. Line numbers are immediately to the left of the verse, leaving open the right side of the page for notes. Available only in hardback; moderately expensive.
>
> *John Milton: A Critical Edition of the Major Works*, ed. Stephen Orgel and Jonathan Goldberg. This edition is the only paperback option for those who want the poetry and prose together. Orgel and Goldberg have modernized Milton's English. The notes are in the back rather than at the bottom of the page, which makes them less accessible but also less distracting. The prose selections are not as extensive as in other editions, nor do the editors include Marvell's and S.B.'s prefatory poems. Very inexpensive.
>
> *The Sixteenth Century / The Early Seventeenth Century*, ed. George Logan, Stephen Greenblatt, Barbara K. Lewalski, and Katherine Mauss (vol. B of *The Norton Anthology of English Literature*). While the selections of the earlier poetry and prose do not match the above editions

(the divorce tracts, *Paradise Regained*, and *Samson Agonistes* are not included), this edition is a very popular choice. The text is thoroughly modernized and the notes unobtrusive yet learned. The font is small but clear; there is not much room on the page for notes. Access to early modern literature generally opens up possibilities for teaching foreclosed by not having, for example, Aemilia Lanyer's "Eve's Apology in Defense of Women" immediately at hand. Includes an instructor image disk (playable on both PC and Mac) and such online resources as a library of images of Adam and Eve. Moderately expensive.

The Early Modern Period, ed. Clare Carroll and Constance Jordan (vol. 1B of *The Longman Anthology of British Literature*). Like the Norton, one trades a larger sampling of Milton's poetry and prose for the opportunity to situate *Paradise Lost* in early modern literature. The "Perspectives" sections featuring excerpts from "Tracts on Women and Gender" and "The Civil War" are very helpful. The text of *Paradise Lost*, edited by Carroll, retains Milton's elisions, capitalization, and italics. Notes are at the bottom of the page; Web resources are included. Moderately expensive.

Complete Poetry

The Complete Poems, ed. John Leonard. The obvious disadvantage of this volume for courses on Milton is that one still needs an edition of the prose (for options, see Herman, "Materials" 3–4), but the very low cost still makes this edition a practical choice. Notes are in the back, and respondents praise them as "solid" and "unobtrusive." Some complain, however, about having to flip back and forth. The text "represents a partial modernization," meaning spelling and orthography have been updated, contractions retained, and punctuation is changed "only when the original pointing might impede a modern reader" (Preface xi).

The Complete Poetry of John Milton, ed. John T. Shawcross. This edition shares the same advantage (low cost) and disadvantage (still need an edition of the prose) as Leonard's. The poems are arranged chronologically, and notes are on the bottom of the page. The text, although inconsistently modernized, as Shawcross admits, "represents the kind of text offered the seventeenth-century reader without being an uncritical duplication of an original printing" ("Textual Notes" 544). The bibliography needs significant updating.

Single-Text Editions

Paradise Lost, ed. Alastair Fowler. Spelling has been modernized, but punctuation has not, so the text preserves the original syntax. Although the edition is generally reputed the most scholarly it is not without its problems. The footnotes sometimes threaten to overwhelm the text; page 41, for example, has three lines of the poem (1.4–6), and the notes consume the rest of the page. Respondents who use this text will either assign it to graduate students or use it for reference. Very expensive.

Paradise Lost, ed. David Hawkes. Directed more for the general reader than the classroom, the text is almost completely modernized (some elisions have been retained), and Hawkes introduces spaces to mark off sections of the poem. Very inexpensive.

Paradise Lost, ed. David Scott Kastan. Spelling, syntax, and punctuation have been brought into line with contemporary conventions. This text comes with an extensive, excellent introduction. This edition started off as a revision to Hughes, and so many of the notes replicate those in the original. Available in hardcover, paperback, e-book, and audio download. Very inexpensive.

Paradise Lost, ed. Barbara K. Lewalski (Blackwell). The only edition of the poem that reproduces "not only the original language of the 1674 edition but also the spelling, punctuation, capitalization and italics" ("Textual Introduction" xxxiii). This is an extremely handsome, large book, printed on good paper using a large, readable font, but it is the most expensive single edition.

Paradise Lost, ed. Gordon Teskey (Norton Critical Edition). The successor to Scott Elledge's popular Norton Critical Edition. Spelling and punctuation have been modernized, although Teskey retains some of the original spellings to reflect Milton's pronunciation ("sovran," for example, rather than "sovereign"). The great advantage of this edition is that Teskey includes source material (excerpts from the Bible) and a selection of "classic" and "modern" criticism, although the latter category is weighted heavily toward such figures as Northrop Frye and C. S. Lewis and Teskey leaves out all political treatments of Milton's epic. Inexpensive and available only in paperback.

The versions of *Paradise Lost* in Leonard, Orgel and Goldberg, and the Modern Library edition are also available as single-text editions. All are inexpensive. Leonard's single-text edition is also available in audio and e-book formats.

Additional Noteworthy Editions

Two editions are freely available on the Web: *The John Milton Reading Room*, which presents an original spelling hypertext of the 1674 *Paradise Lost* edited by Thomas Luxon (see Luxon's essay in this volume on the advantages of using *The John Milton Reading Room* rather than a print edition), and Risa Bear's site *Renascence Editions*, which includes an electronic version of the 1667 edition transcribed by Judy Boss. Teachers whose libraries subscribe to *Early English Books Online* (*EEBO*) can find PDFs of the 1667, 1669, and 1674 editions, and it can be invaluable for students (and teachers) to see what the poem looked like in its various incarnations. Shawcross and Michael Lieb have edited an edition of the 1667 *Paradise Lost*, and Dennis Danielson has produced a parallel prose edition that gives an original-spelling edition on the left and a contemporary prose rendering on the right.

Reference Works and Biographies

Teachers and students of Milton can take advantage of several excellent reference works and biographies.[1] *A Milton Encyclopedia*, edited by William B. Hunter et al., remains an essential source of clarifying information on *Paradise Lost* as well as on Milton's other works. While tilted toward theological concerns (one finds such entries as "Angels" and "Arianism," but not "Republicanism" or "The Ancient Constitution") and in need of updating, it remains a useful reference guide. *The Milton Encyclopedia*, edited by Thomas N. Corns, while more compact, answers the need for more current information. In addition to covering all of Milton's works and his family, this volume contains articles on key historical figures, the publishing history of Milton's works, the critical and editorial traditions, and, finally, writers whose works are significantly shaped by Milton's influence. Students and teachers alike can also profitably consult Gordon Campbell's entry on Milton in the *Oxford Dictionary of National Biography*, the successor to the *Dictionary of National Biography* (*DNB*) edited by Leslie Stephen (this resource is available online and in print, although its cost means that only wealthier libraries can afford it), and Albert C. Labriola's entry on Milton in the *Dictionary of Literary Biography*. William Ingram and Kathleen Swaim have produced a concordance of Milton's English poetry, and Gladys Hudson has edited a concordance to *Paradise Lost* specifically.

Milton criticism has grown to enormous proportions, especially since commentary starts with the publication of *Paradise Lost*. While the speed with which items appear online in journals and the *MLA International Bibliography* makes printed bibliographies less essential than before the digital revolution, they are nonetheless useful in tracking very early criticism of Milton's epic. The two most recent such volumes are Earl Roy Miner, William Moeck, and Steven W. Jablonski's Paradise Lost, *1668–1968: Three Centuries of Milton Criticism* and Calvin Huckabay and Paul J. Klemp's *John Milton: An Annotated Bibliography, 1968–1988*. Shawcross's *Milton, 1732–1801: The Critical Heritage* and *Milton: A Bibliography for the Years 1624–1700*, especially the latter's inclusion of remarks occasioned by Richard Bentley's infamous 1732 edition of *Paradise Lost* (in which Bentley proposed that an unscrupulous editor, "knowing Milton's bad circumstances . . . thought he had a fit opportunity to foist into the Book several his own Verses, without the blind Poet's Discovery" [sigs. A2–A3v]). These volumes have been supplemented by Shawcross's *Milton: A Bibliography for the Years 1624–1700: Addenda and Corrigenda*, which contains references to all Milton's works plus all the allusions, quotations, and imitations. These books provide essential references for understanding Milton's contemporary reputation. An equally essential tool for understanding Milton's importance to Romanticism is Joseph A. Wittreich's *The Romantics on Milton: Formal Essays and Critical Asides*. Wittreich organizes this volume by author, not by work, but the index contains copious references to *Paradise Lost*. For more current critical works, one still must consult the *MLA International Bibliography* and the two journals devoted exclusively to Milton: *Milton Studies* and *Milton Quarterly*.

As for biographies, Milton has never lacked for people to write his life story. The standard text for the earliest biographies remains Helen Darbishire's *The Early Lives of Milton*, and both Hughes and Flannagan include several of them in their editions.[2] The standard contemporary biography, William Riley Parker's magisterial *Milton: A Biography*, has been reissued in a revised version edited by Gordon Campbell. Over the past few years, however, Anna Beer, Lewalski, and the team of Campbell and Corns have published excellent biographies that supplement and update Parker's. Beer's is aimed at a general audience, while Lewalski and Campbell and Corns direct their books at specialists and their students.

Audiovisual and Online Aids

The variety and range of online resources has likewise grown enormously, and the Web has become central to teaching, both positively and negatively (one survey respondent said with relief that he retired "before online Changed Everything"). One must distinguish between the public Web, sites available to anyone with access, and the private Web, sites available only to persons or institutions with the resources to pay for them. One has to be careful with the public Web, and several respondents wrote that they discouraged their students from using search engines or *SparkNotes* or going anywhere near the ubiquitous *Wikipedia*. Others included warnings about Web sites run by "denominational religious colleges which tend to make Milton over in their own image." Web sites run by individuals, even individual professors, may disappear at any time, may not be current, and have no assurances of accuracy. But while one must proceed with caution, there is nonetheless a great deal of exceedingly helpful material available online.

Google Images is an invaluable source of images for teachers to use as aids or to adorn their syllabi (e.g., pictures of Milton, Anthony Van Dyck's portraits of Charles I, Robert Walker's portraits of Oliver Cromwell). Many respondents noted that they liked showing students illustrations of *Paradise Lost* included in the 1688 edition or those by William Blake or Gustav Doré. Plugging in

"Paradise Lost" and "1688," for example, provided a link to the online catalog of an exhibit of Milton's texts at Emory University that includes images of the 1688 edition. Similarly, "Paradise Lost" and "Doré" bring one to *ArtPassions* Doré page, where one can view all of Doré's illustrations of literary works, including *Paradise Lost*.

The public Web also serves as a repository for key documents and out-of-print books, such as the 1649 "Statement of the Levellers." The King James Bible is available online through the *Scholars' Lab* at the University of Virginia Library. Christ College, Cambridge University, where Milton studied, hosts two marvelous sites: *Darkness Visible* contains a wide variety of resources for studying the poem, including a picture gallery of illustrations, and *John Milton: 400th Anniversary Celebrations* contains links to the exhibition *Milton in the Old Library* and podcasts for "inter alia, the all-day reading of *Paradise Lost* and lectures by Quentin Skinner and Christopher Ricks." Furthermore, as *Google Books* proceeds to scan earlier books now out of print, some of the main primary sources for the political history of the seventeenth century, such as Thomas Birch's *The Court and Times of Charles I* (1849) and John Rushworth's *Historical Collections of Private Passages of State* (London, 1689), once restricted even in their reprinted forms to research libraries, are now commonly available.

Other useful teaching resources include sites on Renaissance emblems (e.g., Geoffrey Whitney's *A Choice of Emblems*, available through *The English Emblem Book Project*, hosted by Penn State University) and *Lexicons of Early Modern English* (*LEME*), hosted by the University of Toronto. *The Milton Reading Room* provides online editions of Milton's other poems, as does Bear's site *Renascence Editions*. *The Milton Reading Room* also features a bibliography that includes links to some of the articles. Three aggregate sites (i.e., sites that do not provide content but that direct users to sites that do) are especially useful for early modern studies generally and Milton in particular: *Luminarium: Anthology of English Literature* provides a wealth of links to essays and various other online resources helpful for teaching and studying *Paradise Lost*, as do Alan Liu's *The Voice of the Shuttle* and Jack Lynch's *Literary Resources*, which includes subsections on the Renaissance and John Milton. Since individuals maintain these sites voluntarily, one cannot assume that they are always current (the bibliography for *The Milton Reading Room* has not been updated since 2004), that their links work, or that they provide accurate information. Consequently, while these sites can be very helpful, they must be approached cautiously and with an explicit awareness of their limitations.

The databases available through the private Web, on the other hand, require no such caveats. *Early English Books Online* (*EEBO*) and *Eighteenth Century Collections Online* (*ECCO*) constitute spectacular resources for scholars and students. While not complete, *EEBO* contains nearly every book published in England between 1475 and 1700, including the entire Thomason Tracts collection and the multiple editions of Milton's works. Books can be viewed online or downloaded as PDFs. A teacher could, for instance, present to the class the original editions of *Paradise Lost*, and students could compare them with eighteenth-century editions, such as Bentley's (available on *ECCO*), or with contemporary editions. Both the online *Oxford English Dictionary* (*OED*) and the *Oxford Dictionary of National Biography* (*ODNB*) are extraordinarily informative. The *OED* is essential for understanding how words were used in the seventeenth century, and the *ODNB* provides excellent biographical essays of nearly everyone of importance in English history. For researching literary criticism, the best bibliography remains the *MLA International Bibliography* (*MLAIB*). The *MLAIB*'s inclusiveness, however, can intimidate beginning scholars, and so they can start with *EBSCOhost*, which will give a "quick and dirty" bibliography that can be expanded using *MLAIB*. *Literature Online* (*LION*) provides both primary and secondary sources, including *Milton Studies* (from 1997 to the present).

The Norton anthology comes equipped with a companion Web site that, in addition to an overview with links to many classical and early modern sources and analogues to *Paradise Lost* (e.g., Genesis, Augustine, Calvin, and Speght), provides a list of study questions, Web resources, and illustrations. Access, however, is restricted to those who have purchased the Norton. The Longman anthology also comes with electronic resources: an online biography, a list of additional Web resources, a bibliography, a multiple-choice comprehension quiz, and a group of discussion questions.

The survey showed a mixed response to the question of using visual and musical resources. Many respondents said that they did not use any such aids, claiming either the constraints of time or lack of expertise. Others use visual and musical aids copiously, and one respondent said that her course resembled a seminar in art history. Those who used visual aids unsurprisingly pointed to the illustrations of *Paradise Lost* by Blake and Doré and those in the 1688 *Paradise Lost* (available through *EEBO*). One respondent said that he used reproductions of John Speed's maps, especially when teaching book 9, and others used illustrations found on the Web of Italian baroque architecture or the many medieval and early modern depictions of Satan, Adam and Eve, and the fall. Numerous people said that Roland Mushat Frye's *Milton's Imagery and the Visual Arts* provides an invaluable guide for visual analogues to *Paradise Lost*. Others showed movies. One presented *The Girl with the Pearl Earring* to illustrate the differences between Catholic and Protestant aesthetics; another used *Cromwell* to give a sense of the period. Several used the BBC *History of Britain* series as well as Hugh Richmond's short documentary *Milton by Himself*.

Several respondents said that they liked to play baroque music to help situate Milton. Specific composers included Henry Purcell, John Blow, George Frideric Handel, and Claudio Monteverdi. Handel's *Samson*, with its themes of sexual temptation and blindness, works well as a point of comparison for *Paradise Lost*. More current music can also serve this purpose. Angelica Duran reports that every semester, she creates a playlist of twentieth-century songs intended to spur student thinking about the day's themes (e.g., the Rolling Stones's "Sympathy for the Devil" as background for Milton's portrayal of Satan in book 1; Edwin Starr's "War" [also recorded by Bruce Springsteen] as preparation for book 6, the war in heaven).

Required and Recommended Reading
for Students

The type and amount of secondary reading respondents assigned or recommended for students varied widely; some professors assign a great deal and others avoid it altogether. One respondent wrote, "Milton students have enough on their plates without overburdening them with secondary sources." Nonetheless, there are several texts that were repeatedly praised as especially helpful for undergraduates. First, there are the companions: *Cambridge Companion to Milton*, second edition, edited by Danielson; *A Companion to Milton*, edited by Corns; and *A Concise Companion to Milton*, edited by Duran. All contain excellent essays on Milton's contexts, intellectual history, different theoretical approaches, and other works. Other recommended guides include Catherine Belsey, *John Milton: Language, Gender, Power*; Richard Bradford, *The Complete Critical Guide to John Milton*; and Lois Potter, *A Preface to Milton*. David Loewenstein's *Milton:* Paradise Lost is an excellent general introduction to the poem's difficult parts (e.g., Satan, Milton's Eden, Milton's epic ambitions, *On Christian Doctrine*, and Milton's heresies), and many respondents steered their students toward a more venerable text, C. S. Lewis's *A Preface to* Paradise Lost. Many also recommended that students consult the various guides to the historical and literary backgrounds of Milton's England: Loewenstein and Janel Mueller, *The Cambridge History of Early Modern English Literature*; Christopher Hill, *Milton and the English Revolution*; Graham Parry, *The Intellectual Context: The Seventeenth Century, 1603–1700*; C. A. Patrides and Raymond Waddington, *The Age of Milton*; Deborah Shuger, *The Renaissance Bible*; and Nigel Smith, *Literature and Revolution in England, 1640–1660*. Published after our survey was distributed, Nicholas McDowell and Nigel Smith's *Oxford Handbook of Milton* "seeks to incorporate developments in what can broadly be termed historical criticism over the last twenty years" (Preface v) and, while clearly aimed at professors, nonetheless provides excellent essays on such topics as God (Stuart Curran [525–33]), verse rhythm (John Creaser [462–79]), the politics of Milton's epic (Martin Dzelzainis [407–23]), and Eve (Susan Wiseman [534–46]). I highly recommend it.

A small portion of respondents required substantial secondary source readings in their Milton courses, and these works included Danielson, *Milton's Good God*; William Empson, *Milton's God* ("for those students who want to think about Milton against the grain," as one respondent put it); Stanley Fish, *Surprised by Sin*; Neil Forsyth, *The Satanic Epic*; the Christine Froula–Edward Pechter debate in the pages of *Critical Inquiry*; Hill, *Milton and the English Revolution*; Diane McColley, *Milton's Eve*; and Joseph Summers, *The Muse's Method*. One respondent said that he assigned students Fish, Lewis, and Empson to introduce them to the major themes and controversies of Milton criticism. Instructors also often refer to the introductory essays in the various editions they use for Milton's works.

The Instructor's Library

Milton scholarship has grown into a vast enterprise, and the criticism of *Paradise Lost* seems to cover worlds within worlds. The following, therefore, should be taken not as a general survey or exhaustive list of Milton criticism but as a selection of essential, foundational works for dealing with some of the pedagogical challenges involved in teaching Milton's epic. The divisions I have devised are, I admit, somewhat artificial. Investigations of Milton's politics, for example, may cover his use of classical literature and perhaps focus on the question of gender. Nonetheless, I hope the following will work as a beginning for teachers of Milton.

First, we have the general questions of style and genre. Students today often claim ignorance of epic conventions (in fact, much popular culture recycles these conventions), and they might find Milton's verse impenetrable. Christopher Rick's *Milton's Grand Style*, written to refute claims that Milton wrote uninteresting verse, remains one of the best New Critical treatments of *Paradise Lost* and so remains both a model and a resource for teasing out the multiple significations of Milton's lines. Summer's *The Muse's Method* also remains very helpful.

The two best books for identifying Milton's classical allusions and the problems involved in interpreting them remain Davis P. Harding's *The Club of Hercules* (particularly good on allusions to the *Aeneid*) and William M. Porter's *Reading the Classics and* Paradise Lost. While most critics and editors focus on Milton's relationship with Vergil, David Norbrook profitably shifts the focus to Milton's engagement with Lucan's republican epic *Pharsalia* in *Writing the English Republic* (439–67). Other helpful works include Colin Burrow, *Epic Romance*; Patrick J. Cook, *Milton, Spenser and the Epic Tradition*; David Quint, *Epic and Empire*; Isabel Rivers, *Classical and Christian Ideas*; and John M. Steadman, *Milton and the Renaissance Hero*.

Moving from the literary to the historical, studies of Milton's politics have especially proliferated. How does Milton's epic relate to the tumultuous events that gripped England over the 1640s and 1650s, events that Milton directly participated in, first by writing polemical works, then by working for Cromwell's government? Perhaps the best single essay on the politics of *Paradise Lost* is Blair Worden's "Milton's Republicanism and the Tyranny of Heaven." Worden shows how Milton puts into the mouths of fallen angels near quotations from his *Ready and Easy Way*: "It is no news that in *Paradise Lost* the devil has the best lines; but is it realized how republican those lines are?" (235). While Worden does not believe that investing the fallen angels with republican politics makes them admirable figures, by paralleling quotes from *The Ready and Easy Way* with speeches by Milton's fallen angels, his essay provides the key to complicating Milton's politics. The question of Milton's relation to the radicals of the 1650s remains vexed, but Hill's *Milton and the English Revolution* still stands as the classic treatment for the parallels between Milton's epic and such groups as the Ranters. Loewenstein provides an excellent balance in the chapter "Radical Puritan Politics and Satan's Revolution in *Paradise Lost*" (*Representing Revolution* 202–41), arguing that Milton urges caution toward all sides and noting that Satan at one moment speaks "like a radical or militant Puritan who abhors the constraint of a political yoke and at another [speaks] like a royalist or a defender of Lords who would justify the ancient authority of magnific titles and powers" (217–18). Additional scholarship on Milton's politics especially helpful in the classroom includes the essays collected in David Armitage, Quentin Skinner, and Armand Himy, *Milton and Republicanism*; Arthur E. Barker, *Milton and the Puritan Dilemma*; Joan S. Bennett, *Reviving Liberty*; Stevie Davies, *Images of Kingship*; Robert Thomas Fallon, *Divided Empire*; Norbrook, "*Paradise Lost* and English Republicanism" (ch. 10 in *Writing the English Republic* [433–94]); and Mary Ann Radzinowicz, "The Politics of *Paradise Lost*."

The question of Milton's contexts, however, extends further than who runs England and which political philosophy should dominate. To oversimplify, the seventeenth century witnessed the rise of what we today call science (e.g., the invention of the telescope and the replacement of the Ptolemaic universe with the Copernican). The classic treatments of Milton and science are Walter Clyde Curry's *Milton's Ontology* and Kester Svendsen's *Milton and Science*. Their work has been updated by Karen Edwards, in *Milton and the Natural World*, and by John Rogers, in *The Matter of Revolution*.

If students find themselves puzzled by Milton's politics, they are often entirely baffled by the overlapping question of religion. Teaching *Paradise Lost* contextually means that one has to introduce students to the complicated relations between the various forms of Protestantism current in England during this period, as well as confront the perennially thorny question of what to make of Milton's God. Most criticism on Milton, even the essays in the various companions, assume that students already have a basic acquaintance with the issues of the English Reformation and the differences among the various strands of English Protestantism. Those without this background—that is, those who need to know who Cromwell was, what the differences between Episcopalians and Presbyterians are, and why this distinction matters—should consult chapters 5–8 of Herman's *A Short History of Early Modern England*. For those who have acquired this background, N. H. Keeble's "Milton and Puritanism" is an excellent summary of Milton's relation to Puritanism (the term was originally an insult, and its contemporary use remains controversial among historians), as is Stephen B. Dobranski and John P. Rumrich's introduction to *Milton and Heresy*, which investigates "aspects of Milton's works 'inconsistent with conventional beliefs'" (1). Relatively few respondents said that they used Milton's own theological treatise, *De Doctrina Christiana*, as a pedagogical guide for teaching *Paradise Lost*, but for those who want to, Maurice Kelley's *This Great Argument* remains indispensable. Other pedagogically helpful works on Milton and Christianity include J. Martin Evans, Paradise Lost *and the Genesis Tradition*; Michael Lieb, *Poetics of the Holy* and *Theological Milton*; C. A. Patrides, *Milton and the Christian Tradition*; William Poole, *Milton and the Idea of the Fall*; Regina Schwartz, *Remembering and Repeating*; and Shuger, *The Renaissance Bible*. Recently, the conventional emphasis on Milton and Christianity has been balanced by books investigating Milton's relationship with Judaism, in particular Jeffrey Shoulson's *Milton and the Rabbis* and Jason P. Rosenblatt's *Torah and Law*. Even so, the essays collected in Douglas A. Brooks's *Milton and the Jews* show that anti-Judaic sentiment permeates Milton's work and his culture. The essays by Guibbory ("England") and Trubowitz ("People") are particularly relevant to *Paradise Lost*.

The question of Milton's God—and the concomitant question of Milton's Satan—raises numerous pedagogical opportunities for engaging students in the complexities of *Paradise Lost*. As Miltonists know, there are, broadly speaking, two traditions of interpretation. The first takes the negative impression made by Milton's God seriously and proceeds from there. The most famous exponent of this view is Empson, who, in his essay "Milton and Bentley," expanded into *Milton's God*, argued that the portrayal of the Christian deity in Milton's epic is nothing less than monstrous. Students usually find themselves deeply engaged by Empson's arguments, both positively and negatively. Empson's provocative views have sparked many explicit and implicit rebuttals, most notably by Danielson (*Milton's Good God*), Lieb (*Theological Milton*), and Fish (*How Milton Works*). At the same time, more recent critics, in particular Herman (*Destabilizing Milton*) and Michael Bryson (*The Tyranny of Heaven*), have followed Empson's lead. If some critics have started shading Milton's God as perhaps less than absolutely good, others have started looking at Milton's Satan as less then absolutely evil. This development does not hold that Satan is in fact the hero of *Paradise Lost*; rather, as John Carey puts, the point is "to recognize that the poem is insolubly ambivalent, insofar as the reading of Satan's 'character' is concerned, and that this ambivalence is a precondition of the poem's success" (161). Milton scholars and teachers should also consult Forsyth's *The Satanic Epic* for a more complex view of the fallen angel.

Probably the most controversial aspect of *Paradise Lost* concerns Milton's treatment of gender. All too often, students, especially female students, get to "He for God only, she for God in him" (4.299) and slam the book shut. This reaction presents a significant pedagogical opportunity, as the question of Milton's misogyny has been the subject of extensive debate in criticism. Two of the most frequently cited essays in Milton criticism on this topic, Sandra Gilbert's "Patriarchal Poetry" and Mary Nyquist's "Genesis of Gendered Subjectivity," argue that Milton follows his culture in adopting a fundamentally hostile attitude toward women. But this approach was subject to vigorous challenge. Two article exchanges remain essential reading for students and professors alike:

the Pechter–Froula debate in *Critical Inquiry*, and the Marcia Landy–Barbara Lewalski–Joan Malory Webber cluster in *Milton Studies*. While these articles are foundational, they nonetheless tend toward either denouncing Milton as a misogynist or excusing him because early modern culture did not allow anyone to think differently. Diane McColley, however, provided a fundamentally different approach by arguing that Milton's depiction of Eve is in fact positive and revisionary. In the introduction to *Milton's Eve*, McColley describes her project as "an effort to extricate Eve from a reductive critical tradition, as Milton sought to redeem her from a reductive literary and iconographic tradition, and to establish a regenerative reading of her role" (4; McColley gives a shortened, updated version of this argument in "Milton and the Sexes"). These works have generated much essential scholarship on the problem of Milton and gender (see, e.g., Walker, *Milton and the Idea of Woman*; Wittreich, *Feminist Milton* and "'Inspir'd with Contradiction'"; and Martin, *Milton and Gender*).

Paradoxically, given Milton's blindness, *Paradise Lost* is also an intensely visual poem, and it has inspired generations of illustrators. The best treatment of the iconographic traditions that Milton drew on remains Roland Mushat Frye's magisterial and copiously illustrated *Milton's Imagery and the Visual Arts*. Wendy Furman-Adams and Virginia Tufte have cowritten several essential articles on Milton's nineteenth- and twentieth-century illustrators ("Anticipating," "'Earth,'" "'Metaphysical Tears,'" and "'With Other Eyes'"; Furman and Tufte), and Thomas Anderson has written an excellent commentary on the illustrations for the 1688 edition of *Paradise Lost*.

Finally, the reception history of Milton's epic has its own bibliography, and while it may seem that teaching the poem's reception should take a backseat to teaching the poem itself, going over how earlier readers reacted to *Paradise Lost* can provide fascinating insights into both interpretations of the poem and its enduring controversies. Shawcross's *Milton: The Critical Heritage* and *Milton, 1732–1801: The Critical Heritages* provide an essential record of the published responses to *Paradise Lost* from the eighteenth and nineteenth centuries, while Poole's "The Early Reception of *Paradise Lost*" surveys the first responses to the poem. Lucy Newlyn's Paradise Lost *and the Romantic Reader* focuses, as the title suggests, on how the Romantics, who were among the first to regard Milton's Satan sympathetically, revised the accepted views of Milton's epic. A. J. A. Waldock's Paradise Lost *and Its Critics*, John P. Rumrich's *Milton Unbound*, and William Kolbrener's *Milton's Warring Angels* all focus on the poem's shifting interpretations in the twentieth century; Rumrich provides a trenchant critique of Fish's hegemony in Milton criticism.

NOTES

[1] This paragraph is largely borrowed from Herman, "Materials" 4–5.

[2] Hughes includes biographies by John Aubrey, Edward Phillips, and the "Anonymous Life" now attributed to Cyriack Skinner; Flannagan includes Aubrey, Skinner, Anthony à Wood, and Phillips.

Part Two

APPROACHES

Introduction

Peter C. Herman

Why Teach Milton? And Where Is He Taught?

Why teach *Paradise Lost* at all? What do we hope students will gain from the experience of slowly working their way through this poem? Why does this poem deserve such an outlay of time and effort? There are many answers to these legitimate questions, but the first is to dispel the mistaken notion of *Paradise Lost's* unpopularity. One finds references and allusions to Milton's supposedly obscure epic in all manner of places, from highbrow magazines such as the *New Yorker* to graphic novels and even comedy. (In *Earth (The Book)*, the comedian and political commentator Jon Stewart has Milton condemn Satan to an eternity of reading *Paradise Lost* [71].) Clearly, there is something so deeply compelling about the story Milton tells that our culture will not let it die.

There are many reasons for this poem's enduring popularity and continued relevance. The epic genre remains vital (consider the popularity of the movie version of *The Lord of the Rings* or the Harry Potter series), and students respond to how Milton alters the conventions surrounding the epic hero by turning Satan into a kind of Aeneas or Ulysses figure. Even if they do not understand yet the precise reference, readers still respond to Satan's refusal to accept defeat and to the grandeur of his rebellion and evil plans. Milton's religion might seem to constitute a bar for secular-minded students, but the spectacle of Milton essentially putting God on trial (the first speaker, conventionally associated with Milton, asks for divine assistance so he may "justify the ways of God to men" [1.26])[1] compels attention, especially since (this aspect of Milton's poem may constitute a bar for the religious) Milton's treatment of good and evil is far from simple, so much so that it has sparked wildly different assessments (see, e.g., Danielson, *Milton's Good God*; Empson, *Milton's God*). Milton continues to command attention not only because he wrote about liberty but also because his writings about liberty deeply influenced John Adams and Thomas Jefferson. Consequently, "Milton and his writings have been placed, one way or another, at the center of what is meant to be quintessentially American" (Smith, *Is Milton* 4).

But I think the main reason we should continue to teach *Paradise Lost* is that the poem invites its readers to think hard about the primary issues of our lives in ways that continuously challenge rather than confirm accepted ideals. As Joseph Wittreich puts it at the start of *Why Milton Matters*, "A poem that enfolds hierarchies, *Paradise Lost* is equally a poem that destabilizes them" (xvi). In place of an obviously good God and an obviously bad Satan, Milton depicts a truculent God who exists in a heaven that bears a remarkable resemblance to an absolutist monarchy (Worden 236) and an attractive Satan (at least, at the poem's beginning) who seems to have absorbed Milton's writings on the ancient constitution. The fall is not a simple matter of "just say no"; it results from a complex mélange of motivations, including Adam's love for Eve and Eve's sense of intellectual inferiority and exclusion. At almost every juncture, Milton's story goes against expectations by pitting one interpretation against another—such as Adam's and Eve's contradictory accounts of their first meeting (compare Eve's narrative in 4.440–91 with Adam's in 8.452–514) or God's account of the fall ("man will hearken to his glozing lies" [3.93]) compared with the Muse's narrative in book 9—without his always giving us the means of choosing between them. Add to these hermeneutic complexities the sense that Milton talks about the root issues that matter—What do we want in a life partner? How does one deal with the collapse of one's entire life's project? What is the nature of good? of evil?—and you have a poem that continues to speak to students and professors alike, a poem that challenges authority and upends hierarchies. Far from a dull, sexually repressed pedagogue, Milton is "a poet who dares to speculate on the highest and most perplexing matters in the most challenging of literary ways" (Smith, *Is Milton* 6). Finally, *Paradise Lost* seems to encapsulate all the wrenching paradoxes of the human condition, and never more so than at the very end, when Adam and Eve, "hand in hand with wand'ring steps and slow, / Through Eden took their solitary way" (12.648–49). The first couple wanders out of Eden holding hands, but alone. Every time I read those lines to a class, there follows a few minutes of stunned, reflective silence.

Consequently, *Paradise Lost* finds its way into all sorts of courses of all levels. It is the centerpiece of the many semester-long undergraduate courses devoted to Milton's works. Almost every survey respondent mentioned teaching such a course, and many reported that substantial numbers of students signed up to read almost all Milton's works, providing yet more evidence that Milton studies thrive. *Paradise Lost*, however, is far from restricted to upper-division author-specific courses. Milton's epic shows up in such thematic courses as Nature and the Environment, *Paradise Lost* and the English Civil Wars, Epic and Counter-epic, and The Literary Satanic. *Paradise Lost* also fits in well with courses that focus on the problem of gender in the early modern period, where one can teach it alongside works such as the Hic Mulier–Haec Vir texts and Aemilia Lanyer's *Salve Deus Rex Judaeorum*. Numerous respondents reported teaching *Paradise Lost* in survey courses of British literature, early modern literature, or seventeenth-century literature. A few taught Milton's epic in such first-year courses as Introduction to Poetry, Critical Reading and Writing, and Introduction to Literature. One respondent writes about teaching Mary Shelley's *Frankenstein* alongside Milton's *Paradise Lost* in a general education introduction to literature course. The pairing provides an opportunity to glance at the relevant passages on which Shelley bases her novel, suggesting that she is either revising Milton's Satan or reading Milton's Satan accurately by making him more sympathetic. Either way, teaching the pair in this way introduces students to Milton's epic and to how literary allusions work across time.

Respondents were decidedly split on the question of teaching excerpts from *Paradise Lost* rather than the entire poem. While some left this question blank, others reported that they thought teaching excerpts was a very bad idea. Even so, many respondents reported teaching excerpts, especially in introductory and survey courses, where teaching the entire *Paradise Lost* is just not practical, and it is certainly possible to do so successfully (see Berry's essay in this volume). Among those who taught excerpts, certain books were more popular than others (books 1, 2, 4, and 9 are the clear winners, books 6, 7, and 11 the clear losers). But there is no consistency or pattern in which books, or which excerpts from these books, get taught.

Difficulties of Teaching the Poem

Despite the evident presence of *Paradise Lost* in popular culture and various syllabi, the poem can pose a formidable challenge for some undergraduate and graduate students. Interestingly, many teachers reported that the greatest barrier came not from the poem but from the assumptions students hold about its author. "Students usually regard Milton [as] a remote, aloof Puritan," writes one respondent; another reports, "The most serious problem is the misrepresentation of Milton's personality from various negative perspectives," such as his misogyny, pomposity, and authoritarianism. Some students may also be intimidated by the poem's and the poet's fearsome learning and presume that the poem is beyond them. Once they open the book, more potential barriers arise, such as the complexity of Milton's style and sentence structure (especially in this age of 140-character tweets); their unfamiliarity with seventeenth-century contexts, history, or religion; and their equal unfamiliarity with biblical literature and literary history. It would seem that despite the omnipresence of *Paradise Lost*, teaching the book in the twenty-first century can present a nearly impossible task: shaped by a culture that privileges an exceedingly short attention span, some students can find the length and scope of Milton's epic overwhelming, and when they do manage to get through the words, many do not have the necessary background to understand what they read.

Perhaps the best way for students to enter *Paradise Lost*, to get a basic grasp of the poem before one begins to worry about history, backgrounds, religion, or allusions, is to read the poem out loud. Indeed, it is probably a good idea to have students reading aloud throughout the course. It is one thing to sense the sprightly rhythms of "L'Allegro," another to feel them on your tongue. Similarly, the knotty sentences of *Areopagitica* suddenly make a lot more sense when one proclaims them as if the text were an actual oration. Students generally warm to Satan's brilliant rhetoric, and the cold fury of God's speech in book 3 becomes palpable when a student acts it out. Similarly, turning the debate between Adam and Eve in book 9 into an impromptu dramatic performance brings home the passion and anger in these lines. (For suggestions on how to incorporate oral performance into the classroom, see the essays in this volume by Duran and Richmond.)

From there, a wealth of approaches and aids is available for opening up *Paradise Lost*. If one does not have the time to devote entire lectures to literary and historical backgrounds for reading *Paradise Lost*, contexts sections in the Norton anthology (Logan, Greenblatt, Lewalski, and Mauss) and the Longman anthology (Carroll and Jordan) and selections from texts such as Christopher Hill's *Milton and the English Revolution*, Barbara Lewalski's *Life of John Milton*, and Thomas Corns's *A Companion to Milton* can be very helpful (see esp. C. Brown; Keeble; Raymond; Dzelzainis; Knoppers, "Late Political Prose"; Loewenstein, "Radical Religious Politics"). For a quick summary of epic conventions, the entry "epic" in Meyer Howard Abrams and Geoffrey Galt Harpman's *A Glossary of Literary Terms* can provide an excellent guide.

Relating *Paradise Lost* to Milton's other works poses the same problem addressed in *Approaches to Teaching Milton's Shorter Poetry and Prose*: "given the amount of time that *Paradise Lost* requires . . . can one justify taking time away from Milton's epic" (Herman, "Preface" xi)? The question is made more difficult by how one approaches the relation of the earlier work to Milton's epic. Some survey respondents recommended structuring the course so that everything leads up to Milton's epic. One respondent writes, "I try to show how Milton's early work essentially prepares him for writing the great epic." Another departs from chronology by teaching *Paradise Lost* first "and then relat[ing] the other stuff back to *PL*. I find it easier for students to engage with the earlier poetry and with the prose if they know where [Milton's] headed." Thus one teaches the earlier poetry (the Nativity Ode, "L'Allegro" / "Il Penseroso," "Lycidas") in terms of Milton's developing sense of vocation (or in the case of "Lycidas," a crisis in his sense of vocation). Similarly, the prose gets taught as it relates to *Paradise Lost*. Thus one reads the divorce tracts with an eye toward Adam's request to God for a companion and the subsequent relationship between Adam and Eve; *Of Education* in terms of the poem's project of educating the reader; *Areopagitica* for its description of choices and the difficulty of discerning good from evil; and the political prose, *The Tenure of Kings and Magistrates*, *Eikonoklastes*, and *The Ready and Easy Way*, for understanding the politics of heaven and hell. Respondents also suggested using Milton's treatment of Comus in *A Mask* as a gateway for understanding Satan and the Lady as anticipating Eve. Many noted the natural segues from *Paradise Lost* to both *Paradise Regained* and *Samson Agonistes*, and many brought in *De Doctrina Christiana* as a guide for the theological ideas in the epic (these respondents did not address whether the problems with attribution or Milton's decision not to publish the text troubled the relation of *De Doctrina* and *Paradise Lost*). Other respondents, however, cautioned against this teleological approach, since it has the perhaps unintended consequence of making the earlier work valuable only insofar as it anticipates *Paradise Lost*, and this approach imposes a unity on Milton's career that did not exist. One respondent tries to get his students to resist "treating all of Milton's career as an author up to his final great poems" (he admits that he usually fails since "students want to see everything in relation to *PL*"). Another encourages his students "to read backwards from *Paradise Lost*" but also enjoins them "to read *Paradise Lost* in a way that emphasizes the discontinuities and bold reversals of Milton's career. In this context, the poem reveals itself as a destination that, at an earlier phase of his development, Milton could never have imagined reaching. [The poem comes into focus] as both a fait accompli and a total surprise."

These different approaches resulted in differing organizations of courses. Most proceed chronologically, but some start with *Paradise Lost* and work backward. In my Milton class, we start with the early poetry, and the students read the appropriate selection from Milton's prose when we reach the relevant point in *Paradise Lost*.

Theoretical Approaches

Critics have used every approach imaginable as an aid for teaching and writing about *Paradise Lost*. Feminist theory, historicism of both old and new varieties, the mythographic approach, structuralism, Lacanian psychoanalytic criticism, reader-response, postcolonial criticism, men's studies, the debate on style between C. S. Lewis and F. R. Leavis, genre criticism, and deconstruction all have their proponents, and the responses showed that most teachers were highly eclectic in choosing which theoretical paradigms to bring to the classroom. The following is a representative response: "I tend to assign a selection from a range of critical approaches, so that students can see how debates about gender politics, theology, etc. have developed."

While respondents often offer their students a range of approaches, the prescription for the most pedagogically effective approach for teaching *Paradise Lost* is New Criticism, combined with something else: "My students seem to gain the most from good old-fashioned close reading"; "Close reading mediated by questions that interest me"; "close reading and historicizing"; "Close reading and imitation"; "I unabashedly exploit my own undergraduate training in new criticism as I teach explication (which students love and don't often get in other classes) in combination with cultural materialism, new historicism, and feminism." One respondent sums up the enduring popularity of New Criticism when she writes, "Nothing succeeds like close reading."

While almost all the approaches cited by the respondents are familiar, there are two new approaches to Milton that require some explanation: ecocriticism and the new Milton criticism. The former (explored in this volume by Jeffrey Theis) entails interpreting or teaching *Paradise Lost*'s concern for "human responsibility for the shared habitat of the earth, an organic sphere of interactive lives where only the renewable parts of edible plants are specifically designated for human use" (McColley, "Milton and Ecology" 157; see also Hiltner, *Milton and Ecology*; Wilcher, who describes the lineaments and history of ecocriticism generally and how Miltonists have applied it). The obvious advantage of this approach is that it dovetails with contemporary concerns over the environment and global warming, thus demonstrating to the students who might have a hard time understanding the relevancy of *Paradise Lost* that Milton's concerns anticipate ours. Ecocriticism also demonstrates how new approaches to literature, generated by new contexts, open up older texts in novel and surprising ways.

The new Milton criticism (explored in this volume by Herman; see also in this volume the essays by Bryson, Sauer, and Semenza) assumes that Milton is not the poet of certainty found in so much Milton criticism but rather a poet who filled his works with irresolvable doubts and contradictions that are not meant to be resolved (see Sauer, "Neo-Christian Bias"; Herman, *Destabilizing*; Bryson; Wittreich, "'Inspir'd with Contradiction'" and *Why Milton* 141–94). Nigel Smith accurately summarizes the project of this movement when he observes that "the nature and complexity of [Milton's] contradictory energy is not appreciated, even by Milton specialists" (*Is Milton* 7). Rather than domesticating and resolving the contradictory energies of *Paradise Lost*, the new Milton criticism assumes that *Paradise Lost* "speaks through contradictions, tears on its surface and whispers from its wings" (Wittreich, *Why Milton* 127). The pedagogical advantage is that students can see Milton as a man who struggled with complicated issues rather than as a lofty, difficult poet who already has all the answers; the critical advantage is that students not only get a greater understanding of the complexity of Milton's epic but also see how critics and editors from at least Richard Bentley onward have often papered over the contradictions with their own certainties.

The Essays in This Volume

The essays in this volume focus on broad, thematic topics of teaching *Paradise Lost* rather than specific readings of passages or books, providing approaches to teaching the entire poem instead of a particular set of lines. The volume is divided into six sections: "Literary and Historical Contexts," "Characters," "Poetics," "Critical Approaches," "Classrooms," and "Performance and *Paradise Lost*."

Because *Paradise Lost* requires extensive background or contextual knowledge, this volume starts with essays that help set the scene for reading Milton's epic. *Paradise Lost* is a massive expansion, elaboration, and, to a large extent, revision of the story of the fall in Genesis. Therefore, this volume begins with two essays on *Paradise Lost* and religion that encourage students to think critically about this topic. Regina Schwartz suggests several approaches for opening up the relations between Milton's epic and the Bible. The chief task, Schwartz argues, lies in capturing for contemporary students the sense of centrality and freshness that the Bible had for Milton and his contemporaries. Achsah Guibbory approaches teaching the problem of religion from a different perspective. Obviously, *Paradise Lost* tells a Christian (more properly, English Protestant) story, but one we can no longer assume is universal.

Next to the Bible, the most important literary background for *Paradise Lost* is the epic tradition. Jessica Wolfe provides a detailed roadmap for teaching Milton's engagement with this genre (both classical and early modern), offering the lessons that make up her introductory lecture on the topic and then giving specific suggestions on teaching the key epic intertexts for each section of *Paradise Lost*. Abraham Stoll also focuses on the classical tradition, but from a different perspective; teaching Milton's famously slippery allusions, he uses the analogy of a hyperlink to animate Milton's technique for today's students.

Milton's treatment of these textual backgrounds was shaped by the political events that loomed over the composition of his epic: his participation in the English Revolution, or, more accurately, the civil wars, and the failure of this experiment in nonmonarchic government, a development that exposed Milton to mortal danger. Two essays treat this aspect of teaching *Paradise Lost*. Thomas Fulton suggests that we use Milton's civil war prose to help illuminate the presence of contemporary history in Milton's epic. David Loewenstein offers another path, using the debate in hell, Abdiel, and the final books to suggest that we teach *Paradise Lost* as religious radicals would have read it, as an epic poem of restoration through the Messiah, not a king.

The next essays focus on the characters of *Paradise Lost*: God, Satan, Adam, Eve, and Milton himself. Michael Bryson explains how he seeks to help students understand Milton's portrayal of God, looking at the problem of justification and the possibility of dishonesty in God's actions. Gregory M. Colón Semenza outlines how instructors can use Milton's Satan to show how essential revisiting accepted positions is to Miltonic hermeneutics and epistemology. From divine creatures we next move to human beings. Julia M. Walker argues that the best approach for teaching Eve is to follow the Aristotelian middle, that Milton is neither a feminist nor a misogynist. To get a better read on Milton's treatment of the feminine, Walker suggests that the class attend to grammar. On the other side of the equation, Richard Rambuss focuses on redressing the imbalance in classroom and critical discussions away from Eve and toward Adam. John T. Shawcross shows how Milton functions in *Paradise Lost* through his biography, his beliefs and attitudes, and his presence as a writer and demonstrates how each of these three functions can be mined for classroom exercises and discussions.

The essays in "Poetics" focus on Milton's techniques. In this section, the question is not so much what Milton wrote but how he wrote it and what are the thematic and pedagogical consequences. Elizabeth Sauer reminds us that despite the frequent assumption that Milton speaks throughout the poem, *Paradise Lost* has many speakers and many narrators. Catherine Gimelli Martin, after outlining the complexities of Milton's combination of realism and allegory, suggests using a political cartoon (the more recent, the better) to help students understand abstractions. John Leonard seeks to recuperate the teaching of prosody from its reputation for being dull or merely technical, using Milton's sometimes neglected early critics as his guide to explore the "fit quantity" of various passages.

In addition to new historicism and feminism (implicit in many of the previous essays), there are any number of critical and pedagogical approaches to teaching *Paradise Lost*, and some of these are explored in "Critical Approaches." Feisal G. Mohamed looks at the pedagogical opportunities (and pitfalls) of teaching Milton's epic in the context of his earlier prose, specifically, the *Doctrine and Discipline of Divorce, Areopagitica,* and *An Apology against a Pamphlet.* Anthony Welch demonstrates the advantages of using Milton's early editors, Bentley in particular, to help students enter Milton's epic. Wendy Furman-Adams demonstrates how one can use the visual traditions generated by Milton's epic (e.g., the representations by John Baptiste Medina [1688], Francis Hayman [1728], and William Blake [1808]) to help teach the problems of ecology, marriage, and the fall in *Paradise Lost.*

Sean Keilen reintroduces imitation as an approach to teaching Milton. Keilen argues that we have done our students a disservice by focusing on writing about Milton rather than like Milton. If Keilen returns the classroom to the past, Lauren Shohet brings us back to the present, suggesting ways that contemporary works in a variety of registers—ranging from C. S. Lewis's novel *The Magician's Nephew* to the National Lampoon film *Animal House* to Philip Pullman's *His Dark Materials* trilogy—allow students to read and reread *Paradise Lost* in new and provocative ways. Peter C. Herman outlines how the new Milton criticism, which embraces Miltonic incertitude instead of explaining it away, can enliven the teaching of Milton's epic. William Kolbrener draws on the recent upsurge in food studies to illustrate how focusing on the question of eating angels (and he notes that students surely raise this issue) allows one to enter the larger metaphysical questions of Milton's cosmos and the continuity of spirit and matter. Jeffrey Theis then demonstrates the advantages of ecocriticism for teaching *Paradise Lost*, exploring the physical environments of hell, heaven, Eden, and chaos, as well as plants such as the Tree of Knowledge.

While *Paradise Lost* may be taught mainly in the stand-alone Milton course, that is far from the only place where this epic finds its way onto the syllabus, as shown by the next three essays. Boyd Berry provides a roadmap for teaching an abbreviated version of Milton's epic in a British literature survey course. Randall Ingram discusses how to teach *Paradise Lost* (all of it) in a Western civilization course that runs from *Gilgamesh* to the Beatles. Thomas H. Luxon, focusing on *The Milton Reading Room*, shows how one can use the Web to help students overcome their intimidation at the immense breadth of Milton's learning.

The volume concludes with two essays on performing *Paradise Lost*, which we should remember started as an oral, not a written, poem (see Herman, "Composing"). Hugh Richmond outlines his experience having his Milton students create a dramatic production of *Paradise Lost*. Angelica Duran provides instructions on the theory and practice of the increasing popular marathon readings of *Paradise Lost*, which have many advantages.

A Note on the Texts

The textual situation for Milton is very unsettled. There is no longer a single, authoritative edition of Milton's works that all, or even most, scholars agree on for their own use, and neither is there any agreement on which edition of *Paradise Lost* to use in the classroom. Some prefer editions that are completely modernized; others prefer editions with no modernization all. Some prefer something in between. The same range applies to Milton's other works. Consequently, I thought it best not to impose a unanimity that does not exist, and so each contributor uses the edition he or she thinks best. Quotations from *Paradise Lost* and Milton's other works will appear modernized in one essay, with original spelling and punctuation in the next. Each essay has a note indicating the edition used.

NOTE

[1] All references to *Paradise Lost* are to Kerrigan, Rumrich, and Fallon's edition in *Complete Poetry and Essential Prose*.

Teaching *Paradise Lost* and the Bible

Regina Schwartz

The general malaise about the Bible in contemporary secular culture is not shared by Milton. I do not mean that the Bible is unimportant to many of us in secular modernism but that it was vitally important to Milton. Neither do I mean that Milton was a better interpreter of the Bible than we are. What is striking about Milton's engagement with the Bible is that he does not take it as a given, as inevitable, that he climbs inside its narratives as if he were writing them himself and explores why they take certain paths and what other paths they could have taken or what effects are achieved by choosing this image instead of that one. For Milton, the Bible is startlingly fresh. In contrast, today's students tend to fall into two categories. Those who have not read the Bible but have indirectly encountered its stories tend to regard them vaguely as cultural givens, predictable because of their cultural currency, like the plot of "Jack and the Beanstalk" or the design of the American flag. Students who have more familiarity with biblical narratives through church liturgy or Sunday school have a related response: the Bible is not startling to them because it has been given to them in a package, already interpreted, its stories already assigned meanings. I face the same challenge with both groups: how to make the Bible new. I continually marvel that the Bible was new to Milton, especially in an age when it was everywhere, part of everyday life. As Christopher Hill warns, in Milton's age, "the Bible was central to the whole of the life of the society: we ignore it at our peril" (*English Bible* 4). The Bible

> was everywhere in the lives of men, women and children. Not only in the church services they had to attend, but in the ballads they bought and sang, and in their daily surroundings. . . . [A]lmost all houses had hangings

to keep out draughts and to cover the rough walls. These often took the form of "painted cloths," the real "poor man's pictures," among which Biblical scenes seem to have preponderated. In accordance with Deuteronomy XI.20, Biblical texts were very often painted on walls or posts in houses, "probably representing the most common form in which an 'illiterate' would encounter the written word." In addition, walls were covered with printed matter—almanacs, illustrated ballads and broadsides, again often on Biblical subjects. More elusive, "godly tables [tablets]" specially printed for decorating walls and "most fit to be set up in every house," contained texts from the Bible.   (38)

During the civil war, soldiers carried a Bible into battle; before entering the fray, they sang its psalms; in the evening, parents recounted its narratives to their children; during parliamentary conflicts, proponents cited its verses. The Bible was used in Parliament, in pamphlet wars, in education, in courtship, and in conversation to an extent that is hardly imaginable today. And yet somehow Milton's encounter with it was not tainted by familiarity. Rather, in *Paradise Lost*, he engages the biblical narratives, biblical inspiration, and biblical theology as if he were present at their creation, participating in their inception.

Thus I begin teaching *Paradise Lost* by teaching Genesis 1–3. Again, my aim is to make it new for students. The assignment is to read the stories of the creation and fall of man slowly and to write down what questions are left unanswered by the narratives. I explain that students must free up their imaginations to complete this assignment, that there is no right answer, and ask them to bring in at least ten questions each.

The assignment presupposes Erich Auerbach's brilliant insight that the narrative style of the Bible, in contrast to the Homeric style, is to create a vast background that is unlit—details ignored, explanations unaddressed—to fully illuminate the foreground. In his influential essay "Odysseus's Scar," Auerbach analyzes a passage from the *Odyssey*, in which Odysseus returns and Euryclea recognizes him, and compares it with a passage in the narrative of Abraham being ordered to sacrifice his son (23). Auerbach's essay is my pedagogical inspiration for teaching *Paradise Lost*, because Milton engaged the Bible when he wrote *Paradise Lost* by turning his mental spotlight on the dark background of the biblical story to fill it in. He took a story that is three chapters in the Bible and stretched it into twelve books. Indeed, he includes elements from the epic tradition (e.g., councils, war) and classical literary motifs (e.g., invocations, catalogs) to serve the purpose of illuminating—both in the sense of lighting up and in the sense of explaining—his biblical story.

Here is a sample of the questions this assignment produces:

Why did God create the world?
It says that in the beginning, "God's spirit hovered over the water." Why were there waters before the creation?

What does "it was good," an assessment of each day of creation, signify?
   Why would God's work be judged in that way?
Who is God; that is, what is he/she/it like?
"God created man in the image of himself"—what is that image?
"Male and female he created them"—what is this saying about God's
   gender?
Why does God make beasts and birds to be helpmates for Adam if they
   are "not suitable"?
Do Adam and Eve make love? How old are they?
What do they do all day? What do they learn? What do they think about?
Why did God put a tree in the garden that the man could not eat from?
Why was there a talking serpent in the garden?
Where was Adam when the serpent spoke to the woman?
Why did the snake incite the woman to disobey the divine order?

I ask students to read their questions to the class, and I comment on how
many Milton's poem addresses. I have them keep a record of their questions,
adding a few of my own, so they will begin reading *Paradise Lost* with an extensive set of questions, curious to see how Milton will address these issues. I
hope students will come away from this exercise with an appreciation of how
imaginatively engaged Milton was with the Bible, that it was not just a source
but also an imaginative world that he entered and filled in. By beginning with
questions and letting them linger, I aim to encourage students to do the same.
I want them to read Genesis as well as *Paradise Lost* with fresh eyes, to engage
the epic actively, not passively—that is, to read it as if choices were made at every turn, this event, not that one; this dialogue, not another; and this motivation
of a character, not another. *Paradise Lost* is not inevitable; it did not have to be
this way. It could have been otherwise, just as the world could have been created otherwise, with people made in the image of plants instead of God or the
moon made to govern the day and the sun the night. One difference between
reading literature and reading the newspaper is having one's attention heightened to the creative process, the process of making, of choosing, instead of just
receiving information as a given.
   Let's take up one question: What do Adam and Eve do all day? This question
is worrisome, because so much of life is spent coping with difficulty, laboring to
overcome obstacles to achieve something, and students wonder if paradise is too
easy and hence boring. They note that even though Adam is cursed with work
after he disobeys, he and Eve work before then. Milton is taking his cue from
the verse that says God settled the man in the garden to tend it, but he makes
the work of the garden seem enormous, almost infinite. They will not be able to
keep up with it, until they have more hands to help—until they have children.
So why is the upkeep of the garden an issue? Is it a sign that the world was not
so perfect after all? That it was created with more work than two people could
handle? That dividing their labor seemed a sensible way of coping with the
problem? That there is an inherent tension between two imperatives—to tend

the garden and to be together, sharing their love? How are they supposed to prioritize these imperatives? If they have to do so, is the world less than perfect? All this comes to a head, of course, in book 9, when Eve suggests that they work apart, giving the serpent an opportunity he had not dared to imagine, of capturing his prey alone. But in the Bible, it does not say that they were separated; it says that she gave some of the fruit to "her husband with her" (Gen. 3.6).[1] Is this one of those dark places that Milton lit up with his imagination—Adam was gone during the serpent's temptation but then returned? Or does he think he is improving the Bible by changing it in his elaboration of the separation of Adam and Eve? This is not only our concern; the narrator is also preoccupied with the questions of biblical authority and inspiration, with the problem of the relation of his poem to the Bible.

Broadly speaking, then, *Paradise Lost* has a second debt to the Bible: not only its narrative and its language but also its source. Who is the Muse who has so many names and no names?

> Sing, Heav'nly Muse, that on the secret top
> Of *Oreb*, or of *Sinai*, didst inspire
> That Shepherd, who first taught the chosen Seed,
> In the Beginning how the Heav'ns and Earth
> Rose out of *Chaos*:[2]   (1.6–10)

The Muse is found in many places—Oreb, Sinai, Sion, Siloa, the upright heart—and has inspired the story of the creation, the law giving, the consolidation in Jerusalem, biblical prophecy (the brook of Siloa refers to Isaiah), and the eschatological achievement of the interiorization of the covenant:
Or if *Sion* Hill

> Delight thee more, and *Siloa's* Brook that flow'd
> Fast by the Oracle of God; I thence
> Invoke thy aid to my adventrous Song,
> That with no middle flight intends to soar
> Above th' *Aonian Mount*, while it pursues
> Things unattempted yet in Prose or Rhime.
> And chiefly Thou O Spirit, that dost prefer
> Before all Temples th' upright heart and pure,
> Instruct me, for Thou know'st; Thou from the first
> Wast present, and with mighty wings outspread
> Dove-like satst brooding on the vast Abyss
> And mad'st it pregnant: (1.11–22)

This is the Muse who inspired what Moses wrote (i.e., the Bible), and this is the Muse who was present from the beginning, the spirit of God that "dove-like satst brooding on the vast Abyss." When the narrator calls on this Muse, he is reaching back to the source of the Bible, going behind the Bible in his quest for authorization. He might say things the Bible did not say, and he might even say things differently from the way the Bible said them, but the narrator assures himself that this is not competing with or trumping biblical authority. To the contrary, he is tapping into biblical authority, being authorized by the Muse who wrote the Bible. This is a big claim for a poet to make, and just making the claim does not make it work. Perhaps Milton protests too much? Later the Muse will be called Urania, the muse of epic, but with the qualification that "the meaning, not the Name, I call" (7.5), and so the Muse will have many names and no name, like God in the works of Pseudo-Dionysius, the Areopagite, who proliferated the attributions of God in *On the Divine Names* but confessed in his *Mystical Theology* that God cannot truly be named.

This discussion of the Bible as source takes me to the third kind of debt *Paradise Lost* has, biblical theology, or what I call biblical truth or biblical worldview: Milton's understanding of the meaning of life is indebted to the meaning of life according to the Bible. But this idea raises tough questions. What is that meaning? Is it stable or contradictory in the text? Who decides what that meaning is? Is it constant or open to interpretation? Because students want to believe there is one meaning, a right one, and that Milton could find it because he was so clever, these questions deserve time and the consideration of examples in the classroom. Take, for instance, the creation of woman: there are two different accounts of the creation of woman Genesis: "the male and female he created them" version (1.27) and the creation of Eve from Adam's side (2.22). Different interpretive communities cope with these versions differently: medieval misogynists who wanted to make women subservient said because woman was created from man, that man is originary and superior, that woman is dependent on him, and that her job is to serve him. Twentieth-century feminists argue that woman and man were created together, that in Hebrew *helpmate* signifies not serving but being a companion, and that Eve was a worthy companion for Adam when the animals were not. Other contradictions abound: one story of creation begins with God creating the heavens and the earth (Gen. 1.1), and another reverses the order to the "earth and the heavens" (Gen. 2.4); the first articulates an entire cosmos, with the sun, moon, and stars, before man is created last of all, whereas in the second man is created first, and the garden is articulated around him and for him.[3] The latter is the account a community wants to stress when "man is the measure of all things" as he was in Renaissance humanism; the former is the account a community stresses when it wants to embed man in a cosmic context far greater than him, where he does not dominate nature but humbly respects it.

There is not one stable authoritative biblical account of the meaning of life. Milton created his own biblical theology. He is more than a literary critic of the Bible who discerns how it is written and elaborates on it, more than a biblical poet who writes what was unwritten, authorized by the spirit of God; he is a biblical theologian who constructs a world of meaning that he attributes to the

Bible. He wrote about this task in many places. But rather than turn to his systematic theology, *De Doctrina Christiana*, for help, I prefer his discussion of his principles for biblical interpretation in a prose tract on divorce. *The Doctrine and Discipline of Divorce* could have been justifiably titled *The Doctrine and Discipline of Biblical Exegesis* since so much of it addresses how to interpret the Bible. Milton's theology is one of charity: that God only does what is good for us, that he does nothing for our harm and everything for our benefit.[4] So to take Milton at his word—and many critics do not, and we certainly do not have to—God put a prohibited tree in the garden not to ruin the happiness of the human race but to teach humankind something they need to know, to give them the gift of free choice. Opposite readings have been offered: that God is a sadistic tyrant who demanded subservice to his law and punished ruthlessly when he did not get it. This interpretation is not ridiculous; strong readers have read it that way, but such a theology, or antitheology, would have to survive some stubborn details: if God is an abusive tyrant, why does he ask Michael to intermix mercy with justice? To clothe the nakedness of man, presumably to alleviate their shame?

Milton explains that when we try to discern both how to interpret God's will and how to act, we must remember that God never intends ill for us (like bondage to a tyrannical government in the state or the church, or the bondage of a miserable failed union in marriage) nor intends for us to do ill (commit adultery to satisfy the longing for a helpmeet that a failed marriage does not address). Charity dictates Milton's biblical hermeneutics as well as his revolutionary politics, his personal life, and his critique of church government. To drive home the centrality of charity, Milton asks a rebellious Parliament pointedly, "if charity be excluded and expulst, how yee will defend the untainted honour of your own actions and proceedings? . . . If [a whole people] against any authority, Covnant, or Statute, may by the soveraign edict of charity, save not only their lives, but honest liberties from unworthy bondage, as well may he against any private Covnant . . . redeem himself from unsupportable disturbances" (*Doctrine* [Wolfe et al.] 2: 229). Furthermore, in his charity God has made available to human reason the justness and goodness, indeed, the charity, of his laws. While many of God's ways are mysterious, this is not: "hee hath taught us to love and to extoll his Lawes, not only as they are his, but as they are just and good to every wise and sober understanding" (297–98). Thus Abraham had the temerity to question God's actions, because he well understood the principle of charity and understood that God is the giver of charity: "Therefore *Abraham* ev'n to the face of God himselfe, seem'd to doubt of divine justice, if it should swerve from that irradiation wherewith it had enlight'ned the mind of man, and bound it to observe its own rule. Wilt thou destroy the righteous with the wicked? That be far from thee; shall not the Judge of the earth doe right?" (298). Here justice or charity or the right has irradiated the mind of man, and Abraham, having internalized it, is at pains to correct God according to his own principle.

Adam and Eve are invited to understand their command as issuing from a principle of charity, as a gift of freedom, not as a limitation on freedom issuing from a principle of scarcity. Satan understands the command not as a sign of freedom (to reason) but as a deprivation (of knowledge) and a condemnation (to inferiority):

> One fatal Tree there stands of Knowledge call'd
> Forbidden them to taste: Knowledge forbidd'n?
> Suspicious, reasonless. Why should thir Lord
> Envie them that? can it be sin to know,
> Can it be death? And do they onely stand
> By Ignorance, is that thir happie state,
> The proof of thir obedience and thir faith?   (4.514–20)

Milton's biblical worldview—that charity governs our world, that its trage-dies will be redeemed—has a fierce and eloquent opponent in Satan. In the classroom, there is no better way to underscore this difference than to debate it: when students choose sides and heatedly debate the justice of God and the goodness of the providential design, both *Paradise Lost* and the Bible be-come new.

NOTES

[1] All references to the Bible are to the King James translation.

[2] All references to *Paradise Lost* are to Luxon's edition.

[3] Accounts of creation abound both in the Bible and in Milton's epic. For a further discussion of their impact on Milton's theology, see R. Schwartz, *Remembering*.

[4] For further discussion of Milton's thinking on charity, see R. Schwartz, "Milton."

Paradise Lost and the Jews

Achsah Guibbory

Milton's *Paradise Lost* is a Christian epic, presented as the universal story of humankind. The poem stands at a remove from orthodoxy: Milton was a non-conformist and republican poet, and his poem contains heterodoxies—the mortalist heresy that the soul as well as the body dies; the representation of sex as potentially innocent and holy, fit for the angels as well as the unfallen Adam and Eve; and an implicit denial of the Trinity (the Son is not coequal, coeternal, or coessential with God).[1] Yet for all its transgressions of traditional Christian doctrines, *Paradise Lost* remains a distinctly Christian poem, at the center of which stands the Son, as Milton calls him. The Son is first acknowledged in the invocation of book 1, as the narrator points to "one greater Man" (4).[2] In book 3—the most theological book of the poem, featuring the conversation between God and the Son—the Son is announced as the voluntary savior of "Man," who has yet to fall (203). In book 6, the Son defeats Satan in the battle in heaven, retold by Raphael. Indeed, the Son stands at the mathematical center of the epic—driving the rebel angels out of heaven on his chariot at the end of book 6, then appearing in book 7 as the "King of Glory" in his "Chariot" on his "Expedition" to "create new Worlds" (208, 197, 193, 209). He returns to salvific prominence in the last book of the poem: Michael, sent by God, reveals the Son to Adam, who accepts the Son, making him the first Christian;[3] in the final book, Eve learns she will bear the "Promis'd Seed" (12.623).

When I was first taught *Paradise Lost* as an undergraduate at Indiana University in the 1960s, the poem was presented as "our" story—a universal story—much as in grade school in Connecticut my teachers expected all of us (including me, usually the only Jew) to recite the Lord's Prayer daily and, at Christmastime, to sing joyously about the birth of Jesus, "our Savior." But those of us who read or teach Milton in the twenty-first century live in a changed world. It is no longer possible to presume that everyone in the class is Christian—or Protestant Christians. Our classes are filled with students who belong to many different religions—Jews, Muslims, Hindus, Catholics, varieties of Protestants—or none.

So how do we teach the poem, given that certain books—notably books 3 and 12—are especially problematic when it comes to issues of religion? One could downplay the more offensive aspects of the poem, those passages that make it clear the universalism of the poem is a Christian universalism that is actually exclusive. One could, for example, focus only on God's speech about man being created with free will in book 3 (80–134) or pretty much ignore the last two books of the poem, focusing only on the turn to the "paradise within" in book 12 (587). But these omissions distort the poem. I find it better to teach the whole poem, to address the problems head-on, placing them in the context of Milton's other writing and his time or even in the larger context of Christian-Jewish relations, going back to the New Testament.

The question I pursue here, drawing on my experience as a teacher, is how might we teach *Paradise Lost* while recognizing the difficulties raised by the poem's treatment of religious others (which for Milton included Catholics) and specifically by the place and treatment of the Jews in Milton's poem. In teaching what could be called religious literature, I find it necessary to come clean about my identity and acknowledge my own "difference," so my students can see that one does not have to share Milton's religion to read, understand, and even love his poem. I confront the problem of religion right away. I tell them they are likely to be offended by some things in Milton. I also tell them a little about myself—that I am a Jewish woman, with an eccentric Jewish background, who found it necessary to become a kind of expert about Christianity to teach and write about seventeenth-century English literature. In trying to get my students to see the importance, indeed necessity, of learning about other perspectives, I ask how many are Catholic, Protestant (of various denominations, including Quakers), Muslim, and atheist or agnostic. I then encourage them to tell the class something about their worship traditions and to ask questions, because I want to create an atmosphere in which we can discuss religious issues openly, with curiosity about other beliefs but also with respect for one another. Not every teacher may feel comfortable with such a personal approach, but long experience (at both a public state university and a private liberal arts college) has convinced me that this method is a highly effective way to get students to understand the religious differences inscribed in Milton's poem and to be ready to grapple with his complex text.

But more is needed. Students require a historical perspective that does more than give a sense that Milton can connect with us in the present. In preparing my students to read *Paradise Lost*, I inevitably find myself teaching about the history of Christianity (including the Protestant Reformation), which reveals the fluidity and complexity of Christian identities and how Christian identity (one might say monotheistic identity) has always been defined in terms of others. Having talked briefly about our personal religious identities, my students are now better prepared to understand the history of Christianity.

That history involves Christianity's continually redefined relation to Judaism (its ancestor and sibling) as it moved from a persecuted minority in the Roman Empire to a state religion. Milton shared the anti-Jewish attitudes that had been, from the New Testament on, a part of Christianity. One might go back to Paul's epistles to Romans (chs. 9 and 11) and Galatians (ch. 4), which defined an influential binary opposing the gospel (and spirit) to law (and body), true Israel (those who accept the gospel of Christ) to Jews who remain bound to Mosaic and rabbinic law. Paul and the epistle to Hebrews set the stage for Augustine's later contrast between so-called carnal Israel (Jews) and spiritual Israel (Christians). Perhaps one would not want to bring in the gospel of John, which in chapter 8 demonized the Jews as children of the devil, unless one wanted to show the range of attitudes toward Jews in the New Testament, in which Paul stands as a contrast to John in looking forward to the Jews' conversion, hoping that the genealogical children of Abraham would eventually be incorporated into spiritual Israel.

Once we have looked at these foundational Christian texts, I talk about the Reformation—the attempt to restore Christianity to its supposed primitive purity, to privilege the word of God (scripture) rather than human traditions, inward spirituality rather than outward ritual—and how, beginning with Luther, it involved renegotiation of the relation between true Christianity and Judaism (and all things Jewish). Reformers imagined a church that would be purged of popish and Jewish elements.[4] I stress that in England the Reformation did not happen all at once, that some reformers often identified the church with the narratives of biblical Israel (allowing them to identify with biblical Jews delivered from Egypt or Babylon) and that there were anxieties among zealous English Protestants about the threats supposedly posed by Rome and the pope (called the Antichrist by John Foxe and others), Islam (thought to be extending its power north), and Jews (persecuted and expelled from many nations but in the 1650s seeking readmission to England). Even such a brief history encourages students to realize that, then as now, Christian identities were complex and fluid. Protestantism was not simply one thing, and English Protestants were often sharply anti-Catholic and their attitudes toward Jews conflicted—they could embrace the Old Testament as their history while seeing Jews and Judaism as anti-Christian.[5] I tell my students that Milton boldly questioned Protestant orthodoxies such as the Calvinist notion of predestination or belief in the Trinity, insisting on the supreme importance of conscience, but shared many prejudices of other Christians of his time in England. I urge students to recall the anti-Catholic notes in the depiction of Comus in *A Mask* and the digression on the corrupt clergy in *Lycidas*. This context helps prepare students—especially my Catholic students—for *Paradise Lost*, where the description of Pandemonium suggests Saint Peter's (1.710–30), Satan's entry into Eden echoes fears about Jesuit infiltration of England, and Michael's history in book 12 implicitly attacks the Catholic Church for persecuting the faithful.

But Milton's attitude toward Jews and things Jewish was not much more tolerant than his attitude toward Catholics, despite the fact that Milton is England's great Hebraic poet, versed in rabbinic writings as well as Christian Hebraism.[6] I remind my students of Milton's polemical prose where Milton self-identifies as Moses or Jeremiah yet insists that the true church must not model itself on Jewish and Old Testament precedents and that the English people, recently delivered from Egyptian bondage, must not be like the Israelites who wanted to return to Egypt. Thus prepared, my students can tackle Milton's great epic poem without glossing over the troubling spots and with some context for understanding Milton's complicated stance in his treatment of the Old Testament and Jewish Israel.[7]

My teaching has changed over the years, as has my approach. I no longer avoid the roll call in book 1, which gives the various names fallen angels would assume throughout a history that includes not just the pagan (or classical) world but also that described in the Old Testament. These "Devils" (373) include Moloch and the many Baalim and Ashtraroth, all of whom would be "adore[d] for Deities" by the "Nations" (373, 385), but Milton stresses that these false, demonic gods also fixed "Thir Altars by [God's] Altar" (384), that "the Race of *Israel* oft forsook" God, "thir living strength," for them (432–33). Milton mentions how Solomon, "By that uxorious King . . . / Beguil'd by fair Idolatresses, fell / To Idols foul" (444–46), and how Ezekiel "survay'd the dark Idolatries / Of alienated *Judah*" (456–57). The Old Testament history given in this long section tells a story of a Jewish Israel repeatedly prone to "[t]h'infection" of idolatry (483). Milton's poem thus from the first book presents an ambivalent stance toward the Jewish past: the Miltonic narrator identifies with Moses, who received divine revelation, and the prophet Ezekiel, who spied and condemned Judah's idolatry; the poem depends heavily on the Hebrew Bible and a knowledge of Israel's history, and yet the version of Israel's history presented here aligns Jewish Israel with false worship and betrayal of the true God.

When we get to the final two books of *Paradise Lost*, after having spent most of our time on Adam and Eve (the temptation and fall and its aftereffects), my students can now understand why Jewish Israel comes back into the poem, playing an otherwise surprisingly negative role in the history Michael shows and tells to Adam. Jason Rosenblatt shows that the Edenic, prelapsarian books are Hebraic in their monism, the integration of spirit and body, and their indebtedness to rabbinic thinking. In books 11 and 12, however, there is a marked shift. Here biblical, Jewish Israel is essential to Milton's understanding of Christian history and of true religion, but now Jewish Israel exists typologically as a shadow to figure Christian truths, a means to produce the Son as the Messiah, and an other against which true faith and worship is to be defined by Michael. One of the four archangels in Jewish tradition but also "the typologizing angel of the New Testament" (Rosenblatt 218), Michael in book 11 shows Adam the history the Old Testament presents — from Cain's murder of Abel through the Flood, in which "one Man" (Noah) is "found so perfet and so just / That God voutsafes to raise another World / From him" (876–78). From the perspective of Christian values that shape the story given by Milton's Michael, Abel becomes the example of the true worshipper, the martyr for true religion; Noah is the type of Christ. Book 12 has Michael continue the Old Testament story, from Nimrod and Babel, the degeneration of the world that leads God to "withdraw / His presence" and select "one peculiar Nation . . . / From all the rest" to spring from Abraham, the "one faithful man" (107–08, 111–12, 113). We might think Jewish Israel here has been redeemed, along with Abraham, but Milton actually reads Israelite history through the lens of Paul's epistles. While designating Israel "the Race elect" (214), Michael insists on the Israelites' desire to return to Egypt after their deliverance, "choosing rather / Inglorious life with servitude" (219–20), typologically figuring the Jews' eventual rejection of Christ and Christian liberty (and also England's return to the bondage of monarchy in 1660, after its earlier deliverance). The giving of the law at Mount Sinai is described as "informing them, by types / And shadows, of that destind Seed to bruise / The Serpent" (232–34)—that is, the law informs the Israelites (if they could read) of Christ. But Michael goes further, insisting that the law was

> given them to evince
> Thir natural pravitie, by stirring up
> Sin against Law to fight . . .
> . . . .
> So Law appears imperfet, and but giv'n
> With purpose to resign them in full time
> Up to a better Cov'nant, disciplin'd
> From shadowie Types to Truth, from Flesh to Spirit
> (287–89, 300–03)

Having identified the Israelites with Adam's "pravitie," which can only be expunged by Christ, Michael teaches Adam about the Messiah and the shameful death he will suffer, "naild to the Cross / By his own Nation" (413–14). Living long before Vatican II, which repudiated the dogma of the Jews' guilt, and sharing in the near-universal anti-Jewish attitudes of his contemporaries, Milton in this remark should not surprise us, though we could tell our students that a few radicals (particularly millenarians) in Milton's time rejected or at least questioned the notion. Still, it is worth noting that Adam's (and the reader's) preparation to go out into the world is not complete until Milton had Michael teach Adam that the Son is "thy Saviour and thy Lord" (12.544). Adam responds, converted, with a confession of faith: "Taught this by his example whom I now / Acknowledge my Redeemer ever blest" (12.572–73).

Teaching the whole of *Paradise Lost* and trying to contextualize it within the history of religion while respecting the various backgrounds and experiences that our students bring to the text have the advantage of being truer to Milton than doing the kind of expurgations that Milton attacked censors for in *Areopagitica*. An inclusive approach allows students to recognize how the liberal, even ecumenical, impulse in Milton conflicts with his ardent commitment to a kind of religious fundamentalism that compromised his instincts for tolerance. Such an approach does not preclude encouraging students to appreciate the rich beauty of the poem, Milton's capacious imagination, or his courage in exploring the big questions of faith and humanity. Finally, such an approach makes the classroom a place for dialogue and discovery about religious identity and interfaith relations as well as poetry.

NOTES

[1] See, e.g., Smith, *Is Milton*; Turner; Dobranski and Rumrich.

[2] All references to *Paradise Lost* are to Hughes's edition in his *Complete Poems and Major Prose*. I also use Hughes's edition in my teaching because of its extensive selections from the prose.

[3] See Rosenblatt 18–34, ch. 7, and esp. 227.

[4] See Guibbory, *Ceremony*, esp. 28–41.

[5] See Guibbory, *Christian Identity*. On attitudes toward Roman Catholicism and Catholics, see Marotti; A. Milton.

[6] On Milton and the Jews, see Rosenblatt; Shoulson; Brooks; Trubowitz, "Body Politics"; Guibbory, *Christian Identity*, chs. 2 and 8.

[7] See Guibbory, "England."

Teaching *Paradise Lost* and the Epic Tradition

Jessica Wolfe

I teach *Paradise Lost* in three different contexts: a survey of medieval and early modern British literature, a course devoted solely to Milton, and a comparative literature course on classical and Renaissance epic. In the first of these courses, my students arrive at *Paradise Lost* prepared to grasp Milton's distaste for medieval romance and his reverence for Spenser, but they are unfamiliar with many of Milton's classical forerunners and have a limited vocabulary for analyzing epic. So too in the Milton course, where students develop a deep understanding of Milton's early lyric works and of his political writings of the 1640s and 1650s but nonetheless arrive at their reading of *Paradise Lost* largely unfamiliar with the epic poets—Lucan and Lucretius, Davenant and Cowley—whose works help shape the political and religious conflicts of Milton's era. In my course on classical and Renaissance epic, by contrast, students are able to spot Homeric and Vergilian conventions in *Paradise Lost* and to appreciate Milton's debts to Edmund Spenser, Torquato Tasso, and Dante, but they struggle to understand how and why this seventeenth-century English Protestant epic transforms the tradition to which it belongs. I often find that a rather lengthy explication of Milton's political and religious views is necessary to help students grasp how those views motivate Milton's transformation of classical and early modern epic conventions.

Teaching *Paradise Lost* as participant—or rather agonist—in an epic tradition thus requires a twofold process: students must discern the similarities between Milton's poem and its epic antecedents before they can begin to grasp the various ways in which *Paradise Lost* departs from those models and to understand its underlying reasons for doing so. Paramount to this process is that students have a good grasp of the forms of literary imitation that Thomas Greene has termed "heuristic" and "dialectical"—imitation that deviates from, transforms, corrects, or challenges the models it emulates (39–41). In my course on classical and Renaissance epic, students already have a highly developed understanding of heuristic imitation by the time we arrive at *Paradise Lost*; we have seen how Vergil corrects both Homer and Lucretius by imitating them and how Tasso and Spenser rework episodes and conventions from classical epic—council scenes, moments of divine intervention, the *locus amoenus*—to support their own political or spiritual beliefs. In other courses, I prepare for our reading of *Paradise Lost* early in the semester by teaching the concepts of heuristic and dialectical imitation through lyric works—Thomas Wyatt's adaptations of Petrarch's *Canzoniere* serve well, as do the sonnets of Philip Sidney, John Donne, or even Milton, all of which can easily be shown to defy, resist, and transform aspects of a sonnet tradition whose conventions can be summarized more swiftly than those associated with heroic poetry. Such an introduction to literary imitation is crucial in allowing students to comprehend how *Paradise Lost* closely imitates its epic predecessors while deviating from and challenging its sources and models for reasons grounded in Milton's religious and political doctrines as well as in his conception of what, in *The Reason of Church Government*, he calls the "pattern of a Christian hero" (357). As students learn to analyze conventions such as invocations, similes, and ekphrases, they might consider not just what makes these values and conventions epic but also what makes them Miltonic: how, for instance, *Paradise Lost*'s reworkings of episodes from the *Aeneid* reveal Milton's distaste for imperial ideology, how its invocations support his anti-Trinitarianism, or how its epic similes might serve the poem's efforts to dramatize problems of linguistic and theological accommodation.

Paradise Lost *and the Epic Tradition:*
Four Introductory Lessons

Much of the groundwork for teaching *Paradise Lost* in the context of classical and early modern epic can be accomplished through four introductory lessons in my opening lecture, lessons that also serve to refresh students' memories of some of the key figures and narrative structures of works such as Homer's *Odyssey* and Vergil's *Aeneid*.

Lesson One.   The first of these lessons considers the epic tradition inherited by Milton to be plural and conflictive rather than monolithic, and it demonstrates *Paradise Lost*'s complex imitation of those traditions through a handful of examples drawn from the opening book of the poem. One of the most important points I drive home concerns the generic diversity of the poem: like many epics before it, *Paradise Lost* consists of a patchwork of different poetic kinds (georgic, pastoral, complaint, psalm, hymn) and also comprises multiple epic models—not just the "diffuse" and "brief" models distinguished in Milton's *Reason of Church Government* but also varieties of epic including the *nostos* or homecoming (represented chiefly by the *Odyssey*); hexameral epic (as represented by the Book of Genesis and by Du Bartas's *Sepmaines*); etiologies of discord or of civil war (represented by the *Iliad*, Lucan's *Pharsalia*, and Statius's *Thebaid*, among others); epic poems devoted to natural philosophy, such as Lucretius's *De rerum natura*; and dynastic epics, heroic tales of nation-building or of imperial or religious conquest (Vergil's *Aeneid*, Tasso's *Gerusalemme Liberata*, Camões's *Os Lusíados*). As students grasp the diversity of these and other epic models at Milton's disposal, they are better able to dispense with the idea that epic poems—and their heroes—possess a fixed set of characteristics and to discern the ways in which Milton mixes together and at times pits against each other different narrative patterns or moral problems associated with epic. Students are thus invited to consider what kind of epic Milton is writing in terms of his predecessors, as well as what kind of epic Milton is writing at particular moments of his poem: in the argument to book 1, whose theodicy is inspired partly by Zeus's self-defense in the opening lines of Homer's *Odyssey*; in Satan's foundation of a new empire, an ambition that aligns him with Aeneas; in book 7's account of creation, steeped in the hexameral tradition; or in the prophetic vista of the poem's final two books, whose epic qualities are derived from the narrative structure and scope of the Old Testament. The more that students are encouraged to regard *Paradise Lost* as belonging to a heterogeneous genre marked by mixture and conflict, the more fully will they understand how Milton exploits this generic mixture to dramatize competing values and beliefs, competing perspectives (divine and mortal), and competing views of human history.

Lesson Two. Once students grasp how *Paradise Lost* draws on multiple and variegated epic traditions, they are better able to analyze the poem's characteristic *contaminatio*—its tendency to allude simultaneously to multiple sources. In this second lesson on Milton's imitation of classical epic, students should be encouraged to resist simplistic equations between Milton's characters and their classical models. This objective is most easily accomplished in the opening two books of the poem, where the world of classical epic becomes a stage on which Satan plays many parts. Even those students with the most rudimentary knowledge of Homer and Vergil can make out a failed Aeneas in Satan's attempt to found a "nether empire" (2.296), a failed Achilles (or, a failed Rinaldo) in his complaints about his injured merit, and a failed Odysseus in his "circumspection" (2.414) and his rhetorical skill.[1] Students with exhaustive knowledge of even one epic antecedent to *Paradise Lost* will be able to discern a greater diversity of models available to Satan: within the space of five hundred lines in book 2, Milton casts Satan as a reckless and unrestrained Menelaus, a fierce yet obtuse Ajax, an Agamemnon struggling to maintain authority over his assembly, a flawed Sarpedon who fails to grasp the mutuality of honor, a Diomedes who refuses to acknowledge the value of cooperation, and a deviously "prudent" Odysseus who "prevent[s] all reply" by his council so that he may undertake the journey to Eden alone (2.467–68). My chief purpose in exposing the classical allusions enveloping Satan in the poem's opening books is to demonstrate how Milton bequeaths to his villain many of the traits associated with pagan heroism that he dislikes most vehemently—Satan's lust for honor and fame, the excessive worth Satan places on risk and adventure, and his political ambition.

Lesson Three. Milton's use of *contaminatio* in building Satan's character also helps illustrate the character's demonic powers of mimicry. Many of the epic roles in which Satan is cast are later assigned (albeit with crucial variations) to Adam, Eve, or the Son. If the Son, in his triumphant entry into battle at the end of book 6, resembles Achilles, or if Adam, in choosing his wife over immortality, emulates Odysseus, so too does their devilish rival. Particularly for students already acquainted with Spenser's *Faerie Queene*, Milton's tendency to repeat images *in bono et in malo* can provide a useful model for students to ponder the significance of recurring allusions. Such a model can also help students consider why *Paradise Lost* frequently provides both heavenly and demonic versions of epic conventions such as *consilia deorum*, epic catalogs, invocations, and similes, thus "inviting discriminations which are at once literary and moral," according to Barbara Lewalski (Paradise Lost *and the Rhetoric* 23).[2] In parsing the Homeric and Vergilian allusions in books 1 and 2, I stress the dynamism and diversity of the heroic models at Milton's disposal, models that change according to the poem's *peripeteias* or reversals of fortune. As he founds his new empire, Satan may resemble Aeneas, but his insatiable wrath later casts him as a darker version of Vergil's hero, Turnus's ireful executioner at the end of the poem. Similarly, Eve is cast successively as Venus, Dido, and Lavinia to Adam's Aeneas in books 4 through 10. In the poem's final lines, Adam is driven out of his native land and commanded to seek a new "place of rest" (12.647) in a passage that does not replicate the *Aeneid* so much as spiritually reinvigorate it for Milton's Christian audience.

Lesson Four.   Each of the three aforementioned lessons aims to teach students that Milton's conception of epic heroism, like his conception of generic form, is flexible and complex. The fourth and final lesson I lay out in my opening class asks students to consider how *Paradise Lost* dramatizes the challenges inherent in writing a Christian epic—how Milton's theological and moral beliefs may harmonize with his chosen genre in certain respects but conflict with it in others and how Milton makes certain epic conventions cooperate with the theological foundations of his poem.

My introduction to the intersection between classical and Christian elements in *Paradise Lost* is centered on book 4 of Augustine's *On Christian Doctrine*. A few passages help illustrate how Christian ethics and spirituality confound classical ideals of decorum, both because "the Christian orator is constantly dealing with great matters" (4.18–20) and because the language of Jesus and the apostles in the New Testament is subdued rather than grand or majestic, thus conceivably making the low style "[n]ot less but more heroic" than the grand style from Milton's perspective (*Paradise Lost* 9.14). Augustine thus helps make two key points about the rhetorical differences between *Paradise Lost* and classical epic: first, greatness of subject matter does not automatically require a decorum of corresponding grandeur in style, as classical rhetoricians had insisted; second, Milton discovers a distinctly Christian brand of heroism in the low style of characters such as Abdiel, who "nakedly wrestles error to the ground" in precisely the way described by Augustine (Auksi 124). Reference to Augustine's theories of Christian rhetoric help build a contrast between the three styles of classical oratory and the different situation in Milton's poem, where great subjects are often addressed in low styles and where Raphael's advice to Adam in 8.173 ("be lowly wise") might usefully be interpreted in terms of Milton's rhetorical principles.

Many teachers of undergraduates enlist the hermeneutic lessons contained in *Paradise Lost* to teach students how to read the work properly; this technique is especially useful for looking at classical allusions not as imitations per se but as vehicles for demonstrating the limited truth-value of pagan poetry in Milton's Christian universe. One passage in particular allows me to illustrate how *Paradise Lost* helps its readers move from the "shadowy types" found in pagan epic to their full revelation as Christian "truth" (12.303). The passage, at the end of book 1, concerns the rebel angels' account of

> Mulciber; and how he fell
> From heav'n, they fabled, thrown by angry Jove
> Sheer o'er the crystal battlements . . .
> . . . .
> . . . like a falling star,
> On Lemnos th'Aégean isle; thus they relate,
> Erring.   (1.740–47)

An allusion to *Iliad* 1.590–93, where Hephaestus is ejected from Olympus down to Lemnos, the myth becomes, in Milton's handling, a lie that absolves the rebel angels of responsibility for their fall, a fable that legitimates their disobedience as godly and heroic. Although this passage is especially powerful when presented as a parable of misreading, book 1 abounds with other classical allusions and with transformations of epic convention that are saturated with a similar kind of irony. Students who have trudged through the epic catalogs at *Iliad* 2.484 or *Aeneid* 7.641 take special delight in the way that Milton overturns the normal purpose of the epic catalog, preceding his list of fallen angels with the observation that "of their names in heav'nly records now / Be no memorial" (1.361–62).

Lessons for Subsequent Classes

In each subsequent class on *Paradise Lost*, I focus on an aspect or two of Milton's engagement with epic tradition in greater depth, often linking arguments from the introductory lessons to broader interpretive questions raised by the work. In many instances, these questions concern conventions — contrafactuals, council scenes, messenger angels, or epic similes — that Milton transforms into lessons about political and spiritual liberty, about the dangers of conformity, or about the importance of accommodating divine truths to the human intellect. In other instances, I focus on questions whose answers may be located in Milton's creative reuse of his epic models: his representation of Eden, his treatment of passions such as wrath and pity, his attitude toward typical epic virtues such as valor. Each new section of *Paradise Lost* that we approach foregrounds new issues; I do vary the issues, depending on the larger context and aims of the course, but those highlighted below have consistently provoked good discussions and incisive essays.

Books 1 and 2: Epic Similes and the Miltonic Art of Allusion.   Milton's similes, like those of Homer, Tasso, and Spenser, often emblematize the disparity between divine and mortal points of view, either by yoking together images that "don't fit exactly," as Christopher Ricks puts it (127), or, as Charles Martindale explains, by "intensify[ing] and complicat[ing]" the analogies they create (121).[3] By demonstrating the incompatibility of divergent perspectives, Milton's similes identify "our vision as fallen" (Grose 146) and reflect the "incertitude" of our condition by dramatizing the "suspended choices" that confound our fallen reason (Herman, *Destabilizing Milton* 183). These arguments help explain the abundance of similes in the opening two books of *Paradise Lost*, in which Milton repeatedly likens Satan to epic figures and images to underscore his ethical distance from those figures. I unravel these observations through the succession of similes that punctuate Satan's first speech, culminating in the "ponderous shield" and spear of 1.284–94. Resembling the moon as seen through Galileo's "optick glass," Satan's shield reflects his estrangement from heaven and also alerts the reader to the distortions inherent in Milton's representation of Satan as an epic hero complete with shield and spear: the "spotty globe" displays the moon not as it actually appears but as it appears with our limited vision and from our distant perspective. This passage can also serve to introduce the problem of accommodation in *Paradise Lost*, since the telescope is an instrument for meditating on the problem that mortal creatures cannot, as Milton writes in *De Doctrina Christiana*, grasp God "as he really is, but in such a manner as may be within the scope of our comprehensions" ([Patterson] 14: 33). In anticipation of the opening passage of book 9, where Milton identifies his poem as "[n]ot less but more heroic" than its epic predecessors (9.14), I also dwell on the ironies implicit in many of Milton's early comparisons between his characters and their epic forerunners, such as 2.1015–22, where Satan is described as "more endangered" than Jason or Ulysses on their sea voyages, or 4.714–15, where Eve appears "[m]ore lovely than Pandora, whom the gods / Endowed with all their gifts." Attention to the irony of these passages can shed light on Milton's commonplace technique of comparing small things to great: Eve may well be lovelier than Pandora, but the evils unleashed on the world after her fall are much worse than those that issued from Pandora's box. Satan may assume more "difficulty and labor" on his journey toward earth than do his classical models (2.1022), but only Satan remains under the delusion that his journey is more heroic than those undertaken by the heroes of the *Argonautica* or the *Odyssey*.

Books 2 and 3: Council and Deliberation.   The infernal and celestial council scenes in books 2 and 3 demonstrate Milton's manipulations of an especially rich and complex epic convention while revealing how *Paradise Lost* "refuses uncomplicated allegiances and values" in its transformation of epic models (Smith, "*Paradise Lost*" 263). I approach Milton's use of heavenly and infernal councils by examining how his engagement with this epic convention is shaped by contemporary politics. A brief foray into epic council scenes before we read *Paradise Lost* can help students account for the (seemingly) republican values and practices of Pandemonium. In my epic and romance class, I am lucky to have a roomful of students familiar with Tasso's Satan, who convenes an assembly of devils in canto 4 of the *Gerusalemme Liberata* to lament the "great mischance" that has befallen them and to concoct "new strategies" for remedying their situation (4.9, 12). The disparity between Tasso's infernal council and Milton's Pandemonium is immediately evident: the former is presided over by a "rabble of discordances" whose monstrosity and diversity threatens the ideals of political order embodied by Goffredo, captain of Tasso's Christian troops and the poem's allegorical instantiation of right reason (4.5, 9), whereas the latter is characterized not by discord but by a manufactured concord. Even in courses where I cannot fall back on *Gerusalemme*'s exemplary infernal council, I devote a few minutes of my class on book 2 to the argument that Milton transforms his infernal council to play down the threat posed by disagreement and factionalism and substitute for it the more dire threat of conformity.[4]

It is useful when teaching book 2 to remind students that the "Parliament of Hell" genre was a popular vehicle for royalist propaganda during the 1640s in which republican dissenters were presented as satanic antiheroes, "source[s] of schism" who infuse "contentious spirits" into their audiences to "stir up Faction, and Rebellion" (Achinstein, *Milton* 203, 179–88). After having grasped how Milton's Satan does quite the opposite—permitting dissent mainly to stifle or circumvent it—students are in a much better position to see Pandemonium as a distortion of Milton's republicanism, a caricature of his dearest republican ideals or, perhaps, an opportunity for him to meditate on the failures of republican government under the Rump Parliament, recalled in December 1659. Once students are taught to resist simple equations between the infernal council of book 2 and Milton's politics, it will be easier for them to resist interpreting the godly monarchy of book 3 as concealing royalist sympathies. A point that often eludes students is that, while unity prevails in book 3's heavenly council more than it appears to thrive in Pandemonium, the unity of Milton's heaven is produced by means other than devilish conformity of the rebel angels, its unity voluntary, not constrained, and rooted more in love than in fear.

Books 4 and 5: Gods and Mortals.   Attention to the striking transformations of epic tradition in books 4 and 5 helps foreground how certain distinctive elements of Milton's Eden (and, by extension, his view of prelapsarian nature) are designed to support the poem's spiritual or philosophical doctrines. These doctrines include Milton's use of the angel Raphael as a divine intercessor; his monism, as articulated chiefly through Raphael's explication of the scale of nature; and his representation of the Edenic landscape. Most epic poems, both pagan and Christian, have divine intercessors: from Iris and Hermes in the *Iliad* and *Odyssey* to the angel who rescues Guyon at the beginning of *Faerie Queene* 2.8, angels and messenger gods (from the Greek *aggelos*) mediate between gods and mortals. Milton adapts this convention to serve his theology of accommodation: although only after the fall do we feel the fully tragic consequences of the fact that "to God is no access / Without mediator" (12.239–40), Milton's Raphael is appointed not simply to relay messages (as with the messenger gods of classical epic) or to intervene in ways that might compromise Adam and Eve's liberty (as sometimes appears to be the case with divine intercessors in Christian epic) but rather to accommodate "spiritual to corporal forms" and to explain the "invisible exploits" of angels in a manner comprehensible to "human sense" (5.573, 565). In this respect, Milton's angels function somewhat like his similes, demonstrating both the continuum and the disparity between the poem's divine and mortal perspectives. *Paradise Lost*'s reliance on Homer's and Vergil's characterizations of Odysseus, Achilles, and Aeneas, each depicted in their respective poems as godlike men or as descended from a divine lineage, may help students unravel Milton's representation of Adam in book 4. Adam's "hyacinthine locks" (4.301), inherited from Odysseus at *Odyssey* 6.231 and 23.158, where Athena enhances his natural appearance by making his tresses "flow in curls like the hyacinth flower," remind the reader that Adam's physical beauty, like that of his Homeric ancestor, derives from a divine source. Some attention to book 4's many echoes of the earthly paradises of Homer's Alkinous, Tasso's Armida, and Spenser's Acrasia may also help students grasp how Eden both draws and deviates from its chief epic sources to support the Miltonic values of labor, moderation, marital harmony, and the intrinsic dignity of bodies and their appetites. Depending on which texts my students have read earlier in the semester, I might contrast Eve's nakedness to Homer's Nausicaa or to the wrestling maidens of Spenser's Bower of Bliss; I might prompt students to consider whether the coincidence of "spring and autumn" in Milton's Eden, which enjoys "[b]lossoms and fruits at once" (5.394, 4.148), carries the same significance as it does in the earthly paradises that serve as Milton's models, which emphasize abundance and ease at the expense of Miltonic values such as labor, vigilance, and trial.

Book 6: Valor and Strength.   Students are often vexed by Milton's contrast between Adam, "[f]or contemplation . . . and valor formed," and Eve, made for "softness . . . and sweet attractive grace" (4.297–98). One way to complicate Milton's distinction between Adam and Eve, both made in the "image of their glorious Maker" even though "their sex not equal seemed," is to point out that, in the counterepic realm of *Paradise Lost*, neither contemplation nor valor are necessarily what they are cracked up to be. The war in heaven can challenge students to rethink Milton's description of Adam's valor as a distinctly problematic virtue. I like to set forth the counterepic (and, in places, the explicitly mock epic) features of book 6 by placing the war in heaven in the context of passages elsewhere in Milton's poem that undermine an implicitly pagan value system that prizes valor or physical strength over Miltonic values such as obedience. Although book 1 contrasts the "rage" (1.553) motivating the rebel angels with the "[d]eliberate valor" (1.554) that once encouraged "heroes old" to "highth of noblest temper" (1.552), valor proves to have no heroic value unless it is "deliberate"—that is, unless it is the consequence of rational deliberation (or "contemplation")—suggesting that Adam's key virtues are worthless, and perhaps even dangerous, unless tethered to each other. One of the ironies of Milton's war in heaven is that the rebel angels discover that the rules of engagement are radically different from those that govern the battle scenes (both earthly and Olympian) of Homer, Vergil, and other classical poets. Not only do Milton's "elect / Angels" fight for different reasons (6.374–75)—they are "contented with their fame in heav'n" and "[s]eek not the praise of men" (6.375–76)—but the rebel angels also realize that nothing "avails / Valor or strength, though matchless" (6.456–57), since no amount of physical force can defeat their enemy or eliminate their own pain. It is instructive to connect Milton's attention to the limitations of physical strength and valor with the concluding lines of Michael's prophecy, which anticipates the triumph of good over evil "by small / Accomplishing great things, by things deemed weak / Subverting worldly strong" (12.566–68). Equally instructive is to use Milton's critical reappraisal of valor and fortitude during the war in heaven as a vehicle for getting students to consider whether, and to what extent, the episode should be interpreted allegorically: is it a "fight / Unspeakable" (6.296–97) that Raphael nonetheless narrates with epic conventions to accommodate the spiritual to corporal forms? If the combatants of Milton's war in heaven are understood as wearing spiritual rather than literal armor, then strength avails little to those who fail, in the words of Spenser's Una, to "[a]dd faith unto your force" (1.19.3), a formula Milton spells out explicitly in the final book of *Paradise Lost*, where Michael advises Adam that "suffering for truth's sake / Is fortitude to highest victory" (12.569–70).

Although Milton's Son is critical of Satan and his troops, who "by strength / . . . measure all, of other excellence / Not emulous" (6.820–22), Milton's war in heaven does not overturn all the values of its pagan sources. Abdiel's "single" stand against the "revolted multitudes" (6.30, 31), as well as the Son's later entry into the battle, constitute Milton's answer to *aristeia*, the heroic excellence displayed through single combat that may also shape Eve's insistence on solitary trial in book 9. Milton's war in heaven provokes many of the same questions and objections as did its Greek and Roman models for Milton's contemporaries: a battle between immortal opponents who are evenly matched in strength runs the risk of becoming either tedious or absurd as it hangs "long time in even scale" (6.245). Moreover, Milton's war in heaven is self-consciously indecorous: his adversaries have a predilection for flyting matched only by the combatants of the *Iliad*, and their "wind / Of airy threats" (6.282–83) threatens to erode the gravity of the scene, as does the "derision" of the Father laughing at the "vain designs" (5.736, 737) of his enemies, a scornful jocularity that has classical as well as biblical antecedents. Milton's conception of a God who laughs, when studied in comparison with Zeus in the *Iliad* or the God of Psalm 2, provokes heady debates in my class over whether such laughter is intended to denote God's contempt for his subjects, his cruel indifference, or whether Milton's conception of a God that laughs helps justify Milton's recourse to humor, both in his controversial writings and even in certain moments of *Paradise Lost*.

Books 9 and 10: Wrath and Pity, Shame and Repentance.   One especially compelling narrative for students to trace as they work through *Paradise Lost* is the progression of attitudes toward the epic passions of wrath and pity. These passions are set against each other in relief at *Paradise Lost* 3.405–06, where they are imagined as opposing (and yet harmonious) points on the emotional compass comprised by the Father and Son. Although the *Aeneid* is clearly a key model for Milton, I also like to invoke Rinaldo in Tasso's *Gerusalemme*, whose *sdgeno*, or scorn, is represented as a "fierce fighter on Reason's part" (16.34), a passion distinct from and superior to the *rabbia*, or rage, embodied in Argante, just as the scorn of Milton's Abdiel and the derision of his God are legitimate in ways that the anger of Satan or the fallen Adam are not. Homer's Achilles is another touchstone for exploring the range of attitudes toward the passions in *Paradise Lost*: his ruling passion—a wrath that at long last gives way to pity or shame (*aidôs*)—helps explain the broad ethical spectrum occupied by Achilles throughout his various incarnations in *Paradise Lost*, from the most malevolent (Satan's wrath, his sense of injured merit, and his pretense of self-sacrifice) to the most sanctified (the Son's divine pity and his virtuous self-sacrifice, initiated by his Achilles-like, triumphant reentry into battle) to the most mixed (Adam's foolish self-sacrifice, his Achilles-like rage, and his ultimate, ennobling capitulation to pity).[5] This splintering of Achilles into discrete and divergent aspects demonstrates what is both attractive and dangerous to Milton about the passion of wrath, a point worth establishing before the class arrives at the opening passage of book 9, which I present not as an assault on romance (or epic) per se but as a defense of the legitimate "[a]nger and just rebuke" (9.10) of Milton's God as distinct from the gratuitous or motiveless anger that fuels his literary models—the inexplicable ire of Homer's Neptune and Vergil's Juno, the disproportionate wrath of the disespoused Turnus, or the tedious havoc of Arthurian romance. Milton's justification of righteous anger and just rebuke is counterbalanced, however, by the "mutual accusation" into which Adam and Eve descend after the fall (9.1187); their squabbling comes to resemble a more tragic version of the constant bickering between Jupiter and Juno, the Olympian couple with whom they have already been compared, in a more favorable analogy, at 4.500–01.

Book 12: Inspiration, Dream, and Prophecy.   Most students easily grasp the connection between the Miltonic narrator and his sightless counterparts of antiquity, the "Blind Thamyris and blind Maeonides" (3.35), who are invoked at the beginning of book 3 as guides in the poet's ascent from the darkness of Pandemonium to the "Sovran vital lamp" of heaven (3.22). But the invocations to books 1, 3, and 7 also shed light on the difference between Milton's "Heav'nly Muse" (1.6) and the classical muses invoked by Homer, Vergil, and Ovid. Milton voices many of the same anxieties articulated by the Vergilian narrator as his muse guides him to "venture down / The dark descent, and up to reascend, / Though hard and rare" (3.19–21), an imitation of *Aeneid* 6.126–29 that captures the spiritual dangers of being an earthly guest in heavenly climes. Yet Milton distinguishes the "empty dream" (7.39) afforded by the classical Muses from his own source of inspiration, a "celestial Light" that "[s]hine[s] inward" (3.51, 52) to allow the poet to "see and tell / Of things invisible to mortal sight" (3.54–55). The truth-value that the Miltonic poet places on the source of his poetic inspiration is one of several ways that *Paradise Lost* differs in its treatment of prophecy and revelation from most of its classical and early modern epic counterparts save perhaps Tasso, whose true prophets disclose "the deep foreknowledge of God's hidden plan" and whose heroes receive dreams that "reveal . . . heaven's high decree" (4.18, 4.2). Like so many epic poems before it, *Paradise Lost* is preoccupied with the status of dreams, which can be either deceptive (Agamemnon's dream in *Iliad* 2; the "fit false dreame" created by Archimago at *Faerie Queene* 1.43.9) or genuine (Patroclus's appearance in Achilles's dream; Creusa's appearance in Aeneas's dream). Students find it fascinating to explore how Milton might be responding to Penelope's "two gates of sleep" speech at *Odyssey* 19.560–67, adapted by Vergil at *Aeneid* 6.893–96, as he describes Eve's dreams at 5.28–94 and at 12.610–15, the former an "uncouth dream" (which according to Adam is the "[w]ild work" of the "mimic fancy" [5.98, 112, 110]), and the latter a divine communication that provides evidence that "God is also in sleep, and dreams advise" (12.611). Despite the many debts to the epic tradition in the first ten books of *Paradise Lost*, when Michael removes the "film" from Adam's eyes so that he may behold the future effects of the fall (11.412), the poem shifts into a prophetic mode that marks a definitive turn away from the interpretive ambiguities and uncertainties that characterize the prophecies, predictions, omens, and dreams of Milton's epic forerunners.

NOTES

[1] All references to *Paradise Lost* are to the Norton Critical edition of the poem edited by Elledge. I taught this edition of the poem from 1998 until 2005, when the revised Norton, edited by Teskey, superseded it.

[2] The concept of *in bono et in malo* imitation is derived from Augustine, *On Christian Doctrine* 3.25.35–36.

[3] On Milton's use of similes, see also Fish, *Surprised by Sin* 22–28.

[4] On Milton's use of the infernal council, see Hammond 11; Achinstein, *Milton*, ch. 5 (177–223); Pecheux; O. Moore; Lewalski, Paradise Lost *and the Rhetoric* 115.

[5] On Satan as a parody or perversion of Achilles, see Harding 46–47; Rumrich, *Matter* 28; Steadman, *Milton and the Paradoxes* 46. On the Son as an Achilles figure, see Quint 48; Lewalski, Paradise Lost *and the Rhetoric* 61, 126–28. On Adam as an Achilles figure, see Mueller 301–02; Revard, "Milton."

Clues to the Classical Tradition

Abraham Stoll

Milton's classical allusions display the richly interwoven texture of *Paradise Lost*. Following the clues leads the reader across centuries, through multiple texts, and to an appreciation of the way Milton's poem results from his intimate and foundational reading in the classical tradition. So Satan's first words in the poem carry us back to the *Aeneid*: "If thou beest he; but O how fall'n! How changed" (1.84) recalls Aeneas's reaction to the ghost of Hector, "Ah me! what aspect was his! how changed from that Hector who returns after donning the spoils of Achilles" (2.274–75).[1] Hector is ghastly, torn from being dragged by Achilles, "hair matted with blood, and bearing those many wounds he gat around his native walls" (2.277–79), and Milton's allusion implies that Beelzebub and Satan have been similarly deformed by the Son in his chariot. But the allusion can do much more, for example by aligning Satan with Aeneas in this key moment. Aeneas's position is one of ignorance and surprise: he does not know what has happened to Hector and is repulsed by what he sees. Hector, furthermore, visits the sleeping Aeneas precisely as the Greeks are climbing from the belly of the horse to open the gates of Troy—suggesting, perhaps, Satan's obliviousness toward his own inevitable defeat. Or, more provocatively, it can be noted that Hector urges Aeneas to leave the city and to seek the destined walls of Rome—suggesting that Satan is at the beginning of his own heroic journey, toward his own walled destination. These and many more associations gather around the intensely dramatic appearance of Hector, and they make their way into *Paradise Lost* by the combining power of allusion.

Allusions operate in more complicated ways than students first suspect. Milton's allusions bring into the reader's ken not just an isolated moment but also the narrative surrounding that moment, as well as character and poetic effects. In addition, allusions raise important interpretive questions about what has been imitated and what changed, what conflated and what misread.[2] I alert students to the expansive possibilities of allusion with an analogy: the hyperlink. A single word on a Web site opens to another page, which has an entirely different feel and architecture and context. This new page can be explored top to bottom, and whatever is found can be read back into the original site or can lead to a third site and beyond—though the good reader will eventually follow the back button home. As links structure the Web, so allusions structure a tradition, or a set of intellectual habits, that are at the heart of Milton's poetry. Milton could not think through problems or sit down to write a poem outside these habits. *Of Education* captures the situation: simply glancing through Milton's short treatise, crammed with classical authors, reveals the extent to which the classical tradition was the education of the day. Typical of humanist pedagogy, Milton recommends memorizing and reciting epics, tragedies, and orations, which, if they are "solemnly pronounced with right accent and grace, as might be taught, would endue them even with the spirit and vigor of Demosthenes or Cicero, Euripides or Sophocles" (977). The recall and recitation of the language is bound up in accessing the spirit of these authors, and so it is natural that classical texts would emerge from the blind poet's memory and lips to form the very fabric of his poetry.

Every good edition of *Paradise Lost* will alert students to classical allusions, and so it is easy to ask them to pick one allusion and follow the link to the original text. But the excitement of allusion depends a great deal on uncharted discovery—on making the leap from text to text not merely because the footnote or professor has said so but because the reader has felt the contact through his or her own reading and memory. As much as we would like to begin a study of *Paradise Lost* with Homer and Vergil or to assume a familiarity with Ovid and Hesiod, these poets do not fit easily onto the syllabus, nor are they usually familiar to students. And so Milton's allusions too often become a matter of looking over a footnote and perhaps consulting an encyclopedia of mythology—an arid process that leaves students outside the tradition, likely to feel frustration and indifference rather than the pleasures of poetic association. The key challenge in teaching the classical tradition in *Paradise Lost* is to find ways to assist students in getting beyond the encyclopedias, to offer them a clue to a more substantial engagement with the classics, so that they can begin to feel the "spirit and vigor" that Milton the pedagogue pursues.

Ovid is especially useful for this, because the *Metamorphoses* is an episodic poem. Moving from Eve's famous awakening (4.449–91) to Ovid's tale of Narcissus (1: 3.316–510), the student finds a brief story that can be read and understood on its own—no summaries or encyclopedias needed. But Ovid's text is hardly simple. Not just about reflections in a pool, it tells of Narcissus's strangely intertwined relationship with Echo, quickly complicating students' typically unsympathetic notions of narcissism. This dysfunctional relationship can be read back onto Adam and Eve in rich ways, including what the late Earl Miner once pointed out to me in conversation, that if Eve is Narcissus, then Adam is Echo. It is also suggestive that the tale really begins with the story of how prophetic powers were given to Tiresias, with whom Milton compared himself in an earlier episode (3.36). There are many more points of contact between *Paradise Lost* and *Metamorphoses* (see DuRocher), including Milton's obsession with Orpheus as a figure for his own poetic efforts. Orpheus's ascent from the underworld is echoed in Milton's second invocation (3.13–21) and Orpheus's bloody death in the third (7.32–39). Students can be directed to *Metamorphoses* 10.1–85 and 11.1–84, skipping the long song by Orpheus that lies between these passages. Orpheus repeatedly comes to Milton's mind in his musings on the poet's craft, not just in the invocations, but in much of his early writings ("L'Allegro," lines 145–50; "Il Penseroso," lines 105–08; *Ad Patrem*, lines 50–55; "Lycidas," lines 58–63).

Already the simplicity of a single episode has slipped away, as is fitting for poetry that embraces mutability and multiplicity—getting a sense of how Milton
ranges through the classical tradition demands multiple sources. This necessity
is evident in Eve, who elicits from Milton an explosion of comparisons. In addition to Narcissus, she is variously aligned with Pandora (4.708–19), Venus
(5.377–83), Pomona (9.393–96), and Circe (9.518–22), among other figures
present, even in these passages. What do these parallels add to our understanding of Eve? And why did Milton use so many? To give students the opportunity
to discover their own answers, I direct them to the following sources: for Pandora, Hesiod's *Works and Days*, lines 42–105; for Venus, Ovid's *Heroides*, letters
16–17; for Pomona, Ovid's *Metamorphoses* 14.623–771; and for Circe, Homer's
Odyssey, book 10. I have selected these passages not because Milton necessarily alludes to these texts but because they offer an accessible entrance into the
stories. As the source texts multiply, I find it helps to be very organized and to
provide students with a photocopied packet or collated and precise line numbers for each assignment's background texts.

Moving beyond exact textual parallels, students can attempt generalizations
about the classical tradition. One important theme, for example, is the warrior ethos. From the outset, the Hector allusion aligns Satan with Aeneas and
Satan's project with the epic quest. Satan is then repeatedly cast as an epic
hero, as when in flight he is compared with Ulysses steering through Scylla and
Charybdis (2.1019–20). The attractive Satan of *Paradise Lost* gains considerable
charisma from his representation as a classical warrior, as do the fallen angels in
books 1 and 2 when they are cataloged in the manner of the warriors in Homer's
catalog of ships (*Iliad* [Murray] 2.484–877). The opening of Homer's catalog
(2.484–93) and the description of the Trojans and Hector (2.807–23) can give
students a sense of the martial grandeur that lies behind Satan's troops when
they march "in guise / Of warriors old with ordered spear and shield" (1.564–
65). The fallen angels' weapons are the spear and shield (for Satan's weapons,
see 1.283–96)—specifically not the bows and slingshots of the Bible. But for
all this pomp, war and its trappings are fully parodied throughout the war in
heaven, as when the angels' armor itself causes the angels to topple before the
apostates' cannons (6.584–97). What is most Iliadic in book 6 is also most absurd. Eventually Milton declares his argument "[n]ot less but more heroic than
the wrath / Of stern Achilles" (9.14–15), making clear the poem's assertion of
Christian, in place of classical, heroism. So Christians will "arm / With spiritual
armor, able to resist / Satan's assaults" (12.490–92).[3]

A second theme that provides a broad perspective on the classical tradition
is creation. Milton's primary source is the Genesis creation story, of course, but
Paradise Lost contains several fascinating elements from Hesiod's *Theogony*
that subtend the poem like traces from a repressed, chthonic past. Most boldly,
when Satan leaves hell and encounters chaos and night (2.959–67) the poem
swerves into the pre-Olympian cosmos described in *Theogony* (lines 104–210).
Here is a precedent for Milton's decision to include chaos as matter that exists

before creation, contradicting the ex nihilo creation of Genesis. And here is a creation that unfolds not through the fiat of God but through the actions of Earth and through cycles of incest, castration, patricide, and war. The contrast with Genesis is profound and leads students to consider what the Judeo-Christian tradition has done by moving creation away from such wild and bloody origins and, then, what Milton is doing by reinscribing them in *Paradise Lost*. Hesiod's warring Titans are an important precedent for the rebellious angels as well (see Forsyth 30–35); similarly, Percy Bysshe Shelley later compared Satan with Prometheus (*Prometheus Unbound*). To develop the contrast between Genesis and *Theogony*, I point students to a short but very shocking passage in Friedrich Nietzsche's *The Birth of Tragedy*, in which Nietzsche contrasts the active sin of the "Promethean myth" with the passive morality of the fall in the "Semitic myth" (70–72; ch. 9).

The presence of the Greek cosmogony, despite its radically different world-view, suggests that Milton cannot and will not imagine poetry outside the classical tradition's strong precedents. The structural elements of epic in *Paradise Lost* in particular make the point that, for Milton and his contemporaries, great poetry looks like epic. The French neoclassical critic René Le Bossu insists, for example, that "[m]achines are to be made use of all over, since Homer and Virgil do nothing without them" (216). Milton's angels would seem to be the machinery he needs—a neat blending of epic form with Christian theology. Among the many comings and goings of angels, the connection to machinery is made most clearly when Raphael is compared with Mercury, or "Maia's son" (5.285), a scene that can be closely compared with *Aeneid* 4.219–82. In addition to machinery, catalogs, and epic similes, the poem's structural debt to the classical tradition is most prominent in its use of invocations. Milton's invocation in book 1 can be interestingly compared with the opening invocations of the *Iliad*, *Odyssey*, and *Aeneid*. But Milton departs from these primary epic models in crafting three more major invocations, each at the head of a book. After its first, the *Odyssey* has no further invocations, and the *Iliad* and *Aeneid* offer only brief invocations in the midst of the action (e.g., *Iliad* 11.218–20 and 16.112–13; *Aeneid* 7.37–45 and 9.525–28). Milton's invocations are also far more personal than those of his epic models, concerned with his own life and his poetics. Such an expansion of the invocation, in line numbers, in prominence, and in scope, is an unmistakable announcement of Milton's epic intentions and the fact that *Paradise Lost* is a neoclassical poem.

But it is important to rescue the term *neoclassicism* from its usual association with restrictive rules and slavish imitation. Although Le Bossu and others such as Dryden may speak as if writing good poetry is a matter of gathering up the remains of Homer and Vergil, Milton's neoclassicism is a far more natural, vivid, and unstable influence on his poetry. Having recognized the rich presence of the classical tradition in Milton's memory and pedagogy and its shaping influence on his poetic imagination, we can see neoclassicism as a part of Milton's poetic DNA—and as a part that offers as many challenges as it solves. Spirited critical debates go back to Italians such as Castelvetro, Tasso, and Mazzoni, who Milton cites in *Of Education* (977). But one poem very near to *Paradise Lost* neatly captures the creative tensions behind the neoclassical project: Abraham Cowley's *Davideis* (1656). This retelling of the David story in Vergilian style is a good, though unfinished, poem that was published while Milton was composing *Paradise Lost*. What makes it an especially fascinating text, and very useful in the classroom as a means of exploring neoclassicism, is that Cowley attaches his own explanatory notes to his poem, notes that reveal the complex critical positions that lie behind his, and by extension Milton's, epic. To the first line of verse Cowley attaches a note that defends his use of an invocation:

> The custom of beginning all *Poems*, with a *Proposition* of the whole work, and an *Invocation* of some God for his assistance to go through with it, is so Solemnly and religiously observed by all the ancient *Poets*, that though I could have found out a better way, I should not (I think) have ventured upon it. But there can be, I believe, none better; and that part, of the *Invocation*, if it became a *Heathen*, is no less *Necessary* for a *Christian Poet*.   (24n1)

The muse is here called "some God," marking rather dismissively that he is not the Christian God. A look at the genealogy of the Muses in the opening of Hesiod's *Theogony* (lines 1–102) reveals that they come from a fully polytheistic world. For Cowley to invoke them is to risk casting his poem, at its very outset, into such polytheism. Later in the invocation Cowley is explicit in his desire to win poetry back for Christianity, declaring, "Too long the *Muses-Lands* have *Heathen* bin" (5). And yet, despite the determination to be a Christian poet, Cowley, in his note, cannot imagine a better way to begin a poem. Cowley's anxiety is legible, but so too is the overriding influence of the epic form on his poetic imagination.

Milton is similarly equivocal, whether invoking the Spirit or light or Urania, or whether it is "the meaning, not the name" that he calls (7.5). And he is most tentative in his last invocation, in which he suggests the possibility that his inspiration comes not from a Muse but rather entirely from himself: "if all be mine, / Not hers who brings it nightly to my ear" (9.46–47). Milton, like Cowley, invokes the Muse both vigorously and uneasily—a complexity that is born of the seventeenth-century conflict between neoclassicism and the movement for Christian poetry. With sincere theological purposes, Milton rewrites the Bible. But he does so with literary conventions that were, after all, forged in the polytheism of ancient Greece. Scholars have often emphasized the remarkable syncretism of the medieval and Renaissance periods—the ability to blend the classical tradition with Christianity, resulting in, for example, images of Jupiter dressed as a monk and clutching a cross (Seznec 161). But by the time we arrive at Milton, in an English century shaped by Reformation iconoclasm and efforts at ever purer forms of monotheism, we find a poetics that is far more confrontational and far less integrative than syncretism.

Syncretism is readily found in *Paradise Lost*, in scenes such as when Raphael is like Mercury or in the many allusions and poetic structures discussed here. But a more agonistic poetics regularly surfaces to do battle with this integrative approach. The famous example of Mulciber establishes at the outset of the poem Milton's complicated relationship with the classical tradition. Mulciber closes the catalog of gods, which is modeled after the epic form. His fall from the heavens, so familiar from the classical tradition (*Iliad* 1.590–95), aligns neatly with the angels' fall, reinforcing the syncretic assertion that the fallen angels are to be identified with the polytheistic gods. Until it suddenly does not:

> [Mulciber] with the setting sun
> Dropped from the zenith like a falling star,
> On Lemnos th' Aegean isle: thus they relate,
> Erring   (1.744–47)

This sudden rejection, like Cowley's note, both allows the presence of the god and, in a subsequent action, distances the poem from it. I teach this passage not as a temptation of the reader but as a sign of the serious negotiations that go into Milton's use of the classical tradition.

NOTES

[1] All quotations of Milton's works are from Kerrigan, Rumrich, and Fallon's Modern Library edition, *The Complete Poetry and Essential Prose of John Milton*.

[2] For a recent consideration of allusion, see Machacek.

[3] For a more complete discussion of heroism, see Blessington 1–18.

Paradise Lost and
Milton's Revolutionary Prose and Poetry

Thomas Fulton

William Blake's famous statement that "Milton was of the Devils party without knowing it"[1] represents a problem encountered by all students of *Paradise Lost*: just why did Milton cast Satan and his compeers as political revolutionaries? The rebel angels revolt "against the throne and monarchy of God" just as Milton had revolted against the monarchy of England, using language at times so close to Milton's own that critics have offered a wide range of readings to explain it. Some have argued that Milton's satanic self-casting revealed a now repentant royalist, while others, such as William Empson, thought that Milton "identified Satan with a part of his own mind" (*Milton's God* 6).[2] Others still—especially historicists in recent decades—have sought to recover specific parliamentarian resonances in Satan and his troops.[3] These scenes of satanic rebellion represent only part of the epic's rich engagement with English revolutionary history, since the story of the fall and its aftermath also derive from Milton's literary inventions—as well as his experience—during the civil war years.

Although the tumultuous events of civil war history contribute profoundly to the development of Milton's ideas and representations, and a large part of Milton's literary output derives from the civil war period, this portion of his corpus has a relatively small place in most courses on Milton. The problem, simply, is time. A semester's course providing good coverage of Milton's early poetry, his wartime verse, and his major Restoration poems has little space left for much more than *Areopagitica* and perhaps sections of *The Doctrine and Discipline of Divorce*, *The Tenure of Kings and Magistrates*, and *Eikonoklastes*—not to mention *On Christian Doctrine*. To add to this reading sufficient historical scholarship to explain the English civil war as well as some examples of Milton criticism can be impossible. It is helpful, even necessary at times, to provide nutshell accounts of civil war history, but without substantial immersion (or another course in history) students may find themselves struggling with nebulous questions about Milton's engagement with an ever-changing context. Striking this balance is perhaps the greatest challenge in reducing Milton's literary career into a semester, and yet to take the easy way out and omit the civil war prose—once a common practice—diminishes the value of the polemical texts as well as students' ability to help read the epic that inevitably occupies a substantial portion of the course.

The revolutionary prose and poetry can be effectively incorporated by emphasizing close textual analysis of a selection of texts, allowing the problem of context to emerge as needed (see Hausknecht; Herman, "Milton"; Leonard, "*Areopagitica*"; and Skerpan-Wheeler). After working through a few of these wartime or commonwealth texts individually, a great deal can then be achieved through a comparative close reading of Milton's language in the revolutionary context and as it reappears in *Paradise Lost*. This kind of comparison allows students to analyze an author's self-allusions and his reuse of ideas that had been formative early in his career. The comparison of epic with political prose also touches at the very center of concerns that have preoccupied literary criticism as a whole: does poetry transcend history, and do we use different interpretive methods in reading expository prose from what we use in understanding poetry? Once meaning is determined in the seemingly straightforward context of polemical prose—emphasis on *seemingly*—does it operate in the same fashion when it is set in a work of high art? Does poetry have an argument or even a political cause?

To make this kind of comparative study between prose and poetry effective, not only in general courses or advanced seminars on Milton but also in British literature surveys,[4] I have students read some of the prose most pertinent to the epic on separate occasions, in the brief weeks between "Lycidas" (1637) and *Paradise Lost* (1667). I spend two days on *Areopagitica* (1644) and then step slightly out of sequence to teach the first half of *The Doctrine and Discipline of Divorce* (1643/1644).[5] Treating the wartime poetry as part of this section of Milton's career—rather than separating it according to genre or date of publication—allows for a more integral discussion of the relation of these genres to their methods of conveying meaning. It also allows us to explore what relevance this relation has to their material forms (printed pamphlet, manuscript poems). The exploration of the political poems in their wartime context, surrounded by polemical prose, also provides more solid ground for discussions of *Paradise Lost*. The manuscript poem to the Oxford librarian John Rouse and sonnets 11 and 12 show Milton in a very different light from the polemical prose, as does sonnet 15, "On the Lord General Fairfax at the Siege of Colchester," which urges Fairfax to take revolutionary action. The extraordinary contrast between the positive wartime image of London as the "mansion house of liberty" in *Areopagitica* (957) and the "accursed upheaval of our citizens" described in the poem to Rouse (245) suggests the highly rhetorical and contextual quality of Milton's writing. Psalms 80–88, written in April 1648, provide a valuable preparation for *Paradise Lost*, since Milton here translates the Bible toward a political end and shows his embellishments to the original in italics—italics that are, of course, taken away in his embellishment of the biblical account in the epic.[6] The italics recall the use of italics in the King James Version, in which the translators italicized some English words that were not precisely in the Greek and Hebrew but are added to serve an ancillary or a minor grammatical function. Milton's italicized additions are much more substantive. We then turn to read selections from *The Tenure of Kings and Magistrates* (1649) and *Eikonoklastes* (1649). When we later read *Paradise Lost*, students turn again to specific passages in these texts to draw a comparison.[7]

Milton had seen himself in the civil war years as engaged in a tripartite agenda of reform, in which his writings were concerned, as he wrote looking back in 1654, with "three varieties of liberty," "ecclesiastical liberty, domestic or personal liberty, and civil liberty" (*Second Defense* 1094). These categorical divisions fit Milton's seemingly occasional prose with surprising neatness: of his twenty-one printed polemics written between 1641 and the Restoration in 1660, six are on ecclesiastical liberty, mostly composed in the first two years of this period; six on domestic or personal liberty including *Areopagitica*, the most categorically difficult to define; and nine, all written after *Areopagitica*, on civil liberty. A perfect introduction to this history, *Areopagitica* fits most of Milton's categories of liberty: he writes at the outset that the freedom to express one's grievances in the "commonwealth" is the "utmost bound of civil liberty attained, that wise men look for" (928), presenting his argument as an integral part of a package of political liberties toward which he assumes his audience aspires. The now common phrase "civil liberty" was at that point just gaining currency—this is the first attested use in the *Oxford English Dictionary* and among the first occurrences in Milton.[8] "Liberty," used sixteen times in the tract and only twice as "Christian liberty," takes on a form that exceeds the preconditions for free worship, a central argument of *Areopagitica*. In Milton's encomiastic republican terms, England is "foremost in the achievements of liberty" (935).

"Liberty" is also a keyword in *Paradise Lost*, appearing a dozen times, along with "freedom," which appears eleven times, and "free," some forty-eight times. The most central use of "freedom" that closely connects *Areopagitica* with *Paradise Lost* is the freedom to choose, the cognitive freedom essential to Milton's conception of the state of humanity. Milton uses this concept to argue radically in *Areopagitica* that the fall was in fact a fortunate event—or, in technical terms, a *felix culpa* (see Poole, *Milton*). This argument emerges most evidently in the passage that challenges readers to rethink the implications of the fall: "Many there be that complain of divine providence for suffering Adam to transgress. Foolish tongues! When God gave him reason, he gave him freedom to choose, for reason is but choosing; he had been else a mere artificial Adam . . . God therefore left him free" (944). The present participle in "reason is but choosing," which, like that in "knowledge in the making" or the "building," "cutting," "squaring," and "hewing" that Milton describes England to be engaged in, stresses the incomplete and progressive condition of human understanding (Norbrook, *Writing* 135). Here Milton is embellishing and giving Edenic context to his earlier claim in the tract that God gave humanity "the gift of reason to be his own chooser" (1006). This description of reason ultimately derives from the *Nicomachean Ethics*, in which Aristotle describes the nature of true knowledge acquisition in specific metaphysical terms. For him, this intellectual choice is a precondition of true reason, in which apprehension is uninfluenced by passions like anger or physical needs like appetite. As Aristotle writes, "choice is not common to irrational creatures, . . . but appetite and anger are . . . appetite relates to the pleasant and the painful, choice neither to the painful nor to the pleasant. . . . For this reason too, [choice] cannot be opinion. . . . [W]e choose what we best know to be good, but we opine what we do not quite know" (968).[9] Aristotle's conception of choice helps students think through Milton's eventual dramatization of the vital moment — or moments — of choice in the epic, where Eve's "choice" to eat the fruit seems to be depicted as an intellectual decision heavily swayed by appetite and by the marital tiff she had just had with Adam.

Areopagitica's application of the reinterpreted fall toward a political end supplies a host of provocative questions, useful for class discussion and essay topics (see also Mohamed's essay in this volume). Does the epic follow *Areopagitica* in presenting the fall as a fortunate event? If so, in what way is its version of *felix culpa* different? How are the theories of freedom and reason associated with the fall replayed in the epic? How is the language of *Areopagitica* transported into the characters of *Paradise Lost*, and what bearing do the voice and perspective of a particular character have on our conception of the truth-value of their lines?

The first reuse of *Areopagitica*'s formative theory of choice in the epic occurs not in the mouth of Satan or Adam or Eve but in the seemingly less ambiguous mouth of God. Looking down at Adam and Eve and angrily predicting the events to come, God speaks to the Son in an almost defensive manner about how he had done everything he could to set things right. In a single pentameter line, he pronounces against Adam and Eve in a tellingly convoluted verb tense construction: "Sufficient to have stood, though free to fall" (3.99). The syntactically more natural phrasing "sufficient to *stand*, though free to fall" would not, of course, fit the meter, nor would it capture the strange conditional mood one must use when events are paradoxically foreknown but yet not predestinate. God goes on to quote from *Areopagitica*, explaining the endowment of humanity with such freedom: "reason also is choice" (3.108). "Reason is but choosing," argued Milton in a polemical work of nonfiction; "Reason also is choice," argues God. Not unsurprisingly, they have the same idea. Yet God takes his case for Aristotelian rational liberty into a different set of registers. In *Paradise Lost*, but not in *Areopagitica*, Milton makes clear the implications of his radical view on Reformation theology: that humanity is given this choice by God means that Calvin and Luther were wrong about the depravity of the will. As if in dialogue with misled theologians, God continues, fulfilling part of the theodicy of the narrative: "So [they] were created, nor can justly accuse / Their Maker, or their making, or their fate" (3.12–13). God's words become almost comically dismissive, furthering their ironic dislocation from the theological debate they address:

> As if predestination overruled
> Their will, disposed by absolute decree
> Or high foreknowledge; they themselves decreed
> Their own revolt, not I   (3.114–17)

The Reformation theology of predestination is untenable because it prevents rational liberty. Milton has thus taken an argument from *Areopagitica* and used it to uphold an argument associated with the Dutch theologian Arminius, an association that would have been far more controversial in the early 1640s, when the position was seen as central to the Laudian movement away from true Protestantism. William Laud, the persecutory archbishop who steered the Church of England away from Calvinism, became an enemy of the Puritans. He was accused by the Long Parliament of treason in 1640 and was ultimately executed in 1645. The intense opposition to the emerging free-will theology of the English Church can be seen in such Puritans as Stephen Marshall, who preached in 1640, "take heede you understand it not as some . . . [who] set up the rotten *Dagon* of mans *free will*" (22–23). Now safe from the theological battlefield of the civil war period, Milton is in this case free to express himself theologically—even though the same argument implicitly inheres in his formulation in *Areopagitica*. Or so it seems to inhere—this point is valuably framed as a question to students. This example also provides a glimpse of the extraordinary complexity of Milton's positions, often simply and mistakenly associated with those of the Puritans (a nebulous category), when in this case it seems possible that Milton never really adhered to the Calvinist view of predestination (see Campbell and Corns).

God is not the only one to speak Milton's revolutionary arguments. Both Satan and Eve approach the prohibition against eating the fruit of knowledge with language that at times seems culled straight from Milton. One of Eve's strongest arguments for going out alone, against Adam's rather poorly argued stance that she stay by his side, comes from an astonishing twenty-two-line rebuttal that contains the Miltonic argument "And what is faith, love, virtue unassayed / Alone, without exterior help sustained?" (9.335–36). If Eve stayed by Adam's side, she would be the very "cloistered virtue" that Milton could not praise, "unexercised and unbreathed, that never sallies out and sees her adversary" (*Areopagitica* 939).

The prohibition against eating the fruit is, as Satan reflects, "reasonless" (4.516), a prohibition given without reason but also a prohibition paradoxically antagonistic to reason and knowledge. The reasonlessness of the prohibition emerges also in Eve's explanation to Satan:

> But of this Tree we may not taste nor touch;
> . . . .
> . . . the rest, we live
> Law to ourselves, our reason is our law.
> (9.651–54)

In addition to "Tree," both "Reason" and "Law" are capitalized, perhaps meaningfully, in the original. The law that prohibits taking the fruit of knowledge lies outside reason, and therefore the reason that is synonymous with choice, in God's own terms, may be unavailable until the reasonless prohibition is broken. To keep from "knowing good by evil," as Milton writes in *Areopagitica* (939), is to deny the choice essential to human reason and knowledge. Indeed, Satan uses this very argument from *Areopagitica* in his suggestion to Eve that knowledge of "evil" should be "known, since [it is] easier shunned" (9.698–99).

Milton draws a connection between narrative methods and knowledge in his praise of Spenser that looks forward to some of the representational objectives of *Paradise Lost*:

> Assuredly we bring not innocence into the world, we bring impurity much rather: that which purifies us is trial, and trial is by what is contrary . . . which was the reason why our sage and serious poet, Spenser, whom I dare be known to think a better teacher than Scotus or Aquinas, describing true temperance under the person of Guyon, brings him in with his palmer through the cave of Mammon and the bower of earthly bliss that he may see and know and yet abstain.   (939)

Milton implies that the reader also participates in the experience of confronting evil and turning away that Adam did when given choice and that the reader, in making a choice—or in being made to choose—is brought closer to real knowledge. Poetry is a better teacher than philosophy because of its capacity to reenact the choice essential to the acquisition of knowledge. The question of how choice works in *Paradise Lost* can occupy many different conversations in class, from Milton's persistent use of "or" in his epic similes, to his complex use of perspectivism in representing Adam and Eve, to the seemingly deliberate contradictions and ambiguities offered by the narrative.

In *Paradise Lost*, Milton constantly seeks to provoke readers into working out their beliefs for themselves. This approach defies readers such as Richard Bentley who want Milton's text to acquire a fixable status (see Welch's essay in this volume). As Milton writes suggestively in *Areopagitica*, "Truth is compared in scripture to a streaming fountain; if her waters flow not in a perpetual progression they sicken into a muddy pool of conformity and tradition" (952). This statement reflects a larger problem in representation—that the search for truth does not end when we think we have fixed it as such. Milton goes further in *Areopagitica* to criticize in his contemporaries that tendency to fix the truth: "he who thinks we are to pitch our tent here and have attained the utmost prospect of reformation that the mortal glass wherein we contemplate can show us till we come to beatific vision, that man by this very opinion declares that he is yet far short of truth" (955). The idea of pitching our tent in a place of truth captures Milton's broad concern with the idea of letting textual representation stand for a fixed and absolute truth. The concern is reflected in the comical episode in book 11 where Adam wants to go about Paradise erecting little monuments in the places where he conversed with God. Had he remained in his "capital seat" of Eden (11.343), Adam would have built his tent there—to erect monuments of thought that recall the sepulchral remains of conversations. On many levels, Milton continues to paint the event of leaving Paradise as both fortunate and emancipatory.

Milton's contemporaries generally used the story of the fall in a very different way, not only politically, but also as it related to gender relations in Restoration England. Robert Filmer, John Locke's opponent in the *Two Treatises of Government*, wrote that "the desire for liberty was the cause of the fall of Adam" and that therefore we are to understand the lesson of the fall as supporting absolute obedience to the monarchy (*Patriarcha* 2).[10] William Davenant, in *Gondibert*, similarly gestures toward the story of the fall in his suggestion that political "obedience like the Marriage Yoke, is a restraint more needful and advantagious then liberty; and hath the same reward of pleasant quietnesse, which it anciently had, when *Adam*, till his disobedience, injoy'd Paradise" (30).

Milton's contemporaries drew close connections between the "marriage yoke" and the structures of power on a broader scale. Milton draws on these connections in his first divorce tract, *The Doctrine and Discipline of Divorce*. The tract derives in part from his personal experience, but in this case biography may be more obfuscating than helpful, especially in the context of teaching, where Milton's personal history can become distorted and sensationalized. It is worth mentioning, as a way of correcting this tendency, that Milton had made notes on marriage and divorce in his commonplace book before things had gone sour in his marriage. *The Doctrine and Discipline of Divorce* is valuable as a close study of some of Milton's ideas about the Genesis account as well as of his method of reading and embellishing biblical language. While his arguments here and in *Paradise Lost* are hardly feminist (see Walker in this volume), they are valuably understood in relation to the contemporary sentiments against which Milton constructs his positions. His efforts to reform the institution of marriage are conspicuously tied to his efforts to reform the state. Addressing the Parliament as "supreme senate," Milton draws a comparison between the rights of freedom in marriage and civil rights: "He who marries, intends as little to conspire his own ruin, as he that swears allegiance: and as a whole people is in proportion to an ill government, so is one man to an ill marriage" (862). The analogy between the domestic and the political world continues in his statement that "no effect of tyranny can sit more heavy on the commonwealth than this household unhappiness on the family" (862).

Perhaps the most important elements of this divorce tract in relation to *Paradise Lost* are in Milton's complex rethinking of what the scripture means in Genesis 2.18: "It is not good that man should be alone; I will make a helpmeet for him" (*Doctrine* 871). What, precisely, is a "helpmeet"? This is a terrific classroom moment for the *Oxford English Dictionary*, both because it breaks from lexical objectivity to dismiss "helpmeet" disdainfully as a "compound absurdly formed" and because it shows, in its history of use, how the word was invented solely for the purpose of translating the Hebrew of this laconic passage. This crucial description of the relationship between the first woman and the first man thus has a highly indeterminate quality: an invented word comes without a signifying history; it is a word that readers must bring meaning to, rather than one that carries meaning with it. For Milton, it does not connote a relationship defined by sexuality or a relationship of servitude or physical need. Instead, remarkably, it connotes a relationship based on "meet and happy conversation" (871). The desire to have the marital bond defined by a rational, intellectual companionship prompts Milton to rethink Paul's dictum "It is better to marry than to burn" (1 Cor. 7.9); instead of the burning flames of hell awaiting those who have sex without marriage or the burning desire of remaining forever without marriage or sexuality, Milton proposes "a rational burning" (*Doctrine* 875)—the burning for rational companionship. In surprisingly current terms, Milton also argues for "mutual consent" in the decision to marry and divorce (870).

The relationship between Adam and Eve in *Paradise Lost*—the ideal first marriage—often echoes the terms established for marriage in the divorce tracts. Adam describes to God his desire for a mate who is his equal and who will fulfill his needs for a rational companion:

> Among unequals what society
> Can sort, what harmony or true delight?
> Which must be mutual, in proportion due
> Giv'n and received . . .
> . . . .
> . . . of fellowship I speak
> Such as I seek, fit to participate
> All rational delight   (8.383–91)

In *Paradise Lost* Milton frequently embellishes the "help meet" or "helpmeet" of Genesis 2.18, as when Adam explains to God that humans are different in needing companions, "the cause of his desire / By conversation with his like to help, / Or solace his defects" (8.417–19). "Helpmeet" here is reframed as "like to help" and thus to help in conversation as an equal.

The explicitly political element in the triad of Milton's reform efforts during the civil war period emerges with force in *The Tenure of Kings and Magistrates*, printed within two weeks of the king's execution and reissued in an expanded edition within the same year. The tract vindicates not only the king's trial and execution (which occurred 30 January 1649) but also the overturning of the "magistrates"—the majority of members of Parliament—who were forcibly removed from Parliament in Pride's Purge on 6 December 1648. Milton's republican position grants sovereignty to the private individual in overturning magistrates. The radical argument for popular sovereignty opposes major Reformation thinkers, particularly Calvin in his influential reading of Romans 13 in *Institutes*. The most vital passage in *The Tenure of Kings and Magistrates* in relation to *Paradise Lost* is Milton's bold assertion at the beginning:

> No man who knows aught can be so stupid to deny that all men naturally
> were born free, being the image and resemblance of God himself, and

were by privilege above all the creatures born to command and not to obey; and that they lived so till from the root of Adam's transgression falling among themselves to do wrong and violence, and foreseeing that such courses must needs tend to the destruction of them all, they agreed by common league to bind each other from mutual injury and jointly to defend themselves against any that gave disturbance or opposition to such agreement.   (1028)

Milton's statement employs one biblical line to negate another—God's commandment that humans had dominion over the earth in Genesis 1.26 supersedes the doctrine of passive obedience in Romans 13.5. Perhaps more extraordinary is the suggestion that we were born free not to obey as God bid us to obey in the first prohibition against eating the fruit of knowledge. It seems Milton was of the devil's party without knowing it.

In another generation, the critical world asked different questions in comparing Milton's political prose with his verse—if they deigned to do it at all. Here I give a nutshell account of the many connections that can be drawn and of the fruitful conversations that can ensue from these. But it would be of further value, in classroom discussions of these connections, for teachers to give students a sense of the wide range of critical responses that have accompanied political readings of literature. I close with a telling example from Don M. Wolfe's pioneering study of Milton's polemical prose in 1941, published in the same year as John Crowe Ransom's *The New Criticism*. In turning to read the "political implications" of *Paradise Lost*, now a common undertaking, Wolfe relates with a note of apology that he wrote with "some hesitation," since he worried that any reading of the poem as having political implications "would be construed as an unfavorable judgment of the poem as a whole" (ix). It would not occur to an early modernist today to apologize for such a basic historicist reading, but the debate concerning politics and literary value remains alive and well.

NOTES

[1] Blake's full statement reads, "The reason Milton wrote in fetters when he wrote of Angels & God, and at liberty when of Devils & Hell, is because he was a true Poet and of the Devils party without knowing it" ("Voice" 35).

[2] Waldock similarly argued that Milton "was able, in a marked degree, to conceive Satan in terms of himself" (158). For the old view of a "reformed" Milton, see Ross.

[3] The classic and still assignable book on this is Hill, *Milton*. See also Achinstein, *Milton*; Wolfe; Worden. For a provocative and therefore assignable counterposition, see Patterson, "Why?"

[4] In survey courses, I teach only the abridged version of *Areopagitica* in the *Norton Anthology of British Literature* (Logan, Greenblatt, Lewalski, and Mauss).

[5] While *The Doctrine and Discipline of Divorce* is of great value in itself and useful in broadening students' conceptions of the role of Paradise in Milton's polemic, *Areo-*

pagitica provides a better introduction to Milton's prose and to English political history, so breaking the chronological sequence is useful here. The editors of the Modern Library edition *Complete Poetry and Essential Prose of John Milton* have kindly preserved most of the long divorce tract in their selections — much more than desirable for a single day (I recommend assigning up to chapter 10 [857–81]). Unless otherwise noted, all subsequent citations to Milton are to this edition.

6 For a valuable introduction to English psalm culture, see Hamlin.

7 The complete verse and collected prose volumes such as Merritt Y. Hughes's 1957 edition (*Complete Poems and Major Prose*) or the Modern Library edition facilitate turning back to the prose while discussing *Paradise Lost.*

8 Tournu and Forsyth, Introduction 5. Milton first used "civil liberty" in *An Apology against a Pamphlet* (923 24).

9 See also Fulton, *"Areopagitica"* and *Historical Milton*, ch. 3.

10 For further examples, see Filmer's contradictions of Hobbes in *Observations* 187; *Anarchy* 138.

Radical Politics in *Paradise Lost*?

David Loewenstein

One challenge for teachers of *Paradise Lost* is deciding how to talk about the poem's politics. Indeed, in what way—if at all—does this great poem, which retells the story of the fall of humankind, remain politically engaged? In asking students to consider this large question, one can remind them that Milton had been a politically engaged citizen and radical writer for some twenty turbulent years: he deeply immersed himself in the political and religious upheavals of the English civil wars and interregnum; wrote controversial pamphlets justifying political revolution, republicanism, and regicide; and worked for the English government beginning in 1649, when he was appointed Secretary for Foreign Tongues to the Council of State. Some of his most famous political tracts, including *Eikonoklastes* (1649) and his first and second *Defence of the English People* (1652, 1654), were ordered by the Council of State. In April 1660, just weeks before the Restoration, he dared to publish his last great political tract, *The Ready and Easy Way to Establish a Free Commonwealth*, warning the English people of backsliding and subjugating themselves again to the alluring image and power of monarchy: "Is it," he rhetorically demanded of his compatriots, "such an unspeakable joy to serve, such felicitie to wear a yoke?" (448).[1]

Immediately after the restoration of the monarchy, Milton went into hiding, and in June 1660 the Commons ordered Milton's arrest. These were extremely dangerous times for anyone who had openly supported the execution of King Charles I (in January 1649) and who had supported the experimental English Republic. Religious Dissenters—persons who did not strictly adhere to the restored Church of England—were considered seditious, and many were severely punished with fines and imprisonment. Regicides were tried and executed in October 1660, and the body of the great, godly leader of interregnum England, Oliver Cromwell, was exhumed and then ceremonially hanged, drawn, and quartered in early 1661. In approaching the question of politics in *Paradise Lost*, it is therefore important for teachers to give students a sense of the political and religious turmoil surrounding the Restoration, as well as of Milton's precarious circumstances afterward. It is helpful to stress that Milton composed *Paradise Lost* (first published in 1667) between 1658 and 1663, an extremely volatile and transitional period that included the collapse of the English Commonwealth and the restoration of the monarchy and the Church of England.

There are other valuable ways to frame and enrich class discussions about how to consider politics in Milton's great poem. One is to ask students, especially those taking a course on Milton, to read substantial sections of his prose, including *Areopagitica*, *The Tenure of Kings and Magistrates*, selections from *Eikonoklastes* and the *Second Defence*, and the complete second edition of *The Ready and Easy Way*. This approach will immerse students in some of Milton's most passionate and verbally rich writings about political and religious liberty.

One can then ask students to think about how and where the political language of these writings carries over into *Paradise Lost*. What are we to make of the fact that Satan uses provocative political language that recalls or echoes these tracts? He does so often in the early books of the poem, such as when the fallen Satan, in his fiery speeches, refers to "the Tyranny of Heav'n" (1.124) or when Satan addresses the fallen angels thus: "in this abject posture have ye sworn / To adore the Conqueror?" (1.322–23), a rhetorical question that recalls the antimonarchical Milton's scorn for "the perpetual bowings and cringings of an abject people" who servilely adore a powerful earthly king (*Ready and Easy Way* 426). Juxtaposing the political prose and the great poem in this way can stimulate lots of discussion and argument among students. One can ask students, for example, to point to other specific passages in the poem that echo the language of the political prose. Some students will at first conclude, as did some of the Romantic poets, that Satan is a political rebel like the author of *Paradise Lost*. One can then start to probe questions like the following: Does Milton wish readers of the poem to sympathize with the provocative political language of Satan? If not, where does the poem prompt us to think more critically about the ways Satan uses the language of political rebellion and republicanism? I recommend first asking these questions in class without offering a carefully considered answer, to make students aware, early on in our discussion of *Paradise Lost*, that Milton the poet remains deeply interested in interrogating the uses and abuses of political rhetoric.

I also ask students to consider an alternative narrative about Milton and his politics, one that argues that Milton retreated from politics into faith at the time of the Restoration. Many critics today do not accept the notion that the poet of *Paradise Lost* rejected politics and retired into a spiritual world of faith. And yet at the end of the poem, the archangel Michael does evoke, in his visions and narratives of postlapsarian history, the "heavy persecution" of Restoration England, observing, "Truth shall retire / Bestuck with sland'rous darts, and works of Faith / Rarely be found" (12.531, 535–37). To support the contention that *Paradise Lost* may ultimately be a poem more concerned with spiritual and eternal verities than with politics, I give students suggestive passages from Andrew Marvell, Samuel Coleridge, and the distinguished historian of seventeenth-century England Blair Worden. In *The Rehearsal Transpros'd: The Second Part* (1673), a controversial prose text advocating toleration for Dissenters in the Restoration, the poet and polemicist Marvell observed of his friend Milton that "at His Majesties happy Return, J. M. did partake . . . of his Regal Clemency and has ever since expiated himself in a retired silence" (418). Of course, one can make the point in class that Marvell was protecting his friend and therefore being a bit disingenuous, yet one can also use this quotation to ask students to think about the degree to which *Paradise Lost* marks a significant retirement in Milton's writing from political engagement. Similarly, Coleridge's comment about Milton during the Restoration can help frame class discussion about whether Milton's great poem signals a move away from politics: "He was, as every truly great poet has ever been, a good man; but finding it impossible to realize his own aspirations, whether in religion, or politics, or society, he gave up his heart to the living spirit and light within him, and avenged himself on the world by enriching it with this record [*Paradise Lost*] of his own transcendent ideal" (97; see also Worden). These quotations can show students that the question of Milton's political engagement in *Paradise Lost* has been the subject of considerable critical debate and that the poem's politics may be more oblique than overt.[2]

Quotations like these from Marvell and Coleridge also help frame follow-up questions: To what extent did Milton's radical political and religious voice in *Paradise Lost* remain "unchang'd / To hoarse or mute" (7.24–25), especially given the hostile political climate of the Restoration, when the solitary, blind poet had "fall'n on evil days" and "evil tongues" (7.25, 26)? To what degree, moreover, do Milton's politics and religious convictions remain interconnected in his great spiritual poem? Here one can point out that Milton presents *Paradise Lost* as an epic poem of restoration in the provocative sense that religious radicals and Dissenters would have understood it: the "one greater Man" who will "Restore us" (1.4–5), the poet prophesies, is not a Stuart king but the Messiah.

To highlight the poem's keen interest in politics, I suggest looking closely at the impressive political debate that takes place during the "great consult" of hell among the fallen angels (1.798). To what degree do we find evidence of Milton's radical politics in this fallen version of parliamentary debate? One of Milton's early biographers, the seventeenth-century republican John Toland, suggested that "the chief design" of *Paradise Lost* is "to display the different effects of Liberty and Tyranny" (182). One can quote Toland's passage to students and ask them whether the parliamentary debate in hell supports his point. One can also remind students of the revolutionary England Milton envisioned so vividly in *Areopagitica* (1644), when England was refashioning itself as a nation in the midst of civil war. There, Milton yearned for a nation where liberty of political debate and dispute flourished and conflicting viewpoints were aired—a political nation with "much arguing, much writing, many opinions" (554). Certainly "many opinions" are aired during the parliament in hell, and here one can ask students to interrogate especially carefully the language and arguments of these fallen political speakers. The fierce and blunt Moloch, for example, is motivated by a desire for revenge after infamous defeat in celestial civil war; his aggressive warrior ethic recalls Satan's drive for revenge, as well as the outmoded ideology of classical epic that sanctioned revenge. Given the political contexts of Milton's prose, we can recall that godly republican writers also associated the pursuit of revenge with royalist defeat and bitterness. In his proregicide tracts Milton frequently refers to the unrepentant King Charles I's furious desire "to be reveng'd on his opposers" as "he seeks to satiat his fansie with the imagination of some revenge upon them" (*Eikonoklastes* 563). Milton's political prose can help put in critical perspective the motives that drive Moloch's hatred of God and call for revenge.

Yet other fallen angels dismiss Moloch's call for open war and revenge, so that the parliament in hell, instead of overtly dramatizing Milton's radical political positions, quickly becomes an exquisite study in the art and dangers of political rhetoric. The poet's sharpest condemnation is reserved for Belial: under his seductive rhetoric ("he pleas'd the ear" [2.117]), he counsels "ignoble ease, and peaceful sloth / Not peace" as he dismantles Moloch's arguments and suggests that his compatriots refrain from the use of force or guile against the power of God (2.227–28). Indeed, the vigilant reader of the poem, the poet's warning reminds us, needs to discriminate with great care; seductive political rhetoric can easily disarm its listeners. And that is precisely what happens after Mammon argues that the fallen angels can create a magnificent empire in hell: his political speech is greeted with a groundswell of immediate applause, dramatically countered by the mighty figure of Beelzebub, Satan's strongman. The devils' imperial ambitions must not be allowed to be realized by Mammon's appealing plan; rather, Beelzebub's malicious proposal to destroy or conquer earth and its "puny inhabitants" must win the vote. The plan originates with Satan, "the Author of all ill" who "first devis'd" it (2.367, 381, 379). The long political debate in hell has thus been carefully rigged, and Beelzebub flatters the fallen angels as soon as they vote "with full assent" (2.388). Moreover, Satan quickly takes advantage of the political situation and stifles further debate as he accepts his heroic role as political deliverer and emissary to earth: "Thus saying rose / The Monarch, and prevented all reply" (2.466–67). The other fallen angels do not dare dissent, since they dread Satan's "voice / Forbidding" (2.474–75). If students have been reading *Areopagitica* alongside *Paradise Lost* they can see more sharply that Pandemonium, "the high Capital / Of Satan and his Peers" (1.756–57), is hardly a "mansion house of liberty" (*Areopagitica* 554), as Milton famously characterized revolutionary London, a city that thrives on the ferment of political debate and dissent.

Milton provides multiple perspectives on the fallen angels in books 1 and 2 of the epic poem, enabling him to qualify the splendor and heroic posture of the devils and their forceful political rhetoric in ways that reveal his ongoing polemicism with regard to religious politics. The impressive catalog of fallen angels in book 1 (lines 376–522), for example, highlights themes of idolatry and pagan practices (as well as themes of lust and violence) as it looks forward to the decline of the church narrated in book 12. Milton's reference to "gay Religions full of Pomp and Gold" (1.372), in the midst of this narrative of idolatry and idolatrous cults, evokes the Roman Catholic Church as well as the religious ceremonialism encouraged during Milton's age by the powerful Archbishop of Canterbury, William Laud (executed by Parliament in 1645). In his controversial prose, Milton had blasted "these gaudy glisterings" of ceremonial religion (encouraged by Laud in conflict with the English Reformed tradition) when "altars indeed were a fair forwardnesse" and prelates "were setting up the molten Calfe of their Masse again" (*Reason* 828, 771). Ironically, when the devils in the poem complain about the religious rituals of heaven, including singing "Forc't

Halleluiahs" (2.243), they make themselves sound like victims of religious conformity and Laudian ritualized worship (see 2.241–44).

The tense encounter between Satan and the fiery angel Abdiel (his name means "servant of God") narrated in books 5 and 6 likewise dramatizes the politics of the epic in distinctive ways. In the great rebellion in heaven, Satan employs "Ambiguous words" to fuel his resistance and provoke the rebel angels (5.703), reminding us of Milton's depiction, in his antimonarchical prose, of European monarchs who rebel against the King of Kings and derive their power from the Beast of Revelation as "doubtfull and ambiguous in all thir doings" (*Eikonoklastes* 598–99). However rousing it may sound, Satan's political language in the poem is slippery and equivocal (see 5.773–802), and Abdiel responds with fiery zeal and the scorn of the righteous prophet who dares utter the "odious Truth" in the midst of "a World perverse" (11.704, 701). Abdiel characterizes Satan's inciting speech as "argument blasphémous" (5.809), evoking the Beast of Revelation (13.5–6) who opens "his mouth in blasphemy against God" and makes war with the "saints," as God's loyal angels are called in the war in heaven (6.47, 767, 801, 882). Abdiel's response (see 5.826–29) reminds the poem's discerning readers of heaven's special political circumstances — God's kingship is unlike any other kind of kingship and does not resemble an absolutist earthly monarchy. Satan the provocateur accuses God of tyranny but in private (one can recall to students) speaks differently of God's power in heaven: "nor was his service hard" (4.45). Abdiel thus attempts to restrain the dangerous rhetoric of Satan and to counter his astonishing (if exhilarating) assertion that he and his legion are "self-begot, self-raised" (5.860); Satan's primal sin is his desire to exist on his own and to create an identity for himself not created by God.

The affinity between Abdiel, scornfully rejected by Satan's camp, and Milton as daring visionary poet, "with dangers compast round, / And solitude" (7.27–28), is underscored by Milton's description of the fearless "flaming seraph" who is "Encompass'd round with foes" (5.875, 876). Like the poet whose radical voice remains "unchang'd / To hoarse or mute" in the midst of the evil days of the Restoration, Abdiel will not "swerve from truth, or change his constant mind / Though single" and reviled with reproach (5.902–03). Moreover, there is much pointed irony when Satan reviles the faithful seraph as "seditious" (6.152), an inflammatory epithet that evokes the fiery religious and political controversies of the English Revolution and its aftermath. Here one can give students a few telling passages from the English Revolution and Restoration. John Lilburne, the famous radical Puritan and Leveller leader, for example, complained in his *Just Defence* (1653) that it was common to be labeled "factious and seditious, men of contentious and turbulent spirits . . . for no other cause, but for standing for the truth" (452); in addition, the stern Conventicles Act of 1670 attempted to prevent any sectarian insurrection during the Restoration, warning against "dangerous practices of seditious sectaries and other disloyal persons" (*Stuart Constitution* 356).

The language of religious controversy is likewise crucial to the poem's war in heaven; referring to God's other loyal angels, Abdiel speaks ironically to his adversary on the battlefield, throwing the language of sectarianism back in the face of the rebel Satan:

> but thou seest
> All are not of thy Train; there be who Faith
> Prefer, and Piety to God, though then
> To thee not visible, when I alone
> Seem'd in thy World erroneous to dissent
> From all; my Sect thou seest, now learn too late
> How few sometimes may know, when thousands err.
> (6.142–48)

Abdiel's polemical words fuse the discourse of radical religion and nonconformity with the tense political events of Milton's heaven—a dramatic reminder that the political upheavals of the 1640s and 1650s, as well as the fierce backlash after 1660 against Dissenters, had been fueled by religious ferment and acute fears of radical sectarianism. In the poem's mythic heaven, where rebellion leading to the "horrid confusion" of civil war is not generated by the faithful dissenter (6.668), Milton is prompting his readers to reconsider the relations between political rebellion, sectarianism, and civil confusion that orthodox Protestant authorities were keen to link in the previous decades of turmoil.[3]

The poem's final books afford another crucial opportunity to examine Milton's political perspectives after the Restoration. The tragedy of the fall, Milton's epic shows, has disturbing consequences for human history and politics. The archangel Michael presents dispiriting visions and narratives of human history characterized by human tribulation, often evoking the turbulent world of Milton's revolutionary England, as well as the religious tensions of the Restoration. Closely based on the Bible and moving from the time of the expulsion to the time of Christ and beyond, the last two books depict a handful of faithful individuals—such as Enoch, Noah, Abraham, and Moses—who emerge in the midst of dark periods of lawless tyranny, warfare, and heavy religious persecution "in a World perverse" (11.701). Enoch, mentioned as a figure of faith in Hebrews 11.5, in Milton's poem finds himself as the lone "Just Man" (11.681) rising up in a world of Homeric strife and destruction, as he utters "odious Truth" (11.704), speaking (much like Milton in his prose) "of Right and Wrong, / Of Justice, of Religion, Truth and Peace, / And Judgment from above" before being rescued by heaven "to walk with God / High in Salvation" (11.666–68, 707–08). Consequently, in discussing the poem's often grim depiction of postlapsarian history, one can ask students to consider the following questions: To what degree are these prophetic individuals in human history successful in renovating their fallen or backsliding worlds afflicted by political oppression and violence? How do they compare, say, with the politically outspoken Milton of *The Ready and Easy Way*? Milton's Noah is a zealous preacher and just spokesperson, "the only Son of light / In a dark Age" (11.808–09), rising up in a sybaritic, ungodly period of "luxury and riot" and vainly preaching "Against allurement, custom" while "fearless of reproach or scorn, / Or violence" (11.715, 808, 811–12).[4] Nonetheless, as Adam struggles to interpret the history lessons presented to him, his vehement response, especially to the aggressive tyranny of Nimrod, is instinctively republican (see 12.64–71); Adam recognizes, in the words of John Locke, that God's donation in Genesis 1.28 did not give him "Monarchical Power over those of his own Species" (*Two Treatises* 161; see also 141–71). It is notable that Milton, not the Bible, has dared to imagine our first father's response to such matters as absolute power and sovereignty, political servility, natural freedom, and republicanism.

The final books of the poem consequently address a sad consequence of the fall in human history: earthly monarchy and tyranny, along with the loss of inward and outward liberty. Nevertheless, after the often sorrowful lessons of postlapsarian history, Adam can speak of a subversive weakness that would have had pointed resonance for the besieged godly of the 1660s: "by things deem'd weak / Subverting worldly strong, and worldly wise / By simply meek" (12.567–69). *Paradise Lost*, moreover, offers at the end the consolation of the "paradise within" (12.587), a replacement for the lost earthly paradise (certainly "happier far" than the wreckage of the fallen Eden that Adam and Eve leave behind them) and a reminder that the only true church—like God's "living Temples, built by Faith to stand" (12.527)—lies within the self. The paradise within underscores how radically inward Milton has made the epic poem. Yet that internal impulse and Milton's tragic vision do not mean that the radical godly poet withdrew from politics into faith when the English Revolution collapsed; a careful consideration of the political and religious pressures exerted on Milton can help students see that Milton's responses to the Restoration were more varied and conflicted than that. Despite the universal appeal of *Paradise Lost*, its emphasis on the paradise within the individual believer also speaks movingly to a generation of radical Dissenters whose unorthodox views and polemical writings had challenged all forms of external and institutionalized religion as they sought instead—like Milton himself—guidance from the inner spirit or light.

NOTES

[1] Citations from Milton's prose are taken from *Complete Prose Works* (ed. Wolfe); citations from *Paradise Lost* are taken from *Complete Poems and Major Prose* (ed. Hughes).

[2] Various critical accounts of politics in *Paradise Lost* include Hill, *Milton* 365–75; Radzinowicz; Davies; Wilding 205–31; Quint 268–324; Achinstein, *Milton* 177–223; Corns, *Regaining* 126–43 ; Knoppers, *Historicizing* 67–122; R. Fallon; Norbrook, *Writing*, ch. 10; Lewalski, *Life*, ch. 13; Loewenstein, "Radical Religious Politics"and *Representing* 202–41.

[3] For more on the poem in relation to the combative religious politics of the English Revolution and Restoration, see Loewenstein, *Representing* 226–41.

[4] In *Of True Religion* (1673), his last major tract, published around the same time as the second edition of *Paradise Lost*, Milton bitterly laments the English "Nation of late years . . . grown more . . . excessively vitious then heretofore; Pride, Luxury, Drunkenness, Whoredom, Cursing, Swearing . . . every where abounding" (438).

CHARACTERS

The Problem of God

Michael Bryson

By the time we get to book 3 in *Paradise Lost*, students at the urban, secular university where I teach (California State University, Northridge) are usually thoroughly impressed by Satan. There is much to admire, from the point of view of a secular reader in the twenty-first century, and, although I emphasize the differences between a reader contemporary to Milton and us as readers, I do not insist on them at the expense of making *Paradise Lost* more a pedagogical than a literary experience. I do not insist that my students come away from the poem with a particular view of its characters, whether that view is mine, that of another critic, or some construction of Milton's own view. I do, however, insist that they realize that they are free to ask questions, the very thing that C. S. Lewis once opposed, when he sought to "prevent the reader from ever raising certain questions" (*Preface* 69).

That said, I take an approach that might be termed "foundational" to help students understand what Milton *may* (and I am emphatic on this point of incertitude) have been up to in portraying the character God as he does. In teaching the figure of God, or the Father, in *Paradise Lost*, I consistently encounter two issues: my students dislike the character and are often not at all shy about expressing the reasons for that dislike, and my students have next to no knowledge of the Bible, the various strands of Christian theology on which Milton is drawing, or the epic tradition in general. As a result, I engage them in their dislike of Milton's God, explaining to them the history of the often uneasy reactions to the character. In 1737, for example, Alexander Pope criticized Milton for writing a God who sounds like a "School-divine" ("First Epistle of the Second Book of Horace," line 102). William Blake, in his poem "Milton," described the

Father of *Paradise Lost* as the worst sort of tyrant he could personally imagine: "Urizen . . . in chains of the mind lock'd up" (96). Percy Bysshe Shelley painted the character in Satanic terms: "one who in the cold security of undoubted triumph inflicts the most horrible revenge on his enemy, not from any mistaken notion of inducing him to repent of a perseverance in enmity, but with the alleged design of exasperating him to deserve new torments" ("Defence" 498).

For the twentieth-century critic William Empson, Milton's God "could only have been satisfied by torturing somebody else to death" (*Milton's God* 208). I begin by explaining the difference between the representation and that which is being represented. It is all too easy for this basic principle of literary study to get lost when students consider Milton's God and, indeed, much of the scholarship on Milton's God. I write the following quotation on the board: "Man's last and highest parting is when, for God's sake, he takes leave of God" (Eckhart 204). After situating the origin of this quotation in the German sermons of Meister Eckhart, I spend time eliciting ideas from the students as to what Eckhart might have meant. What does it mean to leave God for God, and why is that the highest parting? Looking into Eckhart's meaning helps introduce a discussion of Milton's portrayal of God with the idea of the provisional, posited, and necessarily inaccurate nature of all such portrayals. I then point them to Milton's statement along these lines: "God, as he really is, is far beyond man's imagination, let alone his understanding" (*Christian Doctrine* 133).

I then move on to emphasize the importance of the project—announced in the poem's famous opening—of justifying "the ways of God to men." I take students through a history of the concept of justification, the theological doctrine describing the process through which fallen humankind is either made or declared righteous in the sight of God. Protestant theologies in the traditions of Luther and Calvin interpret justification as God's imputing righteousness to humankind through its faith in the sacrifice of Christ. The older Augustinian view held that justification was the process through which God made unrighteous humanity righteous. Protestant theologies departed from this view, defining justification as involving not a shift in humanity's being but a change in humanity's status. Being declared righteous in the sight of God implies that one is not really or ontologically changed but merely credited with something one does not actually have. In this way, justification might be seen as a kind of spiritual line of credit extended to a bankrupt and uncreditworthy humanity (Bryson 119–23; see also McGrath).

This view of justification is a two-sided whole. The imputation of righteousness is at once an accusation of and an acquittal from unrighteousness. The Kidderminster curate Richard Baxter, a contemporary of Milton's, defines justification in his *Aphorismes of Justification* as "the acquitting of us from the charge of breaking the Law" and argues that "Justification implyeth accusation" (135). Milton's reversal of this definition, therefore, is dramatic: his attempt to "justify the ways of God to men" is actually an attempt to accuse God in order to acquit him. Here I return to Eckhart and to the idea of negative theology—the idea of the God beyond that expressed by Pseudo-Dionysius (Dionysius the Areopagite), Eckhart, and even Luther. I compare the basic idea that images and ideas of the divine are not the divine itself with the basic literary idea that a representation differs from the thing being represented. I want students to see that Milton is trying something radical with his portrayal of the Father—Milton's God is not necessarily good and is being held up for critique, even prosecution, before ultimately being acquitted. I explain this process with a brief account of Elie Wiesel's story of a trial of God conducted at Auschwitz. God was declared guilty—in fact, no one was willing to defend him—and afterward the "court" conducted evening prayers as usual.[1] It is precisely that torn-in-two-directions quality that I try to communicate to students when we look at Milton's portrayal of God in *Paradise Lost*.

With this idea of accusation and acquittal in place, I go on to explore other issues, such as the possibility of dishonesty in the divine (explored in both biblical and epic literature), a prospect raised by the different ways Satan's escape from hell is presented by the narrator and by the Father in book 3. In class, I use examples of Zeus's sending "dreams" and Yahweh's sending "lying spirits" to illustrate both the frequency and effectiveness of divine dishonesty in the literature that serves as a background for the Father in *Paradise Lost*.

In writing an epic poem, Milton is placing himself (as did Vergil) squarely in the tradition of Homer. Thus Zeus serves as a model for the Father. Zeus, in book 2 of the *Iliad*, sends a dream to Agamemnon, to "exalt Achilles" ([Fagles] 2.4):

> Calling out to the vision, Zeus winged it on:
> "Go, murderous Dream, to the fast Achaean ships
> and once you reach Agamemnon's shelter rouse him,
> order him, word-for-word, exactly as I command.
> Tell Atrides to arm his long-haired Achaeans,
> to attack at once, full force—
> now he can take the broad streets of Troy."
>
> (2.8–14)

This information is false, and in acting on it Agamemnon is made to look foolish when many of his men die over the course of the battles from which Achilles has withdrawn. Zeus lies. Milton, however, is writing not merely an epic but a biblical epic. Thus Zeus is insufficient as a model for the Father. For a complete understanding of Milton's character, an encounter with what is perhaps the greatest character in Western literature is necessary—Yahweh must come into the equation. But is it not a truism that God does not lie? Certainly it is, but, like most truisms, this one is not entirely true, and, because we have already covered the distinction between the representation of God in Milton and the ultimately unrepresentable idea of God behind the representation, students can see how even so famous a representation of God as Yahweh can be seen as just that, a representation, and as such a literary model a poet might use.

Yahweh, although described at Numbers 23.19 as "not a man, that he should lie," does lie. The story of the "lying spirit" at 1 Kings 22.20–23 paints a portrait of a deity who is not at all adverse to generating lies and then punishing others for the lies generated: "The Lord hath put a lying spirit in the mouth of all these thy prophets, and the Lord hath spoken evil concerning thee." The "lying spirit" is the *malak* of Yahweh. If *malak* is here understood—as Jeffrey Burton Russell suggests—as "the voice of the God, the spirit of the God, the God himself" (198), then it is Yahweh who lies to achieve his ends. Yahweh's lies, half-truths, and manipulations are plentiful in the scriptures. It is Yahweh who, at 2 Samuel 24.1 "moved David" to take a census of the people of Israel, and it is Yahweh who savagely punishes David and Israel for this census by "a pestilence" that kills "seventy thousand men" (2 Sam. 24.15). Yahweh serves as his own "lying spirit" here, moving David to take the very action for which Yahweh will inflict horrible punishment. It is also Yahweh whose "hand shall be upon the prophets that see vanity, and that divine lies," or, in the translation of the New Revised Standard Version, "If a prophet is deceived and speaks a word, I, the Lord, have deceived that prophet, and will stretch out my hand against him" (Ezek. 13.9 [*Harper Collins Study Bible*]).

Even by the time of the Pauline epistles, the Hebrew god had not lost this reputation for using deception to accomplish his purposes. Although he is universalized as theos, or God, the figure of whom Paul writes to the Thessalonians acts much like the Yahweh of Job, working hand in hand with Satan to ensure that the "Wicked" shall be revealed: "And for this cause God shall send them strong delusion, that they should believe a lie" (2 Thess. 2.11).

To see clearly how Milton subtly weaves manipulations, half-truths, and the "divine lies" of both Zeus and Yahweh into the Father, a reader must take a closer look at the first words Milton gives his character. After being introduced as one who is "beholding from his prospect high, / Wherein past, present, future he beholds" (3.77–78),[2] the Father speaks his first words of the poem:

> Only begotten Son, seest thou what rage
> Transports our adversary, whom no bounds
> Prescrib'd, no bars of Hell, nor all the chains
> Heapt on him there, nor yet the main Abyss
> Wide interrupt can hold; so bent he seems
> On desperate revenge.   (3.80–85)

Here we have a problem that is basic to literature, especially to dramatic literature: the audience is allowed knowledge that characters do not have. In *Paradise Lost* there are only two individuals who see "past, present, future." One of them, if the narrator is to be trusted, is the Father. The other is the reader. The Son is not included. The reader knows something the Son does not know. The reader has seen things the Son has not seen (there is no indication in the poem that the Son has seen the events in hell).

For the reader, Satan has dominated the action up to this point in the poem. His has been the role that most resembles those Homeric and Vergilian epic heroes: the adventurers who encounter or overcome obstacles through cleverness or the assistance of a god (Zeus assists Achilles, Athena assists Odysseus, and Venus assists Aeneas). This motif begins in *Paradise Lost* with Satan's being allowed up off the floor of hell:

> So stretcht out huge in length the Arch-fiend lay
> Chain'd on the burning Lake, nor ever thence
> Had ris'n or heav'd his head, but that the will
> And permission of all-ruling Heaven
> Left him at large to his own dark designs.
>   (1.209–13)

How, I ask my students, does Satan get up off the floor of hell? By his own ability or through his own determination, as the Father implies in his speech to the Son? But the problem with the Father's words becomes clearer when the reader remembers Satan's encounter with Sin and Death — Sin has the key to the otherwise unopenable gate of hell and is inside the gate (2.850–89). Sin is placed inside the gate and given the key by the Father, and though she claims that she has been ordered not to open the door, why is she on the inside in the first place? Why is the one character most likely to be loyal to Satan given the key to hell and put inside hell where he can find her?[3]

I then ask my students to look again at the Father's first words in *Paradise Lost*. Does his description of events match what you have read to this point in the poem? In years of teaching, I have never gotten a yes. The first words of the Father, like so many of the utterances of the figures on which he is modeled, frame a lie or at least a distortion, a manipulation, a half-truth (see also Herman, *Destabilizing* 120–21). But these lies or half-truths are an integral part of the material out of which Milton constructs his character. Interestingly, I have found that students often appreciate the Father more, not less, after reading him in this way.

Another crucial scene with which I ask students to engage is the Father's raising of the Son in book 5. That the Father does it — and how he does it — provides the crucial impetus for the events that follow:

> Hear all ye Angels, Progeny of Light,
> Thrones, Dominations, Princedoms, Virtues, Powers,
> Hear my Decree, which unrevok't shall stand.
> This day have I begot whom I declare
> My only Son, and on this holy Hill
> Him have anointed, whom ye now behold
> At my right hand; your Head I him appoint;
> And by my Self have sworn to him shall bow

All knees in Heav'n, and shall confess him Lord:
Under his great Vice-gerent Reign abide
United as one individual Soul
For ever happy: him who disobeys
Mee disobeys, breaks union, and that day
Cast out from God and blessed vision, falls
Into utter darkness, deep ingulft, his place
Ordain'ed without redemption, without end.

(5.600–15)

The primary problem with the Father's decree—or the primary power of it, depending on one's point of view—is its belligerent tone: the Father seems to be daring any and all to object in even the smallest way. He tells the assembled audience that they have a new "Head"; that everyone has to get down on one knee and "confess him Lord"; that everyone will do this—no one is exempt; and that everyone has to be happy about it—forever. Moreover, anyone who does not comply with these commands will be cast out without any appeal. This is hardly the kind of announcement that can be expected to engender universal cooperation with the Son as he takes up his new position; instead, it is precisely the kind of decree that can be relied on to drive dissent out into the open, to create dissent in the first place, or both.

Milton is already working with the idea of uncovering or causing rebellion as early as his somewhat loose translation of Psalm 2, the biblical text on which the Father's decree in book 5 is based. As Milton translates the lines, "I, saith hee, / Annointed have my King (though ye rebel) / On Sion my holi' hill" (11–13). Though the phrase "though ye rebel" appears nowhere in the original Hebrew text, Milton includes this phrase in 1653, sketching in miniature what he will years later paint in the broad strokes of *Paradise Lost*. The added phrase in Milton's translation of the psalm seems to assume that the raising of the king will engender rebellion and that God is fully aware of that fact. The anointing of the king both creates dissent and drives it out into the open as active rebellion, exactly as in book 5 of *Paradise Lost*. The Father's decree creates animosity where none existed before; it is only after the Father's announcement that "All seem'd well pleas'd, all seem'd, but were not all" (5.617).

The background of the original Psalm 2 implies that animosity already exists at the time of the anointing of the King who sits on the "holy hill of Zion" (2.6):

Why do the heathen rage, and the people imagine a vain thing? The kings of the earth set themselves, and the rulers take counsel together, against the LORD, and against his anointed, saying, Let us break their bands asunder, and cast away their cords from us. He that sitteth in the heavens shall laugh: the LORD shall have them in derision. Then shall he speak unto them in his wrath, and vex them in his sore displeasure.

(Ps. 2.1–5)

In Milton's heaven, however, the reaction to the Father's imperious decree is something new, a time-buying strategy adopted in response to the potentially dangerous changed order of things: "That day, as other solemn days, they spent / In song and dance about the sacred Hill" (5.618–19). No reference is made to seeming in relation to these "other solemn days." Unlike Psalm 2, in which the Israelite king is anointed and "begotten" as the official human vice-regent of Yahweh amidst the hostile and non-Yahwist nations, the coronation scene in *Paradise Lost* takes place not only in a previously nonhostile context but also in an entirely "monotheist" or "Fatherist" context. There are no "heathen[s]" raging or "people imagin[ing] a vain thing." There are no earthly kings who worship other gods here. There are no other gods. Absent the geographic and henotheistic rivalries at work in the original context of Psalm 2, Milton's borrowing of the basic dramatic structure of the psalm serves to highlight the Father's decree as violently and deliberately confrontational.

More important than re-creating the psalm's hostility, however, is the Father's replicating the atmosphere of dominance and submission, of mutual resentment, hatred, and violence in which Psalm 2 had its origin. David—traditionally regarded as the author of Psalm 2—is anointed as the king of a nation of invaders and conquerors, the vice-regent of a god who, as Regina Schwartz writes, establishes a system in which "to be 'a people' is to be God's people is to inherit his land, and if they are not the people of God, they will not be a people, and they will lose the land" (*Curse* 54). The people who "will not be a people" are the Philistines, as well as other residents of the area, such as the Jebusites, the residents of the walled city—Jebus—that is conquered by David and transformed into his capital, Jerusalem. From the point of view of the Philistines, David and his god are usurpers who have taken what is not rightfully theirs. From Satan's point of view, the Father is "a usurping angel" (Empson, *Milton's God* 103), one who has arrogated to himself powers that are rightfully those of all the angels, not just those who, like Henry Bolingbroke in *Richard II*, "know the strong'st and surest way to get."

Numerous other examples of the Father's speeches and of various characters' reactions to the Father create opportunities to teach both *Paradise Lost* and Milton's rich source material to a student audience that is often lacking the background Milton took for granted in his "fit audience . . . though few." The ways in which Milton makes use of biblical, classical, and theological sources and ideas (material that is largely unfamiliar to undergraduates) allow an instructor to show students just how potentially unorthodox and yet deeply rooted in literary, mythological, and even scriptural tradition Milton's portrayal of God in *Paradise Lost* is.

NOTES

[1] In 1979, Wiesel published a play entitled *The Trial of God (as It Was Held on February 25, 1649 in Shamgorod)*, based on a proceeding he witnessed in Auschwitz. Though

the story has been criticized as an unlikely one, Wiesel stands by his insistence that he witnessed such an event, stating as recently as 2008 that "I was there when God was put on trial" (Frazer).

[2] All references to *Paradise Lost* are to the edition of the poem in Hughes's *Complete Poems and Major Prose*. This volume remains the most comprehensive, single-volume text of Milton's poetry and prose and does the best job of staying out of the reader's, student's, and instructor's way in terms of the tone and content of its footnotes and introductory material. Hughes does an admirable job of providing information while being as nondirective or nonprescriptive as possible.

[3] I compare this passage with 10.585–613, where Sin and Death discuss their victims throughout the world, and 10.613–32, where the Father takes credit for Sin and Death, calling them "my Hell-hounds." I also cite 11.61, where the Father takes credit for having "provided death."

The Problem of Satan; or,
How to Teach Satan on His Own Terms

Gregory M. Colón Semenza

The dominant theme of the 1986 *Approaches to Teaching Milton's* Paradise Lost is that complex pedagogical strategies must be employed in "justifying Milton to the modern student" (Crump, "Introduction" 1). *Paradise Lost*, the volume's editor claims, is an endangered poem because of its complexity and the demands it places on students (8). Having taught Milton's epic several dozen times, in a variety of courses ranging from undergraduate surveys and Milton lectures to PhD seminars, I respectfully wish to disagree with that volume's editor. I would say that teaching *The Faerie Queene* is hard. Teaching *The Tragedy of Mariam* is especially hard. But I am amazed by how stimulating, relevant, and provocative *Paradise Lost* seems to most of my students. One reason perhaps is that as a teacher I find extremely problematic the goal of justifying the ways of Milton to my students, partly because I hold open the possibility that Milton's ways may not be justifiable but mainly because such a goal would imply I am confident in my knowledge of Milton's ways. My hunch is that if one teaches *Paradise Lost* like Milton's God — decreeing with certainty what was, is, and will be — then teaching the poem to undergraduates might become a fairly dreadful task; if one teaches *Paradise Lost* like Milton's Satan, however — questioning everything and resisting what must have been, as well as what must be — then studying it can be an enthralling experience for teachers and students.

Satan is a bit of a narcissist, so to teach like him one must focus the class's attention on Milton's greatest character. Doing so comes naturally, I think, since a large percentage of students in any given class — charmed by Satan's powerful rhetoric — will want to do nothing else. And so one must begin by contending with the complexity of this brilliant poetic creation. The problem of Milton's Satan is, of course, the problem of Milton's God. For most college students, whose knowledge of the complex origins and development of both the Abrahamic God and the Judeo-Christian satan/Satan figure tends to be limited, the difficulty of contending with both problems is compounded by the orthodox view of God put forth by traditional Milton scholarship and by most Christian sects: that of an infallible deity whose goodness is figured a priori. In Milton studies, no statement better sums up the orthodox position on Satan than C. S. Lewis's reductive and dismissive claim that "mere Christianity commits every Christian to believing that 'the Devil is (in the long run) an ass'" (*Preface* 95). Indeed, Christianity commits, in the sense of *compels*, Christians to believe such a fact in the long run, but Lewis seems not to have flinched at the irony of his word choices in describing the work of a poet-polemicist who insisted that only "unjust and foolish men" call "heresy whatever appears to them to differ from the received opinions" (*De Doctrina* 362).[1]

If students come more naturally to the Romantic position on Satan than the Lewisonian one, fear of being branded heretical—which more often than not means ignorant or wrong—causes them to check their visceral identification with the infernal rebel. Worse, since the late 1960s, when Stanley Fish's influential *Surprised by Sin* came to define the new orthodoxy regarding the problem of Milton's Satan, students have also been pressured to check their intellectual identification with Satan, since SparkNotes and most of their professors teach them that knowledge of how Milton works commits every reader to believing that Satan is (in the long run) an ass. So for postmodern, pragmatist readers, as for modern Christian ones, identifying with Satan beyond, say, book 4 of *Paradise Lost* also means proving oneself an ass.

In this short essay, I want to focus on how instructors might heighten their students' appreciation, enjoyment, and understanding of *Paradise Lost* by demonstrating how deeply antithetical to Miltonic hermeneutics and epistemology is the notion of a conclusion derived from an a priori position on any particular subject. Fortunately, the William Empson–inspired conclusions drawn over the past decade or so by scholars we might loosely describe as new Miltonists (e.g., Rumrich, Bryson, Wittreich, Forsyth, Herman) have emphatically demonstrated the intellectual and historical validity of the Romantics' complex understanding of Milton's Satan, challenging directly the idea that we are compelled to read Satan or God in any prescriptive way. As I show, Milton—especially the Milton of the prose writings largely ignored by Lewis and Fish—teaches us to resist actively such prescriptive approaches to reading and analysis. Acknowledging the differences between two frequently taught undergraduate courses, the Milton lecture or discussion and the survey of Renaissance or seventeenth-century literature, I emphasize the importance of encouraging students to "scrutinize and ascertain" for themselves how a problem like Satan might be dealt with (Milton, *De Doctrina* 360), instead of bowing to the suffocating strictures of orthodoxy. I should mention, however, that much of what I have come to believe about teaching *Paradise Lost* was learned in a special-topics course I often teach on the literary satanic that begins with *Prometheus Bound* and the book of Job and ends with Philip Pullman's series His Dark Materials. Such a course allows an instructor the time necessary to chart the basic history of the satan/Satan figure, and I have been amazed by how differently students read Milton's epic, and its orthodox commentators, when well-informed of the character's mythological origins, sociopolitical functions, and historical development. For me, then, one key to handling *Paradise Lost* in the Milton or survey course has to do with somehow conveying this wealth of information about Satan without half the class time required to do so.

At a minimum, I insist on setting aside one week (two to three class periods) for discussion of supplementary materials ranging from satanic fiction to satanic scholarship to popular culture texts. (In a survey class, such study can also shed useful light on works like Marlowe's *Doctor Faustus* and Shakespeare's *Othello*.)

Two to three classes may seem like a lot of time, but it is not much when compared with the eighteen years or so of (mainly conservative) religious socialization many American students will experience before the class. Appropriate secondary materials will vary from teacher to teacher, but I select what to assign with four particular goals in mind: to establish that the Christian Satan is largely constructed outside of and subsequent to the composition of the Old and New Testaments; to demonstrate the original functions of the Hebrew "satan" as a sanctioned adversary of humankind and, arguably, even of God; to draw out the Promethean elements of the satan/Satan figure in literature, especially after the Reformation; and to show that Milton was a restless, adversarial, and far from orthodox religious thinker. I choose to introduce most of this material after students have read books 1 and 2 of *Paradise Lost*, which invariably provoke great interest both in the character and in what Milton is aiming to do by introducing such a seductive protagonist. In other words, students begin asking complex questions that the assigned secondary readings can help them answer, transforming materials they might otherwise regard as dry or digressive into powerful glosses on the poem.

Consideration of Satan might begin even before discussion of the poem; try asking students about their impressions of the Christian Satan before beginning work on books 1 and 2. I find that students' perceptions of the satanic are based almost entirely on popular culture or, at best, on symbolic representations of the figure from literary texts such as Dante's *Inferno*. The cartoon figure of absolute evil pervasive in popular culture—often cloven-hoofed and wielding a pitchfork, sometimes engulfed in flames, other times in ice—is as corrupting a factor in student readings of *Paradise Lost* as unexamined assumptions about God. A few students will offer counterarguments to, or qualifications of, their classmates' responses, but, when pushed, even they reveal that their more informed and thoughtful conceptions of the satanic are usually based on complex popular cultural texts such as Martin Scorsese's *The Last Temptation of Christ*, Gary Ross's *Pleasantville*, Kevin Smith's *Dogma*, and Taylor Hackford's *The Devil's Advocate* (whose Satan happens to be named John Milton). In any case, ten minutes of discussion before beginning *Paradise Lost* can clarify the influence of popular culture on students' impressions of Satan and, usefully, prepare them for the shock of learning about the figure's actual beginnings and changing functions over time. Conversely, it can help them appreciate and understand the complexity of many popular cultural appropriations or adaptations of the Satan myth.

On day 1 of the Satan unit, I require students to read the book of Job (I prefer Stephen Mitchell's translation), several other key biblical passages (e.g., Genesis 1–3; Isaiah 14.12–15; and Revelation 12.7–9), and sections of Elaine Pagels's well-known and highly accessible *The Origin of Satan*. If most students' impressions of the devil come from popular culture, these readings serve both to demonstrate how loosely connected such images of Satan are to scripture and to explain some of the historical reasons for the character's development in Christianity. The presentation of the satan in the book of Job as Yahweh's prosecuting attorney—and arguably, God's alter ego in the form of a distinct being—is the most extended portrait of the devil in the Old or New Testament. The satan's wager with God that Job's faith hinges on his possession of wealth and material goods proves prescient in that Job does curse Yahweh during the second test, revealing in the satan a superior understanding of humanity's weaknesses that God can only counter by awing Job back into faithfulness. More important, the satan is described as one of Yahweh's council and, by extension, one of his creations, not as an autonomous entity in a Manichean universe. That the satan is able to provoke Yahweh into torturing his most faithful servant to prove a point also raises serious questions about the limits of the godhead's foreknowledge, psychological discernment, and compassion for humanity—questions students will find relevant to the Father of *Paradise Lost* when they turn to book 3. Finally, the New Testament and early narrativization of Satan's origin and role in the Christian divine scheme is introduced by the Genesis, Isaiah, and Revelation verses and selected passages from Pagels's book or Neil Forsyth's *The Satanic Epic*. Students should leave such a class questioning popular ideas of Satan as the mere personification of evil—or at least the scriptural grounds for such ideas.

For our second discussion of Satan, I usually assign some combination of readings designed to highlight the parallels between the satanic and the Promethean myths. Aeschylus's *Prometheus Bound* is ideal because of its brevity, its composition at approximately the same time as the book of Job, and its depiction of an authority who seeks to withhold certain forms of knowledge from human beings and of a rebel who seeks to grant them access to those things. Also useful are short supplementary passages from Nietzsche's *Birth of Tragedy* or from any similar work attempting to describe the impact of Abrahamic religious thought on Western conceptions and valuations of experiential knowledge. Finally, to reinforce the point that Satan—and Milton's Satan specifically—has often been read within the Promethean tradition, one might discuss briefly both Mary Shelley's and Percy Shelley's appropriations of *Paradise Lost* in, respectively, *Frankenstein* and *Prometheus Unbound*.

An important function of this unit, then, is to encourage students to take deadly seriously Satan's arguments, as do Eve and about one-third of the heavenly host. Without proof of God's primacy, for example, what is the basis for his superiority over the other angels (5.853–64)?[2] Why should certain forms of knowledge—of good and evil or of any higher things—be forbidden to humankind (9.703–05)? Why should God's superior might convince Satan, or us, that his ways are just (1.105–24)? Contrary to the lessons of the orthodox Milton camp, which point students toward an opinion that Satan's actions are unjustifiable and the ways of God justified, parallels between the Promethean and satanic narratives cause students to ask whether humans are better off being more like Michael—who with Adam believes that "to obey is best" (12.561)—or more like Satan, who from his very first line keeps asking "if." From a pedagogical perspective, at least, the question is not whether Michael is correct in declaring obedience the "sum of wisdom" in this fictional God's universe but how much human potential will be lost in our own universe if we choose to agree with him (12.575–76). From the instructor's vantage point, the answers students offer measure something like the distance between deferential students who faithfully copy down everything their professor says and curious ones who interrogate the veracity and usefulness of authoritative claims.

Establishing that Milton would have admired the interrogators and scorned the fawners is much the point of the final day's work, which highlights Milton's frequent and dramatic rejections of orthodoxy on issues ranging from divorce law to state governance to education to, most important, theology. While I always explain to my students the centrality of Milton's belief, throughout his lifetime, that a "fugitive and cloister'd virtue" is not praiseworthy (*Areopagitica* 213), I believe *De Doctrina Christiana* constitutes the most effective teaching tool for conveying information about Milton's radicalism. The full text of the preface and several short chapters on such subjects as God, predestination, the Son, and marriage can be assigned either for a single discussion or to correspond with appropriate passages in the poem, possibly over several class periods. Milton's intention to "scrutinize and ascertain for . . . [him]self the several points of . . . [his] religious belief" famously reveals major deviations from the orthodox tradition in which so many of his critics have sought to stick him, a fact he defensively acknowledges in the work's opening few pages: "I do not expect from candid and judicious readers a conduct so unworthy of them, that like certain unjust and foolish men, they should stamp with the invidious name of heretic or heresy whatever appears to them to differ from the received opinions" (362). Certainly the author who saw the value of interrogating every aspect of his religious belief and questioning all the received opinions would also have believed in the ability of his most candid and judicious readers (fit, though few) to scrutinize and ascertain for themselves the justness of his God or the fallibility of his Satan. Regardless of whether Milton believed that the devil was simply an ass, he certainly would have thought anyone foolish who would choose not to consider the alternatives. The value in our supplementing *Paradise Lost* with materials such as those discussed here is that we encourage our students "not to repose on the faith or judgment of others in matters relating to God," Satan, or even the meaning of great poetry (*De Doctrina* 360). We surrender our authority and reject paternalism to demonstrate that "if" constitutes the origin, and perhaps the sum, of wisdom.

NOTES

[1] All references to *De Doctrina Christiana* and to *Areopagitica* are to Patrides's edition.

[2] All references to *Paradise Lost* are to Teskey's edition.

Teaching Eve: The Grammar of Eden

Julia M. Walker

Teaching Milton's Eve in the undergraduate classroom is at once too easy and too hard. In many ways, Milton is the canon's juiciest target for misogynist bashing (see Woolf, *Room*; Gilbert and Gubar), but to indulge that impulse is to ignore the context of the English Revolution and Milton's place in the history of the rights of women. And, as Gloucester says at the end of *King Lear*, "that's true, too" (5.2.11). So, for teachers of *Paradise Lost*, while it may be profitable—in a limited way—to turn students loose on "Hee for God only, Shee for God in him" (2.299),[1] we cannot afford to ignore the larger benefits of pointing out that Milton's Eve is less responsible for the fall than any of her precursors. A summary of patristic and medieval views of Eve is certainly helpful for contrast, as is a brief tour of the eighteenth- and nineteenth-century women writers who credited John Milton with saving Eve. Instructors will want to supplement these frames with a review of the 1980s debate engendered by Sandra Gilbert and Susan Gubar's *The Madwoman in the Attic*. A number of militant Milton scholars rushed to engage Gilbert and Gubar, serving as indignant apologists for Milton's views on women. But no amount of quoting from the divorce tracts' lines about the ideal equality of male and female minds can outweigh Milton's failure to mention (or imagine?) any specific woman who might marry his mind.

In teaching *Paradise Lost* to the twenty-first-century student, we must not be tempted into cultural or intellectual relativism. To make the case that Milton's Eve is better than Paul's Eve is to clarify, not to absolve, Milton's misogyny. But is Milton—as Virginia Woolf implies—a cultural absolute of woman hating? Absolutely not. Nor is he a feminist. Teachers who try to engage students by setting up false dichotomies—good witch / bad witch, feminist/misogynist—will fall to their own destruction as surely as did Satan and the rebel angels. Although, if there is enough time in the class, it can be very useful to let students fall into either of these twin pits of error and then dig themselves back out, the truth of the matter lies unsurprisingly in an Aristotelian middle. The best proving ground for this is the poem. The two first-person creation narratives—Eve's in book 4 and Adam's in book 8—allow us to sort out culpability and capacity, both cosmic and individual, in a fairly simple matrix. Eve's first actions as she narrates them to Adam, Adam's first actions as presented to Raphael, God's role in each narrative, and Adam's revision of Eve's narrative give us discrete points of exchange from which to evaluate the question of responsibility. As Eve's narrative reveals her limitations, we realize, more in sorrow than in anger, that her capacity is too limited to bear any significant responsibility for the fall. While students may find this reasoning—"the bimbo defense," a student once called it—more objectionable than straightforward Pauline polemics, a careful presentation of book 10 will remind the class that Adam is arguably even less clear-thinking than his spouse. What exiles the couple from paradise is not the binary of their differing genders but the limitations of their shared humanity.

That said, the very bones of language articulate the gender bias we find in Milton's penning of Eve.

Of all the dichotomies we can apply to *Paradise Lost*, the least reductive and most revealing is the grammatical—active and passive, subject and object. This approach to teaching the poem not only has the advantage of giving students a quick fix on its gender dynamics but also offers a low-tech entry into the elevated language of epic discourse. To set up a close reading of the two creation narratives, I find it worthwhile to take the time to look at the assignment of gender to Eden. (The assignment of gender to the cosmos is even more fascinating, but both deeper into the epic and agonizingly complex.) Putting students in teams to identify gendered elements of the landscape is more effective than individual competition, but in either paradigm the tiebreaker arguments about the importance of a "he" versus an "it" can get a class to realize how lucky we are that English nouns can be gender-neutral. Generally, I wait until the end of the exercise to tell them that Milton's choices are not consistent with any language they might expect—not Hebrew or Greek or Latin.

Eden, we learn in book 4, is feminine. Satan comes to the border of Eden, "where delicious Paradise, / Now nearer, Crowns with her enclosure green" (4.132–33), and fewer than one hundred lines later we are told that "*Eden* stretch'd her Line / . . . Eastward" (4.210–11). God set the boundaries of Eden, and here Milton presents a feminine geography circumscribed by a masculine maker, the feminine earth being the raw material for the maker's masculine creation.[2] And yet the geographic features of Eden are identified as both male and female and assigned gender with less attention to poetic tradition and etymology than we generally expect to find in Milton's poetry. One of the first-mentioned topographic features of the garden is "a River large," which went "Southward," "Nor chang'd his course," and "which from his darksome passage now appears" (4.223, 223, 224, 232). There seems to be, initially, no reason for the river's being given a masculine pronoun; the Lethe in book 2 and the "river of blis" in book 3 are both feminine, and the Nile in book 12 is genderless. Other features of the garden—trees, glades, sands, hills, dales—are here left genderless, even if they are given a gender elsewhere in the poem, and nature (elsewhere consistently feminine), art, and earth are here neither masculine nor feminine. Paradoxically, both the inconsistency of Milton's gendering and the lack of logic with which the poet assigns genders make the reader more aware of the problematic relationship between gender and identity in the poem.

God sets the boundaries of Eden, Eden's valley sets the course of the river, and the river creates the feminine lake in the "lap" of a valley (2.254). Or does the widening of the valley into a plain create the lake? The former appears to be the case, at least syntactically, since the river is always mentioned as the source of the lake. But without the lap of the feminine valley, there would be no space for a lake to exist. Where the waters from the river "unite their streams" (4.263) and after they have fallen down "the slope hills dispersed" (4.261), the poet-narrator arbitrarily assigns the pronoun "her" to the lake, replacing the "his" of the river. Milton gives us an elementally feminine universe, but a universe where those elemental feminine forces are circumscribed by masculine principles.

Eve's initial encounter with Eden is rendered problematic by Milton's invocation of the Narcissus story, but as a narrative it lacks the specificity of Adam's in many ways. Even though this narrative is presented as memory, memory which we might expect to be embellished by subsequent knowledge, Eve's speech does not indicate her gender. She quotes the "voice" who will take her to "hee / Whose image thou art, him thou shalt enjoy." That voice gives her two names, Eve and Mother, but these names are not identified as male or female by the voice of God or by Eve, only by our fallen knowledge. Eve also quotes Adam's odd third-person identification of himself, "whom thou fli'st, of him thou art, / His flesh, his bone," but she uses no other gendered pronouns in this narrative.[3] Neither Eve nor God's voice nor Adam marks her as female. She is drawn to the feminine lake; the mirror of that lake gives her the first vision she has of another human form, but she is not allowed to identify herself with that vision, nor does she identify by gender anything that she sees. She speaks of "it," and she is first told of and then shown "he" and quotes God's and Adam's use of the masculine pronoun, but there are no feminine pronouns in this narrative. Only the reader's knowledge of the feminine lake and of fallen sexuality feminizes Eve's identity. Eve herself assigns gender to nothing, and the voices she hears speak only of male-ness, leaving her other-ness unnamed. How, then, can she identify herself as physically different and individual from either Adam or her surroundings? She cannot know herself as separate and particular, as a unique entity in the cosmos, as Adam knows himself. As she is allowed to know her image only in relation to Adam, so can she know her function only in relation to the fruitful earth with which she is associated, not seeing herself as a unique other—which explains why, in book 9, she worries that Adam might enjoy "another Eve" (9.827).

As Eve "yields" to Adam's voice in book 4, satisfying his need for her, so the earth yields to them that which will satisfy their other needs. To honor Raphael's arrival in book 5, Adam sends Eve out to find the fruits of the earth, and the narrative of his order, Eve's activities, and Raphael's response further ties Eve to the fruitful, yielding, feminine earth. Adam orders:

> But go with speed,
> And what thy stores contain, bring forth and pour
> ·
> . . . well we may afford
> Our givers thir own gifts, and large bestow
> From large bestow'd, where Nature multiplies
> Her fertile growth.   (5.313–14, 316–19)

Eve goes forth to gather "Whatever Earth all-bearing Mother yields" (5.338). Earth, identified as "Mother," "yields," as did Eve in her book 4 narrative, and the fruit of that yielding is both implicitly feminine and explicitly under the control of Eve as "She gathers . . . and . . . / Heaps with unsparing hand" and "crushes" and "tempers" the moist and creamy fruits for the feast (5.343–44, 345, 347). Fifty lines later Raphael greets Eve, "Hail Mother of Mankind, whose fruitful Womb / Shall fill the World" (5.388–89). Because Eve yields to the voice of God and the voice of Adam in book 4, she will ultimately yield, as does the earth, the fruit of her womb to "fill the World." The words of Adam, the narrator, and Raphael all associate Eve with the feminine identity of nature and the womb of the world, an association that confirms—or foretells, if we speak of narrative rather than chronological order—not simply Mary but also the feminine cosmos Raphael describes in book 7.

In contrast to Eve, Adam describes the garden into which he awakens, bathed in a sweat that is both generated and devoured by the sun, in terms of gender. Adam feels some connection to the Sun, to which he speaks and which he identifies as male:

> As new wak't from soundest sleep
> Soft on the flow'ry herb I found me laid
> In Balmy Sweat, which with his Beams the Sun
> Soon dri'd, and on the reeking moisture fed.
>
> (8.252–55)

By the streams of Eden dwell all the creatures of Eden, but not the "great Maker," whom Adam also independently identifies as male: "Tell me," he asks the sun, "how may I know him" (8.280). Adam knows that God is male, but this knowledge allows no alternative, nothing other than an exclusively male universe. Unlike Eve, who in her creation narrative displays no knowledge of herself or of gender, Adam speaks of "Myself" and does assign gender—but exclusively masculine. There are no female pronouns in Adam's speech before the creation of Eve. As he describes the naming of the animals, he uses the plural or masculine pronouns ("each Bird stoop'd on his wing" [8.351]). Even when he speaks of pairs of gendered nouns, the pronouns avoid the feminine: "Each with thir kind, Lion with Lioness" (8.393). Lioness is here a name merely; it conveys no awareness of the inherently gendered female. As Marshall Grossman observes about Eve being called "Mother" in book 4 (4.475), the name "is delivered as a style, a title" (152).[4] When God responds to Adam's request to meet his maker, God's speech—as remembered by Adam—likewise acknowledges only the male. In lines 316–33 of book 8 the pronouns are "I," "they," "thou," "thee," and "thine." In lines 339–40 God tells Adam, "To thee and to thy Race I give; as Lords / Possess" Eden. God allowed Adam to name the creatures of the earth, and in line 472, in his sleep of abstract fancy, Adam also names the first female with the first female pronoun; in his own act of creation he names this image as image; as object, not subject, he names "her."

Most of the feminine pronouns in Adam's eighty-five-line narrative about Eve are either in the objective or genitive case. Of thirty-four feminine pronouns, only six are subject pronouns, and three of these six are widely scattered.[5] Moving beyond the obvious implications of subject/object, Patricia Parker points out the more sinister implications of the genitive, which "is always possessed by something it depends upon" (29). This constitutes a remarkably good description of Eve's position in book 8: Eve is returned to Adam "Led by her Heav'nly Maker" with "Grace . . . in all her steps, Heav'n in her Eye" (8.485, 488). "The genitive," Parker continues, "(despite or perhaps because of its associations with both gender and the generative) is always grammatically related to another," as is Eve (29). Adam sees Eve as an object, first as an object to which he has given life, then as an object of desire. With only one major exception, Eve exists here as an object or as a pronoun in the genitive case, which allows her to possess attributes in "her steps," "her Eye," "her Name," "her worth," "Her loveliness," "her presence," and, most significant, the possibility of "Her loss," all of which make her more pleasing as an object of desire. Eve attains the status of subject only in relation to her disappearance. "Shee disappear'd," then back "she came, / Led"; after Adam speaks to her—"She heard me thus"—Eve turns away, but, responding to Adam's pleas, once again "she turn'd" (8.478, 484, 500, 507). Only the first subject pronoun, marked by the alternative spelling "Shee," denotes an Eve acting not in response to Adam or to God, and even there, all Adam has to do is "to deplore / Her loss" and she returns, led by God (8.479–80). Eve's actions are subordinated to those of Adam and of God with a determined consistency we dare not ignore. Her power lies in Adam's response to her, not in her own speech or actions.

By examining the poem's grammar in detail, it is possible to engage students in a close reading of the text while still allowing them to address what they will almost certainly consider the largest issue in the epic. Moreover, placing the question of bias in the context of grammar, instead of in more recognizably realms of editorial word choice, offers students subtle tools for crafting their own versions of paradise.

NOTES

Portions of this essay are adapted, with permission, from the chapter on Eve in my *Medusa's Mirror: Spenser, Shakespeare, Milton, and the Metamorphoses of the Female Self*.

[1] All references to *Paradise Lost* are to Hughes's edition of the poem in *Complete Poems and Major Prose*.

[2] I make these arguments at greater length in *Medusa's Mirror*.

[3] On the relationship between Adam's and Eve's differing accounts of their first meeting, see Sauer's essay in this volume; Herman, *Destabilizing* 53–54.

[4]Grossman is using *style* here as defined in the *Oxford English Dictionary*, def. 2b18: "A legal, official, or honorific title" (qtd. in 167n); see esp. 151–52.

[5]That Milton was well aware of these nuances of grammar is apparent in his *Accedence Commenc't Grammar*, where he discusses the way in which the Latin case is applied in English with nouns—"The *Genitive* is English with this Sign *of*, as *Libri* of a book" (88)—and pronouns (95–97).

Milton's Adam

Richard Rambuss

Over the years (and beginning with the inspiring course that introduced me to *Paradise Lost* during my junior year in college), I have been struck by those classroom scenes in which students take sides with Milton's Eve or his Adam. I am referring not only to debates about which of them, if either, bears more blame for the fall (a question that Adam and Eve themselves vainly contest "[to] no end" [9.1189]),[1] but also to partisanship that is more character driven than morally or theologically informed. Shades here, one might think, of the preference among the Romantic poets and their followers for Milton's fabulous, daredevil Satan over his cold, doctrinaire God. Lately, though, I have found it much less likely for students to come out as members of the devil's party—much less of Adam's camp—than to be advocates for Eve.

For many of my students—undergraduate and graduate, male and female alike—Eve is the more compellingly drawn of the poem's two human characters. She is often thought to have the better part, the better lines—the better *poetry*, as my Milton professor memorably put it when I was an undergraduate. My students tend to make the like case more impressionistically, asserting that Eve seems more interesting to them than Adam does, that she winds up being the more sympathetic character, or even that she is the smarter, the more resourceful, the more resilient of the pair. They typically find Adam to be narcissistic, brooding, boring, humorless, and, notwithstanding all the poem's declarations of his superior intellectual endowment, more prone to getting things wrong. I suspect that mine is not the only classroom in which such characterological appraisals have been put forth. Nor does one have to look hard to find similar judgments in Milton criticism. And it is difficult to discount these impressions given Adam's startling admission to Raphael, near the end of book 8, that he feels inferior to Eve whenever he lays eyes on her. Adam even worries that in creating her from out of his side, with his bone and blood, God may have miscalculated and taken away too much, leaving Adam, postoperative, somehow now the lesser. The first man's unusual, unsettling word for his experience of this divine surgery is "subducting" (8.536).

There is something attractive about seeing Milton, famously charged by Virginia Woolf as "the first of the masculinists" (*Diary* 192–93), as being of Eve's party without knowing it (or, if not Milton per se, then perhaps the "unconscious" of his text). Yet we would do well for a number of reasons to be circumspect about the kinds of advocacy readings I have sketched. Not the least of those reasons turns on formal considerations involving genre. I will allow my undergraduates, if they are so inclined (and they usually are), some scope for psychologizing interpretations of Adam and Eve, provided that they do not impute motives to the characters that cannot be supported with textual references. But I think it is vital that students keep in mind that they are not here studying characters in a play (a generic road not taken, but, we know, one considered by Milton as a way to render the story of "Adam unparadised"), much less a novel. Milton's Adam and Eve are instead, as John Guillory frames it, "rather like characters in classical epic—they are *ethos* rather than *psyche*." "Their behavior," he explains, "is determined by the pressures upon the text at any given moment and much less upon any overarching conception of their psychological individuality" ("From the Superfluous" 72; see also Guillory, "Milton"). Guillory issues this caveat in the course of a trenchant critique of the essentialism that he finds subtending much of the critical debate over the poem's depiction of these two characters and what that might be taken to mean about Milton's sexual politics. "Hence mistakes that critics no longer make about characters in even the most 'realist' fictions," Guillory objects, "appear commonly in discussions of Adam and Eve, and particularly in the reading of Eve" ("From the Superfluous" 72). In his polemic, Guillory goes so far as to declare Milton's Adam and Eve "relatively uninteresting as characters," by which he means "as representations of people." I would put this point in somewhat different terms. Milton's epic may not be especially concerned with turning out Adam and Eve as literary depictions of real people, as abidingly psychologized, individualized deep subjects, but the poem's rendering of the first man and woman (and not only them among its cast of characters) nonetheless abounds in various subjectivity effects—*gendered* subjectivity effects at that.

That proposition leads to another of my hesitations about advocacy approaches to *Paradise Lost* and to the crux of this short essay. I began by noting my students' tendency to gravitate toward Eve and away from, if not against, Adam. Here I should confess that I too have so tended. For me, this inclination—and I realize that this is by no means the case with all my students, or even with my own college Milton professor—had much to do with a certain kind of feminism. When it came to Milton and the classroom, feminist critical practice seemed for a time to have entailed one or the other of two interpretive procedures. (Sometimes—and I now see that this was my own wont—these plans of attack, however conflicting, could be simultaneously prosecuted.) One would thus, with contracted brow, either condemn Miltonic misogyny and lesson students in critiquing the structures of female subordination in a poem that assigns Adam "Absolute rule" over Eve (4.301) or challenge—or at least try to complicate—that notion of Milton and his poem. That is, one would contest the "largely 'masculinist' critical consensus," as Diane McColley, author of a highly lauded, book-length study, *Milton's Eve*, elsewhere puts it, that sees Milton as "conform[ing] to a traditional reading of the biblical Eve as inherently trivial, vain, and inclined to fall" ("Milton and the Sexes" 175). For McColley and other critics of what I call the feminist redemptionist school, Milton does just the opposite. Note, too, McColley's echo of Woolf on Milton in her redeployment of the term "masculinist." In redeeming Milton's Eve from such sexist shortcomings, McColley thereby exonerates Milton from Woolf's charge of masculinism. That allegation now redounds against not Milton but unenlightened Miltonists—against those who, as McColley sees it, errantly find the poet to be reinforcing rather than "shatter[ing]" such pernicious gender stereotypes ("Milton and the Sexes" 175). Other critic-advocates for Milton's Eve, like Christine Froula, proffer Eve herself as a protofeminist (on Froula, see Nyquist, "Genesis" 119).

What about Milton's Adam? Advocacy for Eve routinely aligns either with an outright antagonism to Adam or (more often the case) with a studied indifference to him. When it comes to *Paradise Lost* and feminism (and feminist-oriented gender studies), the discussion is typically all about Eve. The collection of essays *Milton and Gender*, for example, according to the introductory essay provided by its editor, Catherine Gimelli Martin, "aims to reconsider [Milton] in the light of the most recent developments in feminist theory" ("Introduction" 1). Consult the book's index and you will find an ample entry on Eve. The entry is helpfully divided into two subheadings: one for the "biblical" Eve and another for "Milton's character" Eve. There is, however, no such corresponding entry on Milton's Adam, not even a page. (Similarly, there's a sizable entry for "Dalila [Milton's character]," but nothing on Milton's Samson.) The book's concern with maleness, at least as it is registered by its index, is tellingly filed under the headings "masculinism" and "patriarchy," which stand in paired contrast to the collection's affirmative (or at least neutral) headings for "feminism" and "women." The reverberation of that fraught, antagonistic term *masculinism* throughout Milton criticism begs the question of how to name, how to classify, a critical interest, even investment, in male topics. That said, perhaps more remarkable is how the index's entry for "sexuality" directs us to "*see* heterosexuality."

This brings me to my point at last: the way that I approach Milton's Adam in the classroom has shifted significantly in view of the work now being done on gender and sexuality. I am specifically referring to how representations of men and maleness—male subjectivities, male desire, male bodies, male affect, male-male relations—have come to be recognized as complex questions warranting critical analysis and not simply antipatriarchal critique. This is especially (but not only) so in the relatively new enterprise of queer studies. Related scholarship concerned with the history of sexuality—a project that seems to me to have more effectively taken hold in Shakespeare studies than in Milton studies—has taught us that the discourses of male desire and the performances of masculinity are no more monolithic over (or even within) the ages than are those of female desire and femininity. The male subject is also the sex that is not one (see Rambuss 585). We are in the midst of an efflorescence of theoretical, historical, and interdisciplinary work on gender and sexuality, and it can be put to good use making more subtle the discussion of Milton's Adam.

Let me be clear. I am not at all inclined to discount the poem's patriarchal strains. But I have found that there is much more to do in the classroom with Milton's Adam (not to say with Milton's God) than simply recite what rankles about "He for God only, she for God in him" (4.299). The theoretical paradigms of Eve Kosofsky Sedgwick's *Between Men: English Literature and Male*

Homosocial Desire—to name one work that broke new analytical ground on "the male question"—continue to be helpful, I find, in opening other lines of inquiry involving Adam (and male relations) in *Paradise Lost*, even though it is not one of the canonical texts that Sedgwick herein rereads.[2] Her elaboration of a continuum of male homosocial desire, for instance, can provide a Milton course with theoretical leverage on the affective relations in the poem between the Father and the Son; God and Adam (what does it mean to be created "for" God?); the Son and Satan (rivalry is another kind of bond); and especially Adam and Raphael, the "sociable spirit" who makes a sensuously stimulating entrance into paradise in book 5, sent by God to talk with Adam "as friend with friend" (5.221, 229).[3] Linda Gregerson has written beautifully on the symposium-like setting of Adam and Raphael's conversation, parsing the invocations of love poetry that pervade it (163–76). "Nor are thy lips ungraceful, sire of men," Raphael later blazons of Adam (8.218). "Lips" stand for words, but, given that the angel goes on to size up how "all comeliness and grace / Attends" the first man's "image fair" (8.222–23, 221), it is clear that he is not only trafficking in synecdoche. As for Adam's response to Raphael, Peter C. Herman argues that the sire of men prefers the angel's company to Eve's (*Destabilizing* 142). "Desire with thee still longer to converse" (8.252), Adam admits, induces him first to dilate the gripping story of his own waking up into being. Then, to forestall further the departure of his heavenly visitor, he poses his blush-begetting question about whether angels have sex. We have been told earlier in the poem about the angels' trans- and double-gendered capabilities in their corporeal dealings with humans: "For spirits when they please / Can either sex assume, or both" (1.423–24). But Adam only knows the angels to be male. So his question about angel sex is also one about male-male intercourse. Can "spirits masculine" have sex, Adam wants to know (10.890), and if so, how do they copulate? Utter, mutual interpenetration, comes the heavenly answer: "Total they mix, union of pure with pure / Desiring," admits Raphael (8.627–28), "with a smile that glowed / Celestial rosy red, love's proper hue" (8.618–19). Interesting discussions have also emerged in my classes about the eroticism of the poem's male author's relation to his Adam, the exemplar of Miltonic "manly grace" (4.490).

I like to approach *Paradise Lost* in the classroom in terms of the poem's fault lines: the clefts between its proclaimed orthodoxies (such as divine justice and male primacy) and its narrative effects, which often diverge from and sometimes even disrupt the epic's ideology. The sessions that I allot to Milton's Eve continue to serve that pedagogical endeavor well. But I have recently found that a close look at Milton's Adam, particularly from the vantage of what I present in class as the *problem* of desire in Eden, is just as important. Let me then quickly outline one example of how I structure a series of discussions along these lines. Several classes after we have done a close reading of the scene of the newly created Eve at Milton's Ovidian mirroring pool, I direct my students to other moments in the poem when she is the object not of her own desiring gaze, as in book 3, but of Adam's. Here I like to supply them with an additional theoretical apparatus, one adapted from outside literary studies—Laura Mulvey's manifesto on the gaze, "Visual Pleasure and Narrative Cinema."[4]

Mulvey observes that while the woman "is an indispensable element of spectacle in normal narrative film, . . . her visual presence tends to work against the development of a story line, to freeze the flow of action in moments of erotic contemplation" (11). That claim can be brought to bear on Eve's arresting departure scene near the beginning of book 8, once Adam and Raphael's tête-à-tête has turned cosmological and "abstruse" (8.40). This interlude, which interrupts the narration of their conversation for more than twenty lines, seems meant to show that Eve is designed for and indeed prefers divine colloquy as mediated through her husband: an enactment at the level of the poem's narrative of "He for God only, she for God in him." But does this passage, I ask my students, ultimately have that effect? Sitting at first "retired in sight," Eve dramatically rises "With lowliness majestic from her seat" (8.41–42) and walks across the field of vision, staging herself—think of Grace Kelly's riveting entrance scene in Hitchcock's *Rear Window*, one of Mulvey's exemplary filmic texts—as the object of the male gaze. That act of display imbues Eve's ravishing female form with an irresistible cupidinous influence, as "A pomp of winning graces . . . / . . . from about her shot darts of desire / Into all eyes to wish her still in sight" (8.61–63). Just a few lines earlier Eve's demeanor is described as "goddess-like" (8.59), perhaps in evocation of Venus, the goddess of love herself. Then, as we have just noted, the poem cuts across genders in figuring Eve's "winning graces" as armed, as endowed with penetrative arrows of erotic desire. My aim here is to set students thinking about how complexly gendering operates in Milton's poem, even in scenes that appear to be underwritten by the most patriarchal premises. It is also worth calling their attention (if they have yet to notice it on their own) to the phrase "all eyes," inasmuch as it draws the angel as well as Adam desiringly within Eve's erotic visual penumbra. Milton's she-Cupid Eve thus commandeers the gaze in a triangulated spectatorial field constructed between man and angel. In a way that traverses species and genders, Milton's Eve monopolizes just about every gaze in the poem: Adam's, Satan's, and Raphael's, as well as her own.

Adam more directly connects the gaze—here called the "glance"—to power in a later passage in the same book when, in explaining the weak-in-the-knees effect that Eve has on him, he declares himself "in all enjoyments else / Superior and unmoved, here only weak / Against the charm of beauty's powerful glance" (8.531–33). Is this a phenomenological account of the transportive effects of gazing at beauty? Or of beauty—the beautiful one—gazing back at you? Who wields the gaze here? And how is erotic power distributed between the one who looks and the one who is looked at? What happens when both look? Sometimes my students come to the same conclusion that I have about the provocatively ambiguous phrase "beauty's powerful glance": namely, that the indeterminacy of its referent might be taken as the point. Adam confesses to Raphael that whenever he contemplates Eve in "Her loveliness, so absolute she seems / And in her self complete" that "All higher knowledge in her presence falls" (8.547–48, 551); that is, there is a fall before the fall—into desire. Even in prelapsarian Eden, desire—a state that seizes Adam as soon as he awakens into consciousness (8.252, 354–55)—troubles the poem's manifest claims about male dominance, to say nothing of overschematized applications of Mulvey's account of power, pleasure, and the gendered gaze.

The unsettledness of the poem's conceptions of male subjectivity, male authority, and masculine relations (both same-sex and cross-sex) is lost when Milton is simply labeled "the first of the masculinists." McColley notes approvingly the "lively debate on both Dalila and Eve" that has unfolded over the past several decades in Milton studies ("Milton and the Sexes" 181). The time is ripe for a new debate—in the classroom as well as in the criticism—on Adam, a figure who lately seems more interesting to me every time I teach *Paradise Lost*. Feminist critics have been at work since the 1970s, refashioning the way that we read and teach Milton's Eve. What new interpretive vantages onto Milton's Adam, as well as Milton's "Second Adam," as the Son of God is here called (11.383), can other approaches to gender and sexuality afford us? The aim of such an inquiry is hardly to reinscribe Adamic supremacy, much less to offer a new brief for a masculinism proffered in opposition to feminism. Other approaches to gender and sexuality can differ from feminist ones without being opposed to them. Nor, however, do I think that the most interesting way forward lies in "redeeming" Adam or Eve or Adam and Eve as a couple. I would prefer instead that my students think critically about Milton's Adam and Eve in relation to his poem's various epical set pieces of desire—texts that are to be read within a history of sexual (and other) discourses. As for a consideration of how masculinity is constructed, performed, and experienced, there would seem to be few more germane starting points than the Judeo-Christian first man and Milton's canonical literary representation of him.

NOTES

[1] All references to Milton are to Orgel and Goldberg's *John Milton: A Critical Edition of the Major Works*.

[2] See also Halley's discussion of "Milton's homosocial poetics" in "Female Autonomy"; her *Split Decisions: How and Why to Take a Break from Feminism* has been an inspiration for the theoretical tack I suggest here.

[3] Goldberg treats the erotics of their conversation in the chapter "Milton's Angels" in *The Seeds of Things* (189–95). Goldberg also considers here the "angelic couple" of Lucifer and Belial, who, he points out, are bedfellows both in heaven and in hell (197).

[4] Mulvey establishes two gendered positions with respect to the gaze in classic Hollywood cinema: the woman as image and the man as bearer of the look.

Paradise Lost and Milton's Biography

John T. Shawcross

A reader immediately confronts the author of *Paradise Lost* within the first twenty-six lines of the poem:

>   I thence
> Invoke thy aid to my adventrous Song
> . . . .
> And chiefly Thou O Spirit . . .
> . . . .
> Instruct me, for Thou know'st; . . .
> . . . .
>   . . . What in me is dark
> Illumine, what is low raise and support;
> That to the highth of this great Argument
> I may assert Eternal Providence,
> And justifie the wayes of God to men.
>   (1.12–26)[1]

Herein is one aspect of the biographical content in the long epic that constantly appears and fascinates the student, Milton's "overwhelming sense of vocation." That phrase depicts part of the "authorial personality" that James D. Fleming discusses in "Biographic Milton: Teaching the Undead Author." Milton is indeed never dead but lives in his writing in three significant ways: through recounted biographical events and experiences, through beliefs and attitudes that emerge both positively and negatively, and through his presence as writer employing form and literary devices and allusive material. The proem to book 1 evokes from students numerous questions of meaning and reference, all of which relate to the author, who has expressed an egotism that leads him to believe he can achieve "Things unattempted yet in Prose or Rime" (1.16), can enlist the "Spirit" who "from the first / Wast present" to aid him (1.17, 19–20), and has the ability to "assert Eternal Providence" and thereby "justifie the wayes of God" (1.25, 26).[2] Having the class question the meaning and accuracy of this language leads to interesting reactions.

One problem in dealing with this poem is its length and intricate interrelationships, its amplification or revision (even refutation and replacement) of conclusions that a reader may have reached previously. Thus an important approach for the instructor of students first encountering the text is to examine the biographical events and experiences to which the proems in books 1, 3, 7, and 9 refer. The proem to book 3 (lines 1–55) again invokes a divine personage and recounts what the author has presented in the previous two books: "Thee I revisit now with bolder wing" (3.13), having left hell ("the *Stygian* Pool" [3.14]) and chaos. But the self observed in the first proem is here more strongly modified by recognition of the agency of "the heav'nly Muse," the "holy Light" with its "sovran vital Lamp" (3.19, 1, 22). Most important, the reader becomes aware of the physical blindness of the poet, who expresses that condition as deterrent to awareness of the world around him and is thus more emboldened by that "holy Light" to be able to "see and tell / Of things invisible to mortal sight" (3.54–55).

Both proems set up various topics for class reports and for themes that students may pursue: When and why did Milton become blind, and when did he begin and complete this poem? How was the text produced if he was blind? What were Milton's religious beliefs? Who is the "Spirit" of the first proem, and what is its relationship with the "holy Light" of the second? To what or whom do such allusions as "one greater Man" (1.4), "*Sion* Hill" (1.10), "*Siloa's* Brook" (1.11), "th'*Aonian* Mount" (1.15), and "Blind *Thamyris* and blind *Mæonides*, / And *Tiresias* and *Phineus*" refer (3.35–36), and why are they included? Answers provide biographical and philosophical information about the author, as well as about his knowledge, life experiences, and intention in pursuing this epic. This approach will yield answers that provide understanding when students encounter the full text of the poem.

The proem to book 7 (lines 1–39) makes clear that a second half of the poem is now to be engaged ("Half yet remains unsung" [7.21]), with a different general topic: the first half explored the cause for the loss of paradise; the second examines the actual loss and its unending results. Again there is some summary of the previous text, further divine invocation, now to the "Heav'nlie born" "Urania" (7.7, 1) and to the author's blindness, but also directly biographical references to the "evil dayes, / . . . evil dayes . . . and evil tongues; / . . . with dangers compast round, / And solitude" (7.25–28), relieved only by Urania's nightly inspirational visits (a topic offering much to be discussed). The repetition of "evil dayes" requires awareness of numerous political confrontations, through Milton's prose writings and his position in Oliver Cromwell's government; of Milton's imprisonment in 1660; and of the governmental alterations between the 1650s and the 1660s, ushered in by the Restoration. The proem to book 9 (lines 1–47), while iterating briefly what preceded as well as acknowledging the author's "Celestial Patroness" (9.21), announces that in this book "I now must change / Those Notes to Tragic" (9.5–6). The substance of the book will be not that of classical epic but rather "that which justly gives Heroic name / To Person or to Poem" (9.40–41) — that is, if Milton continues to live, his "intended wing" not "Deprest" (9.45, 46), and if his divine instructor continues nightly to make the "vast Abyss" of his darkness within "pregnant" and "Dove-like" (1.21, 22, 21). Querying these expressions produces an overview of the authorial intention for the full poem.

Students are continually confronted by the author, his life experiences, his "combative personality" and "radical politics" (Fleming 24), his religious convictions, and his literary presence. The last proem raises several important questions: What is epic? What is a hero, and who is the hero of this epic? What is Milton hoping to convey to his readers as the means to becoming heroic themselves? An instructor's guidance through such subjects and questions evokes a deep awareness of Milton's philosophical achievement. Examination of the four proems not only establishes the author and his milieu but also offers an overview of the full poem and helps students see how the pieces fit together as the whole work is revealed in all its complexities of narrative and internal references (including its daunting proleptic passages). Class reports, class discussions, and theme topics clearly emerge in the proems to books 7 and 9 and point to the psychological dimension of the author and the reasons for the poem's segmented structure.

The question of Milton's controversial beliefs has arisen since the poem was first published—the hero; the presentation of God, whose words are actually given; the unorthodox relationship between God the Father and God the Son that raises the unorthodoxy of so-called Arianism or subordinationism and the rejection of a trinity; and the treatment of gender and the position of woman. Such problems surface in the proems and underlie students' reading and understanding of the full poem, thereby leading to biographical conclusions about the inner Milton, the thinker behind the writing. The instructor, introducing these aspects of the poem, thus sets up further uncertainties. Among pertinent biographical matters is the existence of the narrative voice (see Sauer's essay in this volume): Is this Milton? Does that voice reflect Milton's ideas, for example, when the narrator seems to divide sexual relationship into only either "wedded Love . . . true sourse / Of human offspring" (4.750–51) or "the bought smile / Of Harlots, loveless, joyless, unindeard, / Casual fruition" (4.765–67)? or when he says that Adam partook of the fruit, bringing Death into the world, "not deceav'd" (9.998)?[3] Students will learn much about the poem (and its interpretation) and the author by pursuing these questions (see the essays in this volume by Bryson; Wolfe; Loewenstein; and Sauer).

The presence of the author, thus "undead" in another important way, may also be established by the instructor's introduction of devices ("limina") employed to get the message across and to create the literary masterpiece that *Paradise Lost* is. The first of two examples that might engross students concerns the following questions: How is the creation of all things achieved? How does *creatio ex deo* (rather than the biblical *creatio ex nihilo*) fit in the existence of chaos as well as sin? What will be the end of time (recalling the purposeful repetition of 1 Corinthians 15.28, that all things will be put under God so "that God may be all in all")? How has Milton driven home this concept and the hope for salvation for humankind with the last words of a character in the poem (that is, the blank verse sonnet that Eve speaks [12.610–23])? A second example poses another set of questions: At what line in book 2 is death introduced? Why is this significant? (The line is 666, recalling the great beast of Revelation 13.11–18, which thus points to the first beast of Revelation 13.1–10, that is, sin, introduced a few lines before.) Milton's use of such devices—repetition, the sonnet, allusion, numerological considerations — tell us much about the author, his thinking, and the intentionality he imbues in his work.[4]

Milton's biography colors the poem in the three ways noted at the beginning of this essay, and the instructor's approaching the poem through those means creates a valuable reading and interpretation of the full poem and the major critical considerations that have been raised since it first appeared in 1667.

NOTES

[1] All references to *Paradise Lost* are to Shawcross's edition in *Complete Poetry of John Milton*.

[2] The instructor should consider with the class that, according to Addison's interpretation of Aristotle, "the Author of an Heroic Poem should seldom speak himself," employing instead "the Mouths of . . . his principal Actors" (9 Feb. 1712). Addison enumerates several of these "digressions" where Milton enters his text (for Addison, one of the poem's "defects"), only to add, "there is so great a Beauty in these very Digressions that I would not wish them out of the Poem."

[3] We should remember, however, that the latter idea is derived from 1 Timothy 2.14 ("And Adam was not deceived, but the woman being deceived was in the transgression"), although it has usually not been cited in criticism or editions of *Paradise Lost*. The specific question of whether the remark in 9.998 is the narrative voice's statement or Milton's "masculinist" attitude is clearly pertinent.

[4] For further examination of an author's presence in his or her writing, see Shawcross, "Poet" and *Intentionality*.

Narrators

Elizabeth Sauer

"Few characters in non-dramatic literature appear as free as Milton's to choose their own story," Gordon Teskey discerned in 1986 (11). My pedagogical approach to *Paradise Lost* in my first-year, senior-year, and graduate courses includes an extensive analysis of the fundamental and vexing subject of narration and narrative perspective. The recommendations for teaching *Paradise Lost* that I propose here challenge the claims to totalization made by various twentieth-century Miltonists. Critics including Anne Ferry, Louis Martz, William Riggs, Arnold Stein, and John Guillory (*Poetic Authority*), for example, suppressed or resolved tensions in the multivocal epic by positing a univocal, ubiquitous poet-narrator who conveys a powerful "impression of conscious control, deliberate artistry, and carefully articulated method" (Ferry 17). I encourage my students to discover how the politics of narration—an act of transgressing boundaries at once literary, narratological, historical, cultural, and political—directly affects any interpretation of the poem. As Joseph Wittreich has observed, the question of narrative perspective is usefully interrogated by a new Milton criticism that "reaches beyond the narrator's voice to narrative voices, and then to the questions of whether some are privileged and, more challengingly, to an assessment of the relative reliability of those often competing voices" (Afterword 243). There is a politics to Milton's poetics, and in *Paradise Lost* the dialogized voice of the poet-narrator and the multiple, often irreconcilable narrative perspectives and creation stories prevent the poem from adding up to one monumental whole.

In teaching students about narrative technique, I address the following contexts and issues:

1. the poet's use and adaptation of the epic convention of an objective, dominant narrator; the relationship between the poet and the narrative voice he
   constructs; theoretical models and vocabularies for broaching these topics
2. the relationship between Milton's poet-narrator and other narrators in *Paradise Lost* and their status in relation to one another (e.g., the destabilizing
   intersections of Adam's and Eve's autobiographical narratives)
3. the correspondences and conversations between Milton's narrators and authorial voices in extraliterary seventeenth-century writings

Illuminating this last approach are the kinds of comparisons drawn by J. Martin Evans, who studies Milton's narrative techniques in the context of narrative
strategies in English colonial histories. Evans characterizes the Miltonic narrator "not [as] a single euphonious instrument but [as] a chorus of individual and
sometimes discordant voices which echo the complex acoustics of Renaissance
colonial discourse" (*Milton's Imperial Epic* 113). To test this thesis, which exploits connections between narration and postcoloniality and expands the exploration and historicizing of voice, I invite students to compare excerpts from
colonialist treatises and geographic compendiums with corresponding passages
in Milton's epic, thus exhibiting interrelations among literary critical, historicist,
feminist, and postcolonial readings.

The Poet-Narrator

First it is critical to consult a glossary of literary terms to define *narrator* and to
identify the types of narration in literary criticism. As a speaker, voice, or character that recounts the events in a literary work, the narrator is usually but not
always involved in the plot. Narratives communicate points of view, whether as
first-person, third-person, omniscient, limited-omniscient, intrusive, unintru-
sive, fallible, or unreliable. To establish the type of narrator used in *Paradise
Lost*, students need to distinguish his words from those of the other characters,
a task complicated by their unfamiliarity with speeches that are not directly and
specifically introduced or enclosed by quotation marks. Learning to distinguish
among the different voices in the poem involves recognizing and interpreting
epithets (e.g., "Portress of Hell Gate" [2.746]; "our general Ancestor" [4.659];
"the meagre Shadow" [10.264]).[1] Students will need to judge the degree to
which the narrator conditions interpretations of speeches delivered by other
characters (e.g., 1.125–27; 1.589b–621) and whether and how his interventions,
apostrophes, and outbursts affect the unfolding of events and the reader's response to them (e.g., 9.404–11).

The structuralist Donald F. Bouchard remarks on the ill-fated journey of the
flawed narrator in the poem by pointing to the "numerous false starts, hesitations, and interruptions" that are "balanced by presumptions, faulty identifi-
cations, accusations, and counter-accusations: beginning nowhere and leading
'God knows where'" (108). According to Bouchard, Milton's formulation of

voice involves the creation of two speakers—the narrator and the Muse, each controlling a different narration in the poem. The narrator's composition is a temporal construction, whereas the Muse establishes through its playfulness a "sort of oblique counter-point to the sequential action of the poem" (110) and creates meaning at the narrator's expense (109). The double-voiced narrations and the disjunctions between signifier and signified unsettle any direct identification of author and narrator. Even in works produced in the first person, as Michel Foucault famously asserted, "neither the first-person pronoun nor the present indicative refers exactly to the writer or to the moment in which he writes, but rather to an alter ego whose distance from the author varies. . . . It would be just as wrong to equate the author with the real writer as to equate him with the fictitious speaker" (112). Wittreich has formulated the relationship between writer and speaker differently: he judges that the prologues to four of the books of *Paradise Lost* "present different versions of the performing self. . . . Just as there are blurrings of characters, protagonists with antagonists, so in the four prologues, with autobiographical detail as the agent, there are repeated blurrings of the poem's narrator and its author" ("Reading Milton" 13). The proems are extractable from the poem and comprise a developmental narrative, although one must note the irony of their increasing pessimism. The last proem is not an invocation at all: the suggestion that the "mortal voice" of the poet may be speaking alone affords the possibility of meaninglessness or bacchic cacophony, an especially destabilizing prospect given that only fallen and satanic characters have soliloquies in Milton's epic (9.41–47).

The relationship between the narrator and the poem raises the thorny issue of intentionalism. Stanley Fish determines that all readings presuppose authorial intention and that "meaning, intention, and biography are inextricable" ("Biography" 15), a position that departs from his reader-response criticism on the power invested in the interpretative community to construe textual significances. Conscious of the incompatibility of these positions in Fish—as is Peter C. Herman in *Destabilizing Milton*—Stephen Fallon chooses to read with intention in mind while acknowledging the "unresolved tensions in the author" that surface unintentionally (*Milton's Peculiar Grace* 12). In my senior undergraduate course, I assign readings from biographies of Milton (Shawcross, *John Milton*, ch. 16; S. Fallon, *Milton's Peculiar Grace*, ch. 8; Lewalski, *Life*, ch. 13; Campbell and Corns, chs. 15–16) and then invite students to observe how the narrator of *Paradise Lost* resembles or differs from his creator as variously characterized by the biographers.

Narrations

As Fallon perceives:

> Milton himself speaks on both sides of the question of whether characters should be taken as proxies for their authors. . . . Milton is always arguing,

> and his arguments are ventriloquized in his characters. In *Paradise Lost*,
> Milton speaks through Adam, Satan, Raphael, Eve, Abdiel, the Son, and
> the Father, in addition to the narrators. Here one could enter mazes of
> self-representation and find no end.   (*Milton's Peculiar Grace* 3)

The question of the narrator's function as an author intermediary is further
complicated by the inclusion of multiple narrators and the entanglement of the
voices of characters choosing and then recounting their own autobiographical
stories. The relationship between the narrator and Satan is a case in point. Even
when Satan does not speak, he often serves as a focalizer whose perspective is
mediated by but also occasionally eclipses that of the official narrator. Closely
connected with narration, *focalization* refers to the angle of perception or the
concrete perceptual point. At the start of book 3, the narrator moves out of hell
with Satan, who surveys the new world through the narrator's mediation:

> his eye discovers unaware
> The goodly prospect of some foreign land
> First seen . . .
> . . . .
> Such wonder seiz'd, though after Heaven seen,
> The Spirit malign, but much more envy seiz'd,
> At sight of all this World beheld so fair.
>   (3.547–54)

In the following book, Satan and the narrator enter the garden together, their
views superimposed: "Beneath him with new wonder now he [Satan] views / To
all delight of human sense expos'd / In narrow room Nature's whole wealth, yea
more" (4.205–07), and a paradisal panorama unfolds for them both, one that
seizes them with wonder that then induces different responses.

   In addition to analyzing the entanglement of the characters of Satan and the
narrator, I invite my students to produce comparative examinations of Sin's autobiographical narrative, Eve's creation account in book 4, and Adam's version
in book 8, in which Eve's genesis story is corrected and by which it is enveloped.
I ask students to address questions like the following: Is a feminist interpretation of Eve's account in book 4 possible? How does our reading of Eve's narrative change in the light of Adam's creation story in book 8? How does Milton's
poet-narrator condition our response to the two autobiographical accounts?
The autobiographical stories of Sin, Eve, and Adam are shaped by the gendered
hierarchy of discourse established by Milton in the poem: Adam's remembering of Eve's story in book 8 indicates that female expression and creativity must
be channeled into male agency to be legitimate. Finally, Milton assigns Adam
rather than Eve a part in the unfolding of Michael's prophetic revelation in book
11 and his narration in book 12.

   The instructional narratives of Raphael and Michael are readily comparable.
The emphasis on reciprocity, illumination, and communication through analogy

in Raphael's account contrasts with Michael's concern with judgment, typology, and dogmatic pedagogy. Further, whereas the retrospective episodes in the *Odyssey* and *Aeneid* are less significant than the primary narrations in the respective Homeric and Vergilian epics, Raphael's and Michael's stories compete in importance and length with that of Milton's blind poet-narrator, whose memory and prophetic powers are limited. His frame narrative embeds the histories of the angelic narrators and of the poem's other speakers structurally but not conceptually. The fragmentation in *Paradise Lost* of the unified teleology of the classical epics as well as of the official Genesis creation accounts — Genesis 1 is foregrounded in book 7, whereas Adam's autobiography in book 8 relies on Genesis 2's account of a gender hierarchy — results in a contrapuntal narrative of multiple histories and creation stories.

Exploration Literature

Balachandra Rajan describes the epic voice of *Paradise Lost* as "the voice of the imperial imagination, of sumptuous orchestration, of metaphorical opulence, the encyclopaedic, outreaching, all-encompassing voice, the voice of the unifying imperative. No one articulates this voice more resplendently than Milton; and no one struggles against it more insistently" (108). Historicized readings of Milton's narrative voice become manageable and meaningful when readers concentrate on a subject like colonial discourse. New historicist approaches that establish dialogues between the poetic and the other voices of early modern history and culture — and that also interrogate notions of authorial agency and intentionalism — open up the poem to the complexities of literary and cultural representations. Reiterating a point by Natalie Zemon Davis, Paul Stevens judges that "sensitivity to the complexity of literary texts has a deeply enriching effect — it makes the historian sensitive to the rhetorical constitution of all her texts" (278). In Milton's epic, moreover, concepts such as multiple narrators, open forms, and the exchanges between the poetic voices and discourses of the early modern period tell us something about how the poem was circulated to speak to past times and how it may be recuperated to speak to ours (Sauer, *Barbarous Dissonance* 161).

Depending on the range of course material, one can usefully compare voice and perspective or focalization in *Paradise Lost* with selections from canonical works on exploration, imaginary and paradisal worlds, and colonization, such as More's *Utopia*, book 3 of Spenser's *The Faerie Queene*, Shakespeare's *Tempest*, and Harrington's *Oceana*. The challenge is to read such writings not just for content but also specifically for representations of voice and perspective, while always attending to the generic differences of the source texts in accounting for the formulations and modulations thereof.

Taking a cue from Evans's chapter "The Narrator" while taking exception to his dissolution of all distinctions between the narrator and Milton (*Milton's Imperial Epic* 170n1), I direct the class's attention to the constructions of voice and point of view in selections from early travel and exploration literature, available through *Early English Books Online*. I begin with the patriotic prose epic *Principal Navigations*, by the first major English geographer, Richard Hakluyt. Characterized by a sweeping geographic and historical reach, *Principal Navigations* features a primary authorial and authoritative voice that soon gives way to the narrations of individual voyagers who attest to their involvement in the travels documented in the voluminous travel narrative. Among the histories I single out is that of Humphrey Gilbert, the founder of the first English colony in North America, who asserts the God-given right to name and claim the land for the English crown (Hakluyt 42). Another historical source is the *New English Canaan*, by the adventurer Thomas Morton, whose colonial narrator is likewise comparable with Milton's. In his "Epistle to the Reader," Morton testifies to his "indevoure to communicat the knowledge which I have gained and collected together, by mine owne observation, in the time of my many yeares residence in those parts, to my loving Country men" (5). Assertions about the assembly of information, an eyewitness ("by mine owne observation"), accurate reporting, and demonstration represent what Michel de Certeau calls the text's "utterative markings" and "modalities" (68). "The most characteristic of the markings," writes Stephen Greenblatt, "is an appeal to the narrator's own presence: 'I have heard,' 'I say,' 'I write,' and above all 'I have seen'" (123). In fact, the discourse of travel largely foregrounds witnessing (122).

The postlapsarian frame of reference of Milton's poet-narrator in *Paradise Lost* results in an overlaying of perspectives and a heavy reliance on metaphors, anachronisms, and negative comparisons, notably in the description of Eden and its prelapsarian inhabitants (e.g., 4.736–47, 765–70). In *New English Canaan*, the paradisal new world is read likewise through a fallen one: the natives, who manage to construct a society resembling Plato's commonwealth, are represented as being uncorrupted in comparison with the English. Morton testifies:

> I have observed that they will not be troubled with superfluous commodities. Such things as they finde, they are taught by necessity to make use of, they will make choise of . . . they passe awaye the time merrily, not regarding our pompe (which they see dayly before their faces) but are better content with their owne, which some men esteeme so meanely of
> (58, ch. 20)

By deliberate and critical contrast to the self-righteousness exhibited by Puritans like William Bradford and John Winthrop—brief excerpts of whose tracts on New England I also review with the class—Morton defends the Amerindians' humanity, discipline, and morality, anticipating the sympathetic position of Roger Williams a decade later. As for *Paradise Lost*, the poet-narrator relies on negations to portray Adam and Eve as guiltless natives of a new world (e.g., 4.312–23) while reserving the account of the fall for the Americanization of the first couple (9.1114–18).

Cosmographie. In Four Books, the massive 1652 chorographical project by the antiquarian and geographer Peter Heylyn, may also have influenced the representation of Milton's geographic surveillance in the poem, both in terms of its encyclopedic resourcefulness and in its underlying philosophy. Part 4.1 of *Cosmographie*, in which Heylyn ascends with the reader to the great heights of Mount Atlas, is a valuable source for interpreting the episode on top of the Mount of Paradise and the long globe-consuming epic catalog in book 11 of *Paradise Lost* (11.383–411). Presented from the vantage point and anti-imperialist critique of the prophetic narrator Michael, the catalog of empires displays to Adam the poetically, spatially configured transcontinental reaches of Asia, Africa, Europe, and also America, which lies beyond the ecliptic or the sun's annual journey.

This essay on narrators is designed to encourage analyses of poetic and narrative strategies that are often downplayed in criticism on *Paradise Lost* and English literature more generally. The point of the interrelated approaches sketched out here is to demonstrate to students how the poem's narrator negotiates the terms of his self-definition as a speaker and his positions of compliance or resistance in relation to the other narrators in the poem and in terms of the authorial voices of early modern culture. These strategies will invigorate literature courses on early modern England by using the epic's voices as a basis for engaging students in productive analyses of *Paradise Lost* and in conversations about the interconnections of literary, historical, and colonialist writings and issues. Here instructors will find models for teaching Milton's epic that increase students' appreciation of narrative perspectives and of the challenges and rewards of identifying some of the multiple points of entry into Milton's resonant, multivocal masterpiece.

NOTES

Research for this essay was generously funded by the Killam Trusts and Canada Council of the Arts, for whose support I am immensely grateful.
[1] All references to *Paradise Lost* are to Hughes's edition in *Complete Poems and Major Prose*.

Approaches to Teaching
Paradise Lost Allegorically

Catherine Gimelli Martin

In what initially appears to be a realist biblical epic, Milton's allegorical characters and scenes often pose puzzling problems of interpretation for teachers and students alike. The most striking examples occur in the Sin and Death episodes of books 2 and 10, but these scenes are not as aberrant as they may at first appear. Although places such as hell, heaven, and chaos are undoubtedly meant to be understood as real places containing real events, they, too, share these episodes' allegorical function of bringing abstract or intangible agents or ideas to life. They all participate in a clearly imagined but nonexperiential reality reported through partly visionary or surreal symbols. Wholly visionary examples include the Son's quasi-apocalyptic Chariot of Paternal Deity, the semisatiric Paradise of Fools, and the bizarre "pontifex" that Sin and Death use to join hell and earth (10.348).[1] Satan's prophetic glimpse of Jacob's ladder at the gates of heaven is especially characteristic because it mixes abstract ideas or meanings, typology or symbolic forecasts of the future, and concrete, realistic details. Sin and Death's bridge performs a similar function: even though it cannot be a concrete place, the bridge, like the rest of Milton's allegorical topography, translates real experiences. Satan begins to understand his exclusion from heaven after seeing Jacob's ladder, confirms the windy or empty status of any alternative heaven in the Paradise of Fools, and, with his children Sin and Death, provides an easy route to hell for all who would follow them. Thus even when the existence of Milton's allegorical places and personae remains dubious at best, they either are given plausible motions or motives or, like the chariot first glimpsed by Ezekiel and the ladder revealed to Jacob in the field of Luz, have strong biblical authority and prophetic power despite their semisurreal functions. Both attributes are equally important in signaling that heaven and earth will never be severed by the approaching fall of mankind, since divine justice and mercy may be delayed but not defeated.

Similar combinations of realism and symbolism occur in the fictional terrain surrounding the gates of hell and Pandemonium. On the one hand, their plausible, easily imaginable, geography asks readers to accept their mimetic status; on the other hand, their description creates abstractions of symbolic proportions. The description of the city the demons set about building in hell matches the fully mimetic, epic descriptions of Troy, Carthage, or Rome in minute detail, yet it still leaves little doubt that Pandemonium is constructed to oppose the City of God. Intervening episodes in Satan's journey achieve much the same effect. Implausibly, Satan manages to set foot on Jacob's ladder, but he symbolically uses this perch to gaze downward to earth, not upward to heaven (3.540–43). As he does so, he is "seized" with wonder, "but much more envy . . . /

At sight of all this world beheld so fair" (3.552, 553–54). Similarly, Sin may un-lock the gates of hell with magical ease (2.878–79), only to be overtaken with realistic consequences. She swiftly opens them to the noise of an appropriately ominous grating and grinding, as

> With impetuous recoil and jarring sound
> Th' infernal doors, and on their hinges grate
> Harsh thunder, that the lowest bottom shook
> Of Erebus. She opened, but to shut
> Excelled her power; the gates wide open stood,
> That with extended wings a bannered host
> Under spread ensigns marching might pass through
> With horse and chariots ranked in loose array;
> So wide they stood, and like a furnace mouth
> Cast forth redounding smoke and ruddy flame.
>
> (2.880–89)

The apparent inconsistencies in this passage once again ask readers to think morally and philosophically, not just naturalistically. If they succeed, they will have far less trouble understanding why the gates of Eden can be physically but not morally barred against Satan. Not only is there no such thing as "fugitive and cloistered virtue" in a freewill universe, there is also no way to eliminate the many temptations or pathways potentially leading to Sin, whose key physically unlocks a portal that she can never close, although she retains the key. Once her temptations are seized, the way forward seems surprisingly easy and smooth, but its aftermath proves just as jarring and grating as the hot, airless darkness that lies below her gates. Afterward, the path only gets wider until furious war-horses loaded with all their gear may easily pass through.

Students familiar with even a few biblical parables involving gates — such as the rich man and the camel or the sheep and the goats (any of which may eas-ily be read in or before class) — can grasp some of these connections but might not be able to follow allegory's continuous and systematic narrative symbolism. For that reason, one might begin at the beginning, with hell, Pandemonium, and the path to earth. That process is not as difficult as it at first seems if stu-dents are properly alerted to the metaphoric structure of common idioms or expressions such as "hold your horses," a type of dead metaphor that great poets easily bring to life. Milton's semiconcealed puns are especially attractive since their pictographic force is not very far beneath the surface. Pandemonium's Greek temple, for example, at once embodies and satirizes the classical military style and republican rhetoric of Satan and all his demons. The satire becomes particularly evident after plutocrats like Mammon take over the construction project and the supposedly democratic conclaves within the temple become increasingly secret and dark. As with the allusion to the biblical parable of the wide and narrow path in the scene with the hell gates above, one need not have a thorough grounding in the source material to understand the satire. Milton's republican idealism may be approached through modern political cartoons, the more current the better. Choosing new ones to suit our shifting ideological climate and debates is always a good idea, but the main thing is to focus on cartoons where the actions of donkeys, elephants, both, or neither—the options are endless—lampoon political programs or stances that conceal patently false claims to heroic virtue and progress. Most students will easily grasp the cartoonist's general idea, so the instructor can direct attention to how all cartoon details enrich our understanding of the point. This practical exercise will give students a chance to make abstractions work semirealistically and intellectually or symbolically at once.

A nonpolitical example, easily reproduced on any blackboard, is a basic baseball scoreboard showing the result of all nine innings and the final score of a game between realists and idealists. In every inning the realists outscore the idealists two, three, or four to nothing, but the final score shows the idealists beating the realists ten to one. What can this mean? The class can be allowed free rein in this guessing game, although the cartoon was obviously written by an idealist to make a relatively simple point: the temporary scores in life's contests do not necessarily predict the final winners and losers. This point is far more relevant to Milton's vision of hell than it first appears: despite their united energies, talents, and brilliance, Satan and his realists may win all the interim battles but not the final war because they misunderstand the point of the game. This lesson is equally appropriate to class discussions of Milton's war in heaven, where Abdiel and the other good angels do not prevail in the short run but are justified in the end. At this point, the class might begin to discuss the practical difference between abstractions such as good and evil, perhaps by reviewing the epic's opening invocation and its underlying question: why does God temporarily permit evil to thrive? The answers vary with each class, but the exercise helps all students grasp the philosophical—and thus allegorical—underpinnings of Milton's epic.

It is also useful to discuss the symbolic background of the demonic council in book 2. Not by accident, the debate focuses on Satan's chief allies: an exponent of heroic but actually bloodthirsty and nihilistic militarism; an exponent of empty rhetoric and wishful, irresponsible thinking; and an exponent of enterprising but mindless materialism for its own sake. Meanwhile, behind the scenes, Satan and Beelzebub represent the manipulative and deceitful uses of supposedly self-sacrificial heroism for self-serving purposes. These allegorical scenes are especially important because the values Moloch, Belial, Mammon, and Beelzebub represent are depicted only through their words and actions, not through the concrete visual symbolism surrounding Satan. Noting this fact can then lead to a review of the range of symbolism in book 1. Although both Satan and his fellow demons also function at a fully mimetic level, allegorically focusing on their besetting sins eases students' transition to the Sin and Death episode to follow. Powerfully combining symbolic or definitive words and actions with classical and biblical images of fallen or satanic souls, this episode provides a summary of Milton's allegorical techniques, although a full understanding of these images must wait until Raphael describes Sin's spontaneous, Athena-like birth from Satan's head in book 5. At that point, students might be directed to James 1.13–15, the biblical source of the symbol and its relation to Death. Finally, at the end of book 2, fallen souls like Satan, Sin, and Death can be compared and contrasted with chaos's Anarch, the spirit of confusion, and his consort, Night, or utter darkness. Their willingness to assist Satan's destructive purposes suggests their alienation from the creative wholeness of heaven or earth, but it also suggests that any permanent state of confusion prevents real action as well as encourages exploitation. Later, however, confusion positively permits divine creativity not from nothing (*ex nihilo*) but from chaos's latent preatomic matter—one of Milton's more prophetic and protomodern cosmic insights.

In book 3, the most useful allegorical episodes to study in detail are probably not those in the Paradise of Fools (unless this of special interest to the instructor) since most of its allusions will be unfamiliar to today's students. The Jacob's ladder episode mentioned above is much more succinct and accessible, and Satan's landing on the sun and his discourse with its presiding angel are indispensable. When properly unpacked, this stage of his journey teaches two important lessons: even angels with Uriel's extraordinary eyes cannot easily detect hypocrisy or evil, and God does not discourage but actually encourages self-sought knowledge. Uriel's encouragement of Satan's exploration of earth is highly ironic, but his advice remains applicable to all angelic visitors, including other stray cherubs wandering off course to discern previously hidden aspects of the universe. This information will help students understand that Satan clearly knows he is lying to Eve when he claims that God forbids knowledge and hides it to increase his power. (Instructors who regard Satan as the poem's hero will have to get around this point as they see fit, but defending his position can be accomplished allegorically as well as naturalistically.)

Book 4 includes more than a few allegorical symbols, most notably the gates of Eden, the tree of the knowledge of good and evil, and the tree of life, all of which Satan misuses for the purpose of sowing evil or proving God's injustice. For that reason God allegorically weighs Satan in the constellation Libra and finds him wanting (too light in relation to Gabriel), a biblical allusion to Daniel 5.27. Milton's treatment of these details is clever but not indispensable, since their full meaning will not be apparent until students have examined the naturalistic and dramatic dialogues of books 8 and 9. Leading up to them, books 5 and 6 can be made interesting and exciting by focusing on Satan's invention of cannon fire, his method of diverting heavenly light, the hubris that results from it, the punishment that awaits, and the fact that evil can erupt in the midst of heaven. These scenes are central to the poem's allegorical development and therefore its meaning, although most students will be less interested in the episode's heroic conventions than in its major characters, their debates, and their actions. Abdiel's debate with Satan particularly shows that true idealists win even when they are outnumbered or outscored ten or a thousand to one. The biblical counterpart of this symbolic lesson is that of the lost sheep sought by the good shepherd even though all ninety-nine others are in the fold: quality or need always outweighs quantity or mere numbers.

From this point on the epic moves into the naturalistic or dramatic mode that characterizes the creation narrative and the events surrounding Adam and Eve's fall; immediately afterward, however, there is a rapid return to allegory. *Pace* Anne Ferry, Milton returns to allegory here not because he regards it as a fallen narrative mode but because the fall's consequences are too enormous to be told except in a highly compact mode. The birth of Sin's daughter Discord initially signals Milton's resumption of allegory, although her presence is first glimpsed in Adam and Eve's mutual guilt, resentment, and retreat from responsibility. The allegorical character Discord thus serves mainly to convey the rapid spread of rage and ruin throughout the earthly cosmos, its inhabitants, and its climate. Like her birth, the surrounding events of the fall have no natural explanation except as a kind of contagion whereby Sin and her children infect everything around them and make it ripe for her son Death. The good angels are conventionally directed by God to alter earth's climate and expel the human couple from Eden, but Milton chooses to give the symbolic actions of Satan, Sin, and Death substantial weight throughout book 10. Sin and Death first promote the work of their father by creating an unpleasantly "hot, cold, moist, and dry" path between earth and hell (2.898). The unexpected repercussions of their victory are later clarified in another major allegorical episode as Satan's triumphant cohort suddenly finds his victorious rhetoric turned into the hissing sounds of serpents or (in another sense) of bad actors who cannot perform the parts they have assumed. Students already familiar with symbolic actions may be expected to work out the meaning of these actions on their own, including the meaning of how and why ashy apples continue to tantalize the demons—though some discussion of the mythic Tantalus will help here. A particularly good exercise might be to ask students to find or create a cartoon or graphic-novel-type illustration of what is happening in this episode.

Similar exercises will help students understand the most symbolic or nonbiblical scenes in books 11 and 12: Milton's "lazar house," which is full of those sickened by their cravings (11.479); the sons of Seth, who gain the attractive women they want only to lose what they truly prize, a healthy relationship with God and Nature; and their sons, the giants in the earth who gain the conquests they desire only to lose all their manhood, valor, integrity, and willpower. Noah's Flood then intervenes to lessen this reign of Sin and Death, but book 12 appropriately shows how it will continue long after Christ's coming, even until the final end of the world as we know it. At this point students might be asked to interpret Milton's meaning in terms of contemporary politics, spirituality, or philosophy. Whether or not students believe in his story or in the biblical account, what modern examples can they find of deceptive desire leading to ruin and regret? Why do even secular people often long for either an end to the world as we know it or drastic reforms to end greed and corruption? How likely is the success of such reforms, given our fallen nature and the interim failures of idealists? Within this general framework, instructors may stress, for example, the epic feminization of evil or point out its entanglement with male hubris and desire, to expand the poem's philosophical underpinning in a modern direction. Focusing on allegorical images does not foreclose alternative interpretations but instead enables an engagement with their complexity, ambiguity, and meaningfulness.[2]

NOTES

[1] All references to *Paradise Lost* are to the version of the poem in *The Complete Poetry and Essential Prose of John Milton*, edited by Kerrigan, Rumrich, and Fallon.

[2] For further reading, see S. Fallon, *Milton*, esp. ch. 6; Ferry; Fletcher; Martin, *Ruins*; Treip.

Fit Quantity of Syllables

John Leonard

Prosody in the classroom has the reputation of being dull, and it will be if it is taught as a matter of arid technicalities. As Alastair Fowler notes in the introduction to his Longman edition of *Paradise Lost*, "Who but a prosodist cares how often an nth foot is inverted?" (24). But Milton's note on the verse, prefaced to *Paradise Lost* in 1668, suggests that there might be another approach. Milton speaks of "delight": "true musical delight . . . consists onely in apt Numbers, fit quantity of Syllables, and the sense variously drawn out from one Verse into another" (352).[1] Several of these terms are ambiguous, and the temptation for the bewildered teacher is to mutter something evasive and hurry on to other topics. That would be a mistake. An earnest inquiry into Milton's meaning at this point can deliver some of the most rewarding classes on *Paradise Lost*. There is nearly unanimous agreement about the meaning of "the sense variously drawn out from one Verse into another." "Verse" means the individual line, and "variously" refers to the placement of the caesura within it. (Milton famously places his pauses anywhere in the line, and seldom in the same place in two consecutive lines.) But "apt Numbers" and "fit quantity" have long been a problem. First, there is the question of what they are apt and fit *to*. Second, there is the question of what Milton means by "quantity." ("Numbers" is not a problem; it refers to the number and arrangement of syllables in a line of accentual-syllabic verse.) Most modern editors who have dared to venture a gloss have assumed that "apt" and "fit" signal conformity to the decasyllabic norm of iambic pentameter. Several editors (myself included) have glossed "quantity" as "number" and so encouraged the notion that "apt Numbers" and "fit quantity of Syllables" mean the same thing.

I now think that this interpretation is wrong. I have come to change my mind in the course of writing *Faithful Labourers*, a long reception history of *Paradise Lost*. Early editors (until about the middle of the nineteenth century) had a different understanding of "apt Numbers" and "fit quantity." They took "apt" and "fit" as advertisements of Milton's intent to make his verse apt and fit *to the things described*. They took "quantity" in the prosodic sense (familiar since the sixteenth century) of syllabic length (duration not stress). I now think that the early editors are right and that modern editors have led students astray. The early editors are certainly more interesting. Their interpretation allows for great variety (which goes better with "variously drawn out"). The modern interpretation threatens to reduce Milton's rhythms to a deadening norm and so deliver him into the hands of a hostile critic like F. R. Leavis, who speaks of "the foreseen thud in the foreseen place" (45). Here I concentrate on one feature of Milton's verse: "fit quantity." I look at various places in the poem where Milton makes expressive use of the length of his syllables, using early commentators to bring out his felicities. Early critics have much to teach us about how to teach

Paradise Lost.[2] In my classes I refer to early critics by name and encourage students to read them. Not every instructor will want to do this, but all classes on *Paradise Lost* should allow the poetry to be heard, and attention to "fit quantity" can attune the ears of both teachers and students to Milton's "true musical delight."

If, as I have claimed, the prosodic sense of "quantity" was readily available, why have Miltonists been so reluctant to acknowledge it? The answer is not far to seek. Critics have been inhibited by an understandable but irrational fear that the prosodic sense of "quantity" will intrude the whole irrelevant classical apparatus of bacchics and amphibrachs and cretics rare. The fear is groundless. Sixteenth-century poets like Sidney experimented with classical meters in English, but the experiments led nowhere and Milton is certainly not reviving them. But he is alive to syllabic length.

I suggest starting with Richard Bentley's notorious 1732 edition (*Milton's Paradise Lost: A New Edition*), not because it gets things right, but because it gets them usefully wrong (Empson, "Milton and Bentley" 141). Bentley does not gloss "apt Numbers" or "fit quantity," but in his preface he observes of the received text that many "Numbers seem embarass'd" (a1v). Several of his most execrable emendations are unblushing attempts to rescue Milton from metrical embarrassment. Milton: "Silence, ye troubl'd waves, and thou Deep, peace" (7.216). Bentley: "He rather gave it in this Order; *Silence, ye troubl'd Waves, and* Peace, *thou Deep*" (225). The beauty of the original is that it does what it describes: the long vowel of "peace" is as calming as oil on water. Bentley is deaf to this effect. He hears only a violation of accent ("DEEP, peace") and assumes that the text is "embarass'd" because that scoundrel "the editor" has put his spondaic foot in his mouth. In a sense, Bentley is right. "Deep" does have the heavier accent, but "peace" prevails over the prosodic turbulence by imposing the calm of "fit quantity."

Bentley finds what he takes to be another maladroit trochee when Mammon offers hope in hell:

> great things of small,
> Useful of hurtful, prosperous of adverse
> We can create, and in what place so e're
> Thrive under evil, and work ease out of pain
> Through labour and indurance.   (2.258–62)

"Better Accent," Bentley grumbles, "if thus inverted, *And out of Pain work Ease*" (66). *Ti-tum, ti-tum, ti-tum.* By moving "ease" to the end of the line, Bentley makes hell more laid-back — like paradise, where work served only "To recommend coole *Zephyr*, and made ease / More easie" (4.329–30). But Mammon does not say that hell will be easy; he says it can be eased. His policy demands "labour and indurance" and "long process of time" (2.262, 297). His rhythms accordingly take time. Bentley objects to an inversion of "Accent," but to my ears "ease" stands out not so much by accent as by quantity. Milton employed a similar effect in *A Mask*. Comus, proffering his cup, promises the Lady "Refreshment after toil, ease after pain" (line 687). Here too "ease" comes in an inverted fourth foot, and here too it drawls languidly. The effect is bewitching, almost hypnotic. It has been plausibly suggested that Comus echoes another tempter, Spenser's Despair:

> Is not short payne well borne, that bringes long ease,
> And layes the soule to sleepe in quiet graue?
> Sleepe after toyle, port after stormie seas,
>   Ease after warre, death after life does greatly please.
>   (1.9.40)

Here too there are suggestive inversions, and both occurrences of "ease" are long. In the first, "short payne" is explicitly contrasted with "long ease," while in the second, the anadiplosis "seas / Ease" is calculated to stretch "ease" out. We might have expected "Peace after warre," but a plosive at this pivotal moment would break the spell. Suicide seems all the more peaceful for being "Ease." Mammon too casts a spell over his audience with "ease out of pain." Bentley's "Better Accent" breaks the spell, but his note can help us hear it.

Thomas Newton is arguably the best editor Milton has ever had. His 1749 edition of *Paradise Lost* notes many instances of "apt Numbers" and "fit quantity":

>   So eagerly the fiend
> Ore bog or steep, through strait, rough, dense, or rare,
> With head, hands, wings or feet pursues his way,
> And swims or sinks, or wades, or creeps, or flyes. (2.947–50)

"The difficulty of Satan's voyage," Newton notes, "is very well express'd by so many monosyllables as follow, which cannot be pronounced but slowly" (1: 149). Ernest Sprott in *Milton's Art of Prosody* cites "fit quantity" to account for this effect. He identifies "rough" and "hands" as words that have a "retarded tempo" (100). Sprott is one of very few modern commentators to recognize that "fit quantity" means "not a fit number of syllables in the line . . . but fit length or weight of syllables" (44). Sprott's observation is in some ways finer than Newton's, since Newton had made no distinction between the monosyllables. Sprott thinks that "rough" and "hands" stand out in being "retarded . . . not accented" (109). It is possible to disagree. One can read lines 948 and 949 with six heavy stresses each. Sprott's point in distinguishing accent from quantity in these lines is to insist on a dogmatic rule that there can only be "five accents in the line" and "cannot ever be more" (109). The point is dull (and wrong), but we should not let that blind us to the critical advantages that Sprott's scansion delivers. It is Newton who tells us why it works so well: it conveys "[t]he difficulty of Satan's voyage." Stresses alone would not be enough. Recall Leavis on Milton's alleged "monotony": "the foreseen thud in the foreseen place," "an automatic ritual, responding automatically with bodily gestures — swayed head and lifted shoulders," a "swaying ritual movement back and forth" (45). That might be Beavis and Butthead headbanging to heavy metal. Newton and Sprott help us see that Milton's verse does not move in this way. Satan begins by trying to head butt his way through chaos ("With héad . . ."), but his predictable thuds founder as the "rough" patches retard him (". . . hands, wíngs or féet"). By a deft use of "apt Numbers" and "fit quantity," Milton suggests the variety of chaotic materials Satan must traverse and the various means of locomotion he must use to get through them.

William Cowper's "Fragment of an Intended Commentary on *Paradise Lost*" was written in 1791–92 and published posthumously as an appendix to his translation of Milton's *Latin and Italian Poems* (1808). Cowper, himself an accomplished blank verse poet (arguably the best between Milton and Wordsworth), has no doubt that "fit quantity" refers to syllabic length:

> [T]hough our syllables are not strictly reducible to the rules either of Greek or Latin prosody, they are nevertheless all long or short in the judgment of an accurate ear, and . . . without close attention to syllabic quantity in the construction of our verse, we can give it neither melody nor dignity. . . . The more long syllables there are in a verse, the more the time of it is protracted, and consequently the pace with which it moves is the more majestic.   (187)

Cowper's point is not that Milton routinely moves at a snail's pace, but that he uses "fit quantity" to achieve epic stateliness and to match sound with sense:

> As when from mountain tops the dusky clouds
> Ascending, while the North wind sleeps, o'respread
> Heav'ns chearful face, the lowring Element
> Scowls ore the dark'nd lantskip Snow, or showre;
> If chance the radiant Sun with farewell sweet
> Extend his ev'ning beam, the fields revive,
> The birds thir notes renew, and bleating herds
> Attest thir joy, that hill and valley rings.
>   (2.488–95)

"The reader loses half the beauty of this charming Simile," Cowper writes, "who does not give particular attention to the numbers."

> There is a majesty in them not often equalled, and never surpassed even by this great poet himself; the movement is uncommonly slow; an effect produced by means already hinted at, the assemblage of a greater proportion of long syllables than usual. The pauses are also managed with great skill and judgment; while the clouds rise, and the heavens gather

blackness, they fall in those parts of the verse, where they retard the reader most, and thus become expressive of the solemnity of the subject; but in the latter part of the simile, where the sun breaks out, and the scene brightens, they are so disposed as to allow the verse an easier, and less interrupted flow, more suited to the cheerfulness of the occasion.

(213–14)

The effect that Cowper describes is achieved partly by internal rhyme ("low-ring," "Scowls," "showre"). The "movement" is especially slow in "North wind sleeps"—three syllables that can easily take as much time as the six syllables "that hill and valley rings." The difference is not that the earlier phrases have a heavier stress. No word in the simile is stressed more ringingly than "rings"—but it "breaks out"; it does not "retard the reader."

So far I have emphasized words of "retarded tempo" (Sprott), but Milton's fit quantities are not always slow; some turn swift their various motions. Edwin Guest, in his monumental *History of English Rhythms* (1838), mentions Milton often and gives several fine examples of his expressive rhythms. Guest notes how Milton uses long vowels to decelerate his verse and short ones to accelerate it. Cowper emphasized the "majesty" of "slow" syllables; Guest pays equal attention to the sprightliness of short ones. He notes how Milton, like Shakespeare, "affected the short vowels, and particularly the short *i*, when he had to describe any quickness of motion," as in the following passage from *Paradise Lost*:

> So warnd he them aware themselves, and soon
> In order, quit of all impediment;
> Instant without disturb they took Allarm,
> And onward move Embattelld, when behold
> Not distant far with heavie pace the Foe
> Approaching gross and huge.   (6.547–52)

"In order, quit of all impediment": the good angels move so quickly that the line (in both senses) is full before we know it. After this, the rebel army's "heavie pace" seems all the more "gross and huge." As Guest notes, the effect is possible because Milton pays "attention to his quantities" (111). Later in his book, Guest gives a superb description of Milton's "apt Numbers" that will be quoted by numerous nineteenth-century editors:

> By "apt numbers" I understand that accommodation of the sound to the sense, which Pope's hackneyed line has made familiar, as one of the rules of criticism. Perhaps no man ever paid the same attention to the quality of his rhythm as Milton. What other poets effect, as it were, by chance, Milton achieved by the aid of science and of art; he *studied* the aptness of his numbers, and diligently tutored an ear, which nature had gifted with the most delicate sensibility. In the flow of his rhythm, in the quality of his letter-sounds, in the disposition of his pauses, his verse almost ever *fits*

the subject; and so insensibly does poetry blend with this—the last beauty of exquisite versification, that the reader may sometimes doubt whether it be the thought itself, or merely the happiness of its expression, which is the source of a gratification so deeply felt. (530)

This description is excellent on "apt" and "fit" and "numbers," and it is clear from his earlier comment on "quantities" that Guest appreciates what Milton does with "fit quantity of Syllables." But Guest never makes the connection with that specific phrase. When he does turn to it (right after the passage just quoted), he offers a quite different explanation. He thinks that Milton is declaring his intent always to adhere to the common pronunciation of particular words and never to yield to the exigencies of meter and admit such pronunciations as "súpreme" or "óbscure." No sooner has Guest put this dubious rule in Milton's mouth than he is forced to admit that readers "will be disappointed if they look to Milton for its observance" (530–31). This is very odd. Guest has given us an incomparably superior illustration of "fit quantity of Syllables"—one that actually works—but he never puts two and two together to see that his own close readings offer a much better theoretical explanation of "fit quantity" than the one he eventually alights on.

I conclude with another nineteenth-century critic, John Addington Symonds. His excellent (and now unjustly neglected) study *Blank Verse* was first published in 1879 as an appendix to his *Sketches in Italy* and subsequently brought out as a single volume in 1895. The chapter on Milton is brief, but full of good things, and it is especially good on the way that "apt Numbers," "fit quantity," and enjambment work together. After the fall, Eve tells Adam that she will

> importune Heaven, that all
> The sentence from thy head remov'd may light
> On me, sole cause to thee of all this woe,
> Mee mee onely just object of his ire.
> (10.933–36)

Symonds warns us not to try to impose neoclassical scansion onto that last line:

It is obvious here that scansion by feet will be of little use, though we may grant that the line opens with a spondee followed by a trochee. Its intention is understood as soon as we allow the time of two whole syllables to the first emphatic *me*, and bring over the next words, *me only*, in the time of another two syllables, by doing which we give dramatic energy to the utterance. (92)

The "dramatic energy" that Symonds rightly perceives is a result of "fit quantity," and it is all the more dramatic after the "apt Numbers" two lines before: "from thy head remov'd may light / On me." *That* "me" *is* heavily stressed, and Eve's burden is heavier for coming after "light." She means "alight," but she is also grimly aware of the adjectival sense, as Adam had been when he stooped under his own burden: "On mee as on thir natural center light / Heavie" (10.740–41). In both cases, "light" is a pun. The word occupies an accented position, but the stress is mimetically light and so shifts a heavy burden onto the beginning of the next line: "light / Heavie"; "light / On me." The stress on "me" is especially strong for the pause that immediately follows. Coleridge, in a letter to William Sotheby (letter 698; 28 Apr. 1808), noted that Milton "never" pauses "at the second Syllable"

> except when he means to give an unusual Importance to the words—and even then most often a trochaic, not a Spondee or Iambic—
>
> > "And now his Heart
> > Distends with pride, and, hard'ning, in his strength
> > *Glories:"*   Book I. 572.—
>
> But when it is an Iambic, it always has & is meant to have some great effect—see book I. from Line 585 to 615—after all this grand preparation of the imaginative power—
>
> > "He now prepared
> > *Tŏ spēak:*—whereat their doubled ranks they bend, &c."
> >   (qtd. in Wittreich, *Romantics* 182–83)

Eve's "On me" has a "great effect" of Coleridge's "iambic" kind. It is a perfect instance of "apt Numbers" and "the sense variously drawn out from one Verse into another." A lesser poet would have ended Eve's speech with line 935, but Milton adds one more line, masterfully shifting from "apt Numbers" to "fit quantity": "Mee mee onely just object of his ire." As Symonds recognizes, the power of that "first emphatic me" comes not solely or even primarily from emphasis but from quantity—"the time of two whole syllables." Having stooped under her burden ("light / On me"), Eve now composes herself to repeat her offer, and the verse too extends itself with Atlantean shoulders: "Mee mee onely."

I do not mean to suggest that there is just one right way of reading *Paradise Lost*. My point is that an alertness to "fit quantity of Syllables" as well as "apt Numbers" can help us hear the "dramatic energy" that Symonds rightly praises. There is no better way for students to appreciate *Paradise Lost* than to read it aloud, and there is no better way to read it than with "true musical delight; which consists onely in apt Numbers, fit quantity of Syllables, and the sense variously drawn out from one Verse into another."

NOTES

[1] All references to *Paradise Lost* are to Flannagan's edition in *The Riverside Milton*.
[2] For more on how to use early editors, see Welch's and Kolbrener's essays in this volume.

The Analogical Approach to *Paradise Lost* and Milton's Prose: Uses and Abuses

Feisal G. Mohamed

Many of Milton's perennial themes appear in both his prose and his poetry. But that is not to say that the various expressions of those themes are identical. The application of something like the analogical approach to scripture is a temptation to be resisted in reading Milton's works, and we do well to explore the function of each iteration within its text and in its immediate historical context. That is, our teaching should be informed by scholarship refining our knowledge of Milton's interventions in his period and treat the prose as more than a gloss on the poetry. In the following I take a look at three moments that invite comparison of *Paradise Lost* with Milton's prose and suggest questions that might be raised in discussion and course assignments to examine Milton's complexities as poet and statesman. These examples are drawn from the Modern Library's *Complete Poetry and Essential Prose*, edited by William Kerrigan, John Rumrich, and Stephen M. Fallon, which to my mind has supplanted Merritt Hughes's *Complete Poems and Major Prose* as the finest undergraduate text that provides both poetry and prose.[1]

Hail Wedded Love

The apostrophe on wedded love as Adam and Eve arrive at their shady bower in book 4 recalls the ideal of companionate marriage developed in the divorce tracts. Marriage in these lines is opposed to physical passion and associated with humanity's highest faculties. It is "Founded in reason, loyal, just, and pure"

(4.755) and as such drives away "adulterous lust" (4.753), recalling the claim in *The Doctrine and Discipline of Divorce* that with the spread of companionate marriage "places of prostitution will be less haunted, the neighbor's bed less attempted" (863). As Alan Rudrum noted some time ago, the passage also evinces the invective tone of these most controversial of the prose works, so that even late in his career, and in writing epic, Milton comes to the subject of marriage striking polemical blows in an earlier debate that had gained new relevance with the excesses of the restored Stuart court, which did not entirely measure up to the divorce tracts' ideal of "sober and well ordered living" (863; see Rudrum). The torrent of invective is unleashed especially by the word "revels," the Edenic signification of which is opposed to its courtly counterpart:

> Here love his golden shafts employs, here lights
> His constant lamp, and waves his purple wings,
> Reigns here and revels; not in the bought smile
> Of harlots, loveless, joyless, unendeared,
> Casual fruition, nor in court amours
> Mixed dance, or wanton masque, or midnight ball,
> Or serenade, which the starved lover sings
> To his proud fair, best quitted with disdain.
> These lulled by nightingales embracing slept.
> (4.763–71)

The passage is a showcase of Milton's flawless ear. The liquid sounds of its location of idealized love in Eden abruptly vanish in the disdainful catalogs punctuated by the grating *t*'s and *d*'s culminating in "best quitted with disdain." Those harsh sounds vanish in turn as our attention is drawn back to Adam and Eve, a return producing the truly lovely description beginning at line 771 that is held together by soft consonants and sibilance.

But we realize in reading this apostrophe on love at its purest that its idealization of the Edenic couple and its poetic loveliness have been used in part for polemical effect. That realization might raise several questions about the relationship between Milton's Eden and his divorce tracts. Does our perception of Eden change when we see that Milton is speaking in part in the voice of his earlier controversial prose? Are there differences between the view of marriage presented here and that presented in the divorce tracts? If discussion of that question turns to the subject of gender, we might notice Milton's exclusively male "Relations dear" (4.756), how the term "wanton" in 4.768 recalls the description of Eve's "wanton ringlets" in 4.306 and with it the unequivocal statement on Edenic hierarchy of 4.299, "He for God only, she for God in him," that is later reinforced by Raphael and the Son (8.570–75, 10.145–51). What are the terms of that hierarchy in the fallen world of the divorce tracts? In *Paradise Lost* as in Genesis a postlapsarian Adam is given dominion over Eve but is also a corrupt head unreliable in directing her toward God. How might the tension between Eve's subjection and her independence inform our reading of the postlapsarian books of *Paradise Lost*, which Barbara Lewalski has described as an "Eviad" (*Life* 485–86), and be compared with the consistently masculinist view of marriage in the divorce tracts? In an essay on gay marriage, Martha Nussbaum points to Milton's divorce tracts as a key moment in the intellectual history of marriage, because of their claim that the state should not interfere with the pursuit of companionship proper to marriage, which is also a pursuit of high ideals (46–47). Do the texts themselves support that view? Or is companionate marriage in the tracts and in *Paradise Lost* a rhetorical convenience necessitated by Milton's wish to emphasize the spiritual lives of male subjects?

Foolish Tongues!

That last question leads us to a second moment where the prose invites comparison to *Paradise Lost*: the dismissal in *Areopagitica* of those who would second-guess divine disposal in allowing Adam freely to stand or fall: "When God gave him reason, he gave him freedom to choose, for reason is but choosing; he had been else a mere artificial Adam" (944). The note in the Modern Library edition rightly invites us to compare this passage with *Paradise Lost* 3.95–128, where the Father tells us in his punishing style that all creatures were created free, that "reason also is choice" (3.108), and that without free reason creatures would be automatons exercising a meaningless obedience. But the passage also sets limits on free reason: "I formed them free, and free they must remain, / Till they enthrall themselves" (3.124–25). Such enthrallment makes our obedience dependent on grace rather than a reason that has become vitiated: "Man shall not quite be lost, but saved who will, / Yet not of will in him, but grace in me / Freely vouchsafed" (3.173–75). We might again ask how the prelapsarian condition compares with the postlapsarian world with which the prose concerns itself.

The epic also illustrates, however, that unfallen reason is free but limited. Interpreting Eve's dream in the opening scene of book 5, Adam provides a speech that both shows and tells us of prelapsarian reason: though reason is the "chief" faculty, it rests in sleep and allows its subordinate "Fancy" to wake and "imitate her," producing "wild work" (5.110, 111, 112). "Evil," Adam concludes, "into the mind of god or man / May come or go, so unapproved, and leave / No spot or blame behind" (5.117–19). We find a counterpart to that statement in *Areopagitica*, which claims that we must necessarily come into contact with evil in our postlapsarian search for the good: "perhaps this is that doom which Adam fell into of knowing good and evil, that is to say, of knowing good by evil" (939). Adam's discursus on human faculties is impressively logical—and is one of the places where we see that Adam and Eve are not dimwits before eating from the Tree of Knowledge—but we must notice that Adam gets wrong the question that he seeks to answer: "evil whence?" (5.99). Eve's dream did not arise from her own fancy; it was planted by an external agent. Reason alone cannot discover the workings of that agent, which must be revealed in books 5–8 by a divinely appointed angel, Raphael.

In *Paradise Lost*, then, reason is supplemented by revelation before the fall and after, and we learn that postlapsarian reason is corrupted to the extent that obedience depends on the promptings of grace. Those limits on reason invite us to take a second look at the epistemology described in *Areopagitica*, where we might especially notice that truth is not a human discovery so much as an irruption of the divine into the world: "Truth indeed came once into the world with her divine Master and was a perfect shape most glorious to look on" (955). How are reason and truth related in *Paradise Lost* and in *Areopagitica*? Given that *Areopagitica* intervenes in a public policy debate on prepublication censorship, how do we read its statements as opposed to those in *Paradise Lost*?

Two video texts might be brought into the classroom to suggest the ongoing relevance of these issues. The first is a talk by Christopher Hitchens delivered at the University of Toronto's Hart House — in which one hall has around its circumference a long passage from *Areopagitica* in gold letters — in the wake of the Danish Muhammad cartoon controversy. Hitchens begins by citing Milton as one of the fathers of the modern Western tradition of free speech and proceeds to dismiss religion out of hand in a way that Milton might have found discomfiting, to say the least. Another is a talk by Alain Badiou that describes democratic openness as necessary to the work of philosophy but also claims that philosophy becomes undemocratic in its discovery of truth, which becomes a positive obligation for every rational mind. This argument seems closer to the spirit of Milton's *Areopagitica* than the kind of free exchange of ideas with which it has sometimes been associated. How might these present-day engagements of reason and truth be brought into dialogue with *Paradise Lost* and *Areopagitica*?

A Self-Patterning of the Best and Most Honorable Things

After several pages of self-restraint, I begin this example by breaking the promise to stay within the confines of the Modern Library edition. The third example comes from *An Apology against a Pamphlet*, in which Milton, defending himself from the charge of sexual license, states that the man who would write well "ought himselfe to bee a true Poem, that is a composition, and patterne of the best and honourablest things" (890). The phrase sums up well Milton's aim in his self-construction, which tends to argue for the purity of his composition, personal and written. We are quite aware in the autobiographical moments of the controversial prose provided in the Modern Library edition that Milton is engaged in ethos-based rhetoric, a tactic that uses the rhetor's personal qualities for rhetorical effect — Cicero's *Pro Murena* is a famous classical example. The preface to the second book of *The Reason of Church Government* makes the removal of the bishops much more than a movement of London shopkeepers: Milton advertises his education and social standing and his now international reputation as a scholar and poet and pledges to be the English Vergil (that he ultimately makes good on the pledge should not blind us to its naked chutzpah at a point in time when he had published very few literary works, and those relatively anonymously). The obverse of ethos as rhetorical device is of course the ad hominem attack, to which Milton responds in *The Second Defense*; here he tells us that his eyes remain clear in his blindness, that he takes pride in his swordsmanship, that he is more middling in height than short, and that far from being shriveled his skin is more smooth than one would expect of a man in his forties.

As Milton proceeds on the topic of his blindness in *The Second Defense*, he points to such "ancient bards and wise men" as Tiresias and Phineus who were compensated for their physical blindness with prophetic vision (1080). That statement is echoed in the invocation to book 3 of *Paradise Lost*, which also points to "Tiresias and Phineus prophets old" (3.36). Here, too, Milton describes internal sight as compensation for blindness:

> So much the rather thou celestial light
> Shine inward, and the mind through all her powers
> Irradiate, there plant eyes, all mist from thence
> Purge and disperse, that I may see and tell
> Of things invisible to mortal sight.   (3.51–55)

This brief passage is packed with emphasis: it thrice shows Milton's favorite device of enjambment into emphatic statement separated by a caesura and points repeatedly to the internal location of sight—"inward," "mind," "there," "from thence."

If reading the prose invites us to consider the rhetorical aims of Milton's self-construction, then this close proximity of *The Second Defense* and *Paradise Lost* might lead us to ask similar questions of the epic. Claudius Salmasius was, alas, not the last to ridicule Milton's blindness, which would be a running theme among his Restoration detractors, most famously Roger L'Estrange in *No Blind Guides* (see also W. R. Parker, ch. 13). How do the autobiographical moments in the invocations to books 3 and 7 evoke Milton's career as a controversialist? To what end is Milton deploying that career, or his self-image, in the epic? Does an awareness of the presence of his controversialist persona change the way in which we read his declared artistic aspirations, both in *The Reason of Church Government* and in the epic's distinction of itself from other epics in the opening invocation and in the proem to book 9?

These intentionally broad outlines can be adapted to several instructional approaches. The kind of questions posed here might encourage students to come to a knowledgeable and sophisticated understanding of Milton and train them in a critical use of primary sources that is sensitive to text and context in political pamphlets and literary works. Not to be satisfied with a flat connecting of dots, smart inquiry will scratch beneath surface parallels in exploring a dynamic mind energetically at work in a wonderfully chaotic age.

NOTE

[1] When teaching a single-author course on Milton, I also make Lewalski's *Life of John Milton* a required text, since it is enormously valuable as a source of biographical information, history of the period, and spotless critical readings.

Editing Milton with Richard Bentley

Anthony Welch

What can our students learn from Milton's early editors? In the case of Richard Bentley, we might at first expect, scarcely anything. Best known as a pioneering eighteenth-century philologist and classical scholar, Bentley lives in infamy among Miltonists for his 1732 edition of *Paradise Lost* (Milton, *Milton's Paradise Lost: A New Edition*). Puzzling over passages in the epic that he felt were unworthy of Milton, Bentley concluded that a scheming amanuensis or editor had tampered with the poem on its way into print. Since this villain had marred the text "so vilely . . . that *Paradise* under his Ignorance and Audaciousness may be said to be *twice lost*," Bentley set about reconstructing the poem that Milton had actually composed (a1v). His "corrected" *Paradise Lost* is a masterpiece of pedantry. His more than eight hundred conjectural emendations are often flat-footed, literal-minded, and bent on making the poem conform to Augustan standards of literary taste. Bentley smoothed out its meter and simplified its syntax. He banished what he viewed as inconsistencies in its plot. He forced clarity upon ambiguity. He altered Milton's sixth book because he found that the devils had used the wrong recipe for gunpowder (6.513n).[1] In book 4, uneasy that the angels could find Satan "Squat like a Toad" in Eve's bower, he changed the lines to reassure the reader that "NO REAL TOAD DURST THERE IN-TRUDE" (4.810n). Probably the most famous of Bentley's interventions is his new version of the poem's final lines: "THEN hand in hand with SOCIAL steps their Way / Through *Eden* took, WITH HEAV'NLY COMFORT CHEER'D" (12.648n).

This sampling of Bentley's work highlights his most obvious attraction for teachers of Milton: students tend to react to his edition with glee. His battle of wills with Milton's nefarious editor can be an engaging way to set forth critical issues in *Paradise Lost*—whether, for example, the poem's ending offers its readers enough "heav'nly comfort." But there are many more reasons to bring Milton's early editors and commentators into the classroom. Like other forms of literary criticism, their remarks on the poem ask students to read with another's eyes, to expose themselves to alien perspectives and habits of thought. More particularly, they bring a valuable historical dimension to the experience of reading Milton; students learn that the poem's meaning is not a fait accompli but a dynamic process acted out over time. New technologies have enabled teachers to trace that process with their students at close range. Those whose college libraries subscribe to electronic databases like Chadwyck-Healey's *Early English Books Online* (*EEBO*) or Gale Cengage's *Eighteenth Century Collections Online* (*ECCO*) have access to a treasure trove of early responses to Milton's epic. Key editions and commentaries include those by Patrick Hume (1695); Joseph Addison (1712); Zachary Pearce (1733 [dated 1732]); Jonathan Richardson, father and son (1734); Thomas Newton (1749); and Henry John Todd (1801,

1809, 1826, 1842).[2] Those without *EEBO* and *ECCO* can find selections from these works in James Thorpe; John T. Shawcross, *Milton: The Critical Heritage* and *Milton, 1732–1801: The Critical Heritage*; Timothy C. Miller; and, most recently, Earl Roy Miner, William Moeck, and Steven W. Jablonski. Bentley's *Paradise Lost* is available in a 1974 facsimile reprint edition.

A great advantage of working with Milton's early readers—and his editors in particular—is that they pondered each of his words so carefully. Glossing exotic terms, explicating knotty passages, they offer a model for sensitive close reading of *Paradise Lost*. To grapple with their commentary is to share their patient, searching scrutiny of Milton's poetry, word by word and line by line. Students find themselves describing the effects created by the poem's language and measuring their responses against those of other readers. Why did Bentley feel the need to replace Milton's "darkness visible" with "A TRANSPICUOUS GLOOM" (1.63n)? Why was Hume uneasy over Milton's use of the adjective "rigid" when the Father calls for a volunteer to "pay / The rigid satisfaction, death for death" (3.212n)? What was at stake when Bentley, Pearce, and Newton wanted the notorious account of Eve's relation to Adam—"shee for God in him"—to read "she for God AND Him" (4.299n)? Why did Satan's plan to "incarnate and imbrute" his "essence" in the serpent prompt such a flurry of editorial comment (Hume 9.165n; Bentley 9.166n; Pearce 9.163n)? These questions linger over nuances of word choice and syntax that students tend to hurry past in pursuit of more abstract questions. When we show them that Milton's early readers lavished attention on these local details, we convey to our students that every word matters in a poem where the subtlest choices have wide-ranging implications. Milton's early commentators serve not to teach the correct or conventional reading of a given passage but to raise questions and challenge students to think for themselves. By exploring cases where we feel that the editors got Milton wrong, we make clear that literary interpretation can be uncertain and contentious. Students are justly relieved to learn that Milton's poetry has never been easy, even for skilled readers whose intellectual world was much closer to the poet's.

I have also found these early voices useful for their close scrutiny of the epic conventions that often perplex modern readers. Their shrewd and sometimes skeptical remarks on Milton's similes, epic catalogs, and the like are a helpful reminder to today's students that the form and style of *Paradise Lost* struck even its first readers as alien and artificial. Long before T. S. Eliot complained that Milton's catalogs of exotic names were "dictated by a demand of verbal music, instead of by any demand of sense" (159), Bentley found nearly opposite reasons to grumble over the long list of fabled pleasure gardens that introduces Milton's paradise: "in stead of painting out their several Beauties, as a Pretense for their rivaling Paradise; you give us their bare Names, with some fabulous Story to them, not denoting at all any Beauty" (4.268n). Bentley was especially unhappy about Milton's allusions to classical or chivalric fictions as analogues for religious truths. He dismissed a long reference in book 1 to Arthurian and

Carolingian story as "Romantic Trash" (1.580n). He changed Milton's description of the golden fruit of paradise from "*Hesperian* Fables true" to "*Hesperian* APPLES *true*" (4.250). Elsewhere he struck down an analogy between Milton's paradise and the *Odyssey*'s garden of Alcinous, asking, "What *Deliciousness* can exist in a Fable? or what Proportion, what Compare between Truth and Fiction?" (9.439n). Newton shared some of Bentley's qualms: "tho' we cannot agree with Dr. Bentley in rejecting some of these lines as spurious," Newton wrote of the chivalric catalog in book 1, "yet it is much to be wish'd that our poet had not so far indulged his taste for romances, of which he professes himself to have been fond in his younger years, and had not been ostentatious of such reading, as perhaps had better never have been read" (1.575n).

These concerns prompt a range of questions. What could Bentley mean, I ask my students, by "Romantic Trash"? Why might one apply that term to Arthurian literature? Why might such allusions be viewed as a sign of poor "Judgment" in Milton, an "indulgence" associated with youth? At this point we might follow Newton back to the poet's "younger years" and his famous defense of "lofty fables and romances" in the *Apology for Smectymnuus* (*Complete Prose Works* 890–91). How has chivalric romance in *Paradise Lost* changed that earlier coloring? Why would Milton have made a place for "Romantic Trash" in hell? Why, indeed, does he allow his devils to invent the first of all heroic songs (2.546–55), which, in their concern for virtue, fate, and free will, so closely parallel his own? Such questions can set the terms for a conversation about the antiromance of books 1–2 (Burrow 263–75), about Milton's changing attitude toward chivalric fictions and their protocols of heroism (Williamson; Lewalski, "Milton: Revaluations"), or about the shifting relations between Scripture and fable in Milton's late epics (Kerrigan 125–87; Guillory, *Poetic Authority* 94–145; Patterson, "*Paradise Regained*"). When pushed to make sense of elements in *Paradise Lost* that met with early censure or sheer bewilderment—a task that often means rising above narrowly literalistic or pietistic readings of the poem—students teach themselves how passages that at first seem unyielding to critical analysis can enable key insights into Milton's purposes.

These examples are fairly remote, but many familiar passages and problems in *Paradise Lost* can be unlocked for students in the same way. Teachers might bring the early commentators into a discussion of Milton's semiautobiographical proems (Richardson and Richardson 3.32n, 7.26n; Newton 3.1n, 9.1n), the allegory of Sin and Death (Addison 11–12, 55–56; Newton 2.648n), the dialogue in heaven (Hume 3.342n; Addison 58; Todd 3.80n), gender relations in paradise (Bentley 4.634n, 8.576n; Todd 4.304n), or the fall of Adam and Eve (Richardson and Richardson 9.744n, 997n; Newton 9.531n, 794n).[3] These remarks take provocative stands on issues of abiding interest to Milton scholarship and cast light not just on *Paradise Lost* but also on our ongoing relationship with the readers who came before us.

For the reception of *Paradise Lost* is in many ways a history of literary criticism. Evolving responses to Milton's style, his theology and politics, his treatment of gender and sexuality, and his stance toward the literary past reveal at least as much about his readers as about the poem that they set out to interpret (see, e.g., Oras; Griffin; Wittreich, *Visionary Poetics* and *Feminist Milton*; Rumrich, *Milton Unbound*; Kolbrener). Teachers of survey courses can use the epic's *Nachleben* as a case study in the history of reading, a way to map shifting cultural configurations over the last three centuries. Many of us already make this connection when we discuss Samuel Johnson's disparagement of *Lycidas* or William Blake's attraction to Milton's Satan. Teachers may wish to point students toward specific historical controversies to pose questions about literary influence and canon formation (Miner and Brady; Shawcross, *Milton and Influence*; Guillory, *Cultural Capital*), the aesthetics of the sublime (L. E. Moore; Reiss 301–37), the politics of literature and nationhood (Maltzahn, "Acts" and "Whig Milton"; Patterson, *Nobody's Perfect* 99–138), the quarrel of the ancients and the moderns (Walsh; Levine 245–63), or changing paradigms of authorship and originality (Goldgar; Newlyn 223–56). Pursuing the concerns that readers have brought to *Paradise Lost* over time vividly shows how and why we value Milton and challenges students to recognize that they have a share in the evolving meaning of the literary past.

An approach that might interest instructors who have access to *EEBO*, *ECCO*, or similar resources asks upper-level undergraduates or graduate students to write an essay in which they edit a passage from *Paradise Lost*. Using the databases to survey the work of Milton's early editors and commentators, students should offer in a concise form whatever details a reader might need to come to grips with their chosen text, glossing difficult words, supplying biblical and other allusions, sketching differing interpretations, and so on. The editors' annotations can be supplemented by the *Oxford English Dictionary*, William Ingram and Kathleen Swaim's *Concordance to Milton's English Poetry*, James H. Sims's *The Bible in Milton's Epics*, and other such reference sources. As a component of this variorum exercise, students should compare their choices with those of some recent editors of *Paradise Lost* (such as those listed in part 1 of this volume). They can then contrast the questions asked of the poem by its early readers with the priorities of its modern editors. Weighing the commentators' views, measuring how much information ought to be included for the reader and in what order, and even perhaps taking on a pugnacious, adversarial posture like Bentley's, these students will not only learn to know their small patch of the poem intimately but also find it changing before their eyes as it passes from one generation of readers to the next.

We all struggle in our teaching with underprepared students and insufficient time. In my view, bringing historical voices into the conversation does not crowd out other approaches to Milton but reframes and enriches them. Integrating early readers of Milton into the teaching of *Paradise Lost*, whether in class discussion or in a structured essay assignment, can provide a model for how to give this great poem the lingering, word-pondering care that it demands. Just as important, when we acquaint our students with Bentley and his peers, we teach them that they are joining a long, vigorous, and sometimes fractious history of interpreting Milton, even as they, like Bentley, try to imagine the poem anew.

NOTES

[1] References to *Paradise Lost* are from *Complete Poems and Major Prose*, edited by Hughes. Annotations by Bentley and other editors are cited by the line number keyed to the footnote in their edition.

[2] Each of Todd's four editions contains minor revisions and additions; a Harvard University Library copy of the third edition (vols. 2–3; 1826) can be accessed online through *Google Books*. Addison's commentary is included here both because it attempts to survey Milton's entire poem book by book and because large parts of it were incorporated into the editorial annotations of Newton and others. References to Addison's remarks, which first appeared serially in eighteen issues of the *Spectator* between 5 January and 3 May 1712, are to page numbers in the collected edition of these essays, printed in 1719 as *Notes upon the Twelve Books of* Paradise Lost.

[3] Other editorial comments that can be useful in the classroom include Bentley's notes to 1.287; 2.636; 3.121, 444; 4.983; 7.24, 463; 8.28, 71; 9.15, 166.

Visualizing *Paradise Lost*: Artists Teaching Milton

Wendy Furman-Adams

It is no coincidence that *Paradise Lost* is one of the most illustrated works in European literary history; probably no work is more difficult to imagine visually—representing, as it does, three realms "invisible to human sight" (3.55): heaven, hell, and the prelapsarian landscape of Eden.[1] Yet paradoxically, as Roland Mushat Frye demonstrated long ago, Milton was a profoundly visual poet—imagining these realms in dazzlingly visual detail (9–39). What wonder if artists—challenged by the difficulty and piqued by the visual wonders of Milton's poetry—have attempted since the first illustrated edition of 1688 to interpret the poem visually? As teachers of Milton, we are fortunate that they have done so. For their work can speak powerfully to visually oriented twenty-first-century students, helping them make sense of Milton's epic in ways they would struggle to do otherwise. My Milton course has become almost as much a course in art history as in literature, since I use the work of dozens of artists—earlier artists whose work Milton could have known, as well as some of the over 150 later artists who have illustrated *Paradise Lost*.

As students grapple with these images—discovering what artists foreground in a given biblical or Miltonic scene, what they play down or leave out—their attention is drawn back to Milton's text by way of comparison. Is the natural world merely a backdrop for human and divine activity, as it is represented by Francis Hayman in 1728 and William Blake in 1808, or is it the subject of the poem, as it is represented by John Martin in 1824–27?[2] Does Eve really continue making lunch as Raphael arrives at the bower, as John Baptiste Medina represents her in 1688, or does she stand "to entertain her guest from Heav'n" (5.383), as later artists show? Is Adam's fall—suggested by Eve—*the* fall in the poem, as most artists, including many of Milton's illustrators, represent it? Or is Eve, like Adam, an independent agent, "Sufficient to have stood, though free to fall" (3.99), as represented by Martin and the twentieth-century artist Mary Elizabeth Groom?

These questions (and others I cannot take up here) have enormous significance in our readings of the epic—readings that, like artists' interpretations, have developed over time. To read the history of artists interpreting Milton is to read the history of literary interpretation as well, from anthropocentric to ecological readings, from patriarchal to egalitarian readings, from theological to political readings. Each artist illuminates some aspects of Milton's own vision while suppressing others, challenging students to arrive at "re-visions" of their own, in their effort to understand this most complex and multivalent of poems.

Eden as Place and **Paradise Lost** *as an Ecological Text*

One important crux in recent Milton studies is the ecological strain in *Paradise Lost*—a strain not much noted by the poem's illustrators until about 1825, after which point it became quite dominant. I begin by showing my students a 1728 illustration by Hayman and one by Blake from 1808, both representing Raphael's visit to Adam and Eve's bower in books 5–8. I ask students to describe what they see, paying particular attention to the scale of the angelic and human figures relative to the surrounding natural environment. They notice that although Hayman's landscape is beautifully and naturalistically rendered—with a dappling of light and shade upon foliage and ground—his Adam is more than half as tall as the tree against which he leans, suggesting that he is indeed the center of a universe that exists primarily as a stage for human activity. Human activity, moreover, is defined primarily by male discourse, as Eve stands "retired in sight" behind the groaning luncheon board (8.41). Somewhat differently, Blake's majestic figures are arranged so as to remove all reference to literal space and instead locate the viewer in an eternal symbolic universe outside the illusory dimensions of this world.

Next I show my students some of the places of *Paradise Lost* as represented by Martin between 1825 and 1827, and again ask them about scale. They could hardly respond more differently to Martin's representations than they do to Hayman's or Blake's. Here the natural world becomes the subject of the work, as well as the subject of Raphael's discourse—a discourse intended to remind Adam and Eve that their connection with God and proper dominion within nature depends on their understanding that all things differ "but in degree, of kind the same" (5.490). That Raphael's visit is largely concerned with nature itself is clear in Martin's representation, in which the world extends outward from Adam and Eve's bower toward an infinity beyond the hills that dissolve, by the miracle of mezzotint, into cloud and sky. At the moment represented by Martin, moreover, Eve leans on Adam as an equal auditor, and indeed most ecological readings of the poem foreground Eve as well.

Martin also differs from most other illustrators in representing Eve at the mirror pool, a scene in which our first mother tentatively explores her relation to the natural world. In her consciousness of her surroundings, she stands—like a nineteenth-century naturalist, just as women for the first time began working alongside men in that role—somewhat apart from the phenomena that surround her. But she is also clearly a part of the scene she observes, reflected in the pool as she reflects on her reflection. Although her scale relative to the natural world is slightly larger here than in the scene of Raphael's visit, my students note that she does not tower over it as Adam does in Hayman's design or as she does in Blake's.

On the other hand, as the innocent Adam and Eve work modestly within nature as important but integral parts of a whole, Satan, like a mad nineteenth-century industrialist, imagines himself entirely in charge, confusing dominion

Fig. 1. John Martin, *Bridge over Chaos* (1825–27), from *The* Paradise Lost *of John Milton* (London: H. Warshbourne, 1853). Special Collections Library, University of Southern California.

(a term, Hiltner has taught us, suggesting housekeeping within the *domus*, or house, of nature [*Milton* 26]) with domination. Martin's terrifying image of the villain's bridge over chaos (fig. 1) never fails to elicit a collective gasp. When I ask the students what accounts for their reaction, they often refer to the swollen, light-eclipsing tunnel as indicative of a terrible rape. They also generally arrive on their own at Beverley Sherry's observation: this image embodies Martin's prophetic judgment of the excesses of his own industrial age ("John Martin's Apocalyptic Illustrations" 133)—a "completing," perhaps, "of the mortal sin / Original" (9.1003–04).

Prelapsarian Marriage: Paradise Lost *as Feminist (or Antifeminist) Text*

Just as books 4 and 7 have moved to the foreground since the advent of ecological and place-centered readings of *Paradise Lost*, books 5 and 8 have gained prominence as we think about Milton's complex view of gender and marriage. Here too illustrators have arrived ahead of the critics, to aid our students in grappling with the poem's complexity. In their discussion of the primal marriage, readers have historically tended either to play up the hierarchical pole or, conversely, to focus on the underlying deep structure of mutuality—a tension at the very heart of Milton's epic.

On the subject of gender, it is especially helpful to start at the beginning: with Medina's 1688 synoptic illustration to book 5 (fig. 2). Partly because his business was to illustrate numerous scenes within a single plate, Medina occasionally conflates related but distinct moments in Milton's text. Working in 1688, he might have felt Milton's distinctions to be of little importance, but their importance has since grown on readers and on illustrators. In class we discuss the entire design: Adam and Eve's orisons; the angel's Annunciation-inspired arrival (as if in direct answer to their prayer); and the background scene, most important for us here, of Raphael's arrival at the bower. I point out to my students that in the epic, when the angel arrives at the couple's "sylvan lodge," Eve "*Stood* to entertain *her* guest from Heav'n" (5.377, 383; emphasis mine), underscoring the fact that Raphael is her guest as well as Adam's. Adam, after all, has requested his presence in exactly such terms:

> vouchsafe with *us*
> Two only, who yet by sov'reign gift possess
> This spacious ground, in yonder shady bow'r
> To rest.   (5.365–68; emphasis mine)

In Medina's visual rendering, however, although Adam and Raphael already have arrived at the bower, Eve is pictured, out of phase, at a point earlier in the narrative — exactly the moment when

> for drink the grape
> She crushes, inoffensive must, and meaths
> From many a berry, and from sweet kernels pressed
> She tempers dulcet creams.   (5.344–47)

She seems "on hospitable thoughts" so "intent," so concerned with "What choice to choose for delicacy best" (5.332, 332, 333), that she turns to the shadows of domestic care, away from the light of the approaching angel. At best she becomes a Martha figure (Luke 10.38–42), at worst a household drudge.[3]

During the 1930s, however, two women artists produced remarkable correctives to this earliest representation of Milton's dinner party, distorting the narrator's account as much as Medina, but in opposite directions.[4] In 1936 Carlotta Petrina stretches Milton's text considerably, to show Adam and Eve equally engaged in preparing and serving lunch to a pensive-looking Raphael. And in 1937 Mary Elizabeth Groom moves exactly opposite to Medina, sending out both Adam and Eve, along with their two dogs, to greet the approaching angel.[5] (In the poem, only Adam walks forth to meet him [5.350–70], while Eve rises to greet him on his arrival at the bower [379–87].) These are small details, and my students, at least, tend not to read as closely as Milton requires. But looking at various representations of the scene forces them back to the text, to discover what the narrative implies about gender and marriage in paradise: neither quite

Fig. 2. John Baptiste Medina, illustration of *Paradise Lost*, book 5, from the first illustrated edition of *Paradise Lost* (London: printed for Jacob Tonson, 1688). William Andrews Clark Memorial Library, University of California, Los Angeles.

as egalitarian a picture as Petrina's and Groom's, nor quite as patriarchal as Medina's.

Blake makes Eve's role problematic in a very different way: by placing her at the center of his design, under the fatal tree "whose mortal taste / Brought death into the world, and all our woe" (1.2–3). I work through this profound image with my students, helping them discover a complexity equal to but different from Milton's own.[6] But for Blake, even as Eve becomes a special agent of redemption, she is also set apart from her husband and the angel (represented as parallel in their shared masculinity) as a special agent of the fall—a pattern we shall also see in illustrations to book 9.

Groom's representation of the dinner scene is one of her richest contributions to our classroom discussion of gender. The question I begin with here underscores the inextricable connection of form and content, medium and message: who sits or stands at the apex of Groom's formal triangle, as opposed to Blake's, and why? Students note that Blake gives Eve the raised and central position, from which she serves lunch to the two male figures (made equal by their position relative to her), while presaging the fall—through both her position under the snake-wound tree and the ambivalent gourd in her hand. In sharp (and deliberate) contrast, Groom places the angel at the center—"minister[ing]" at the table of salvation to a couple who sit in a parallel position and attend equally to his saving discourse. Raphael (whose name means "Yahweh heals") becomes, indeed, a type of Christ at Emmaus,[7] as our first parents represent, through prevenient grace, a new humanity to come, in which there will be no male and female (Galatians 3.28). Yet, in their equality before God, Adam and Eve are nonetheless differentiated in sexual terms that allude to the Bible's most joyous celebration of both gender equality and married love: the Song of Songs.[8] As Catherine Belsey has argued, if *Paradise Lost* is not a feminist poem, it can be read on behalf of feminism (59). And in this one brilliant image, Groom manages to convey the full truth of that observation.

The Fall: Moral Agency and the Gender of Reason

If the ecological and marital strains in *Paradise Lost* are among those of most interest to contemporary students, no discussion can possibly avoid a consideration of Adam and Eve's temptation and fall—the ultimate gender minefield in Western culture, if not in the poem. It is a site, not surprisingly, to which hundreds of artists have been drawn, offering a range of visual readings that suggest what the poem is about at its deepest level. Traditionally—as I show my students with images by Renaissance artists like Masolino, Michelangelo, and Raphael—the "fall of man" means the fall of Adam, with Eve cast as the feminine avatar of a feminine serpent.[9] As I project Raphael's well-known image (fig. 3), for instance, my students enjoy their shocked discovery that the snake's feminine face exactly mirrors Eve's. They are likewise indignantly empowered

Fig. 3. Raphael Sanzio (1483–1520), *Temptation of Adam* (Stanze de Raffaello, Vatican Palace). Reproduced by permission of Art Resource, New York.

by their ability to read Adam's temptation in his posture: subordinate to his sinister, serpentine—clearly never innocent—wife. This work, like most produced during the Italian Renaissance, posits woman as the cause of man's undoing and so serves as a marvelous introduction to Adam's misogynic outburst against Eve in 10.867–908.

But to what extent, I ask my students (who already know something about Milton's early marital history), does this speech reflect the poet's considered view of the fall? How has Milton in fact represented the primal wound of the earth and of humankind? First, I point out, far from representing Eve only as wily temptress for whom the serpent serves as mere accomplice if not metaphor, he gives Eve a temptation scene lasting 339 lines (9.494–838), during most of which she remains "yet sinless" (9.659). The serpent—Satan—is resplendently, even phallically, male. And Adam withstands temptation for only 143 lines (9.856–999). Both falls clearly "count" for Milton, with Adam's only "completing . . . the mortal sin / Original" (9.1003–04).

Yet many of Milton's illustrators have ignored Milton's carefully calibrated dual representation, returning instead to iconographic tradition and its mysogynic roots. Blake (fig. 4) resists Renaissance iconography of the fall by representing Eve's transgression rather than Adam's. As my students notice, however,

Fig. 4. William Blake, *The Fall* (1807). Reproduced by permission of the Huntington Art Collections, San Marino, California.

Blake does not represent our first mother innocent and tempted, but rather in the throes of a voluntary and sexualized act of disobedience with the serpent.[10] Adam, moreover, appears only as the innocent perceiver of the "wound" the earth suddenly feels (9.782); Blake never represents him as the man who, tasting the fruit himself, will judge Eve to be "exact of taste" (9.1017).

How very different is the approach of Groom (fig. 5), who follows Milton to the letter in representing two separate falls: first Eve's, then Adam's. Milton's

Fig. 5. Mary Elizabeth Groom, *Eve's Temptation*, from John Milton, *Paradise Lost* (London: Golden Cockerel, 1937). Reproduced by permission of the Golden Cockerel Press and the William Andrews Clark Library, University of California, Los Angeles.

Eve, in Groom's design, is faithfully represented. When Satan surprises her, she stands, as the poet tells us, in the midst of her flourishing roses, where—"yet sinless"—she is busy propping them, not narcissistically "longing to be seen / Though by the Devil himself" (10.877–78). Groom captures an early moment of the serpent's attack—when Eve is surprised not so much by his flattering address to her as "sov'ran Mistress" as by an encounter with a talking snake—or perhaps even the first instant, when he "Curl[s] many a wanton wreath" until "His gentle dumb expression turn[s] at length / The eye of Eve to mark his play" (9.517, 527–28). My students cannot find a trace of cupidity in her face: she appears kind, frank, and free of the guile she cannot, in her innocence, see in Satan: "Hate . . . under show of Love well feign'd" (9.492). Even when, in Groom's next design, Eve becomes Adam's tempter, she retains her touching humanity—reminding us (with the puffed-up serpent in the foreground) of the justice in her later plea (also represented by Groom):

Foresake me not thus, Adam, ...

. . . .

Between us two let there be peace, both joining,
As joined in injuries, one enmity
Against a foe by doom express assigned us,
That cruel serpent.   (10.914, 924–27)

These few images must stand in for many to suggest the contentious but compelling issues *Paradise Lost* continually raises for my students, once artists have helped them, literally, to frame their questions. "All art," Petrina has said, "is of its own time." Thus illustrators build a bridge across four centuries, from the poet's mind to the minds of our students—empowering them to see the epic for themselves, in ways that illuminate both Milton's time and their own.

NOTES

[1] All references to *Paradise Lost* are to the edition in Kerrigan, Rumrich, and Fallon's *Complete Poetry and Essential Prose of John Milton.*

[2] Hayman's *Raphael's Visit to Adam and Eve* can be seen in *Paradise Lost* (London, 1749), at the William Andrews Clark Library, University of California, Los Angeles; Blake's *Raphael's Visit to Adam and Eve* at the Museum of Fine Arts, Boston; and images by Martin in *The* Paradise Lost *of John Milton* (London: H. Warshbourne, 1853), at the Special Collections Library, University of Southern California. Other artists I use to consider ecocritical questions in Milton are Jane Giraud and Mary Elizabeth Groom. For purposes of this essay, ecocritical approaches can be defined as those that take up the natural world—the *oikos*, or "house," of nature that lies at the root of both the word *economy* and the nineteenth-century term *ecology*—as a central concern. Ecocritics both study and critique an instrumental view of nature that imagines its phenomena to exist primarily for the use and gratification of human beings. Many ecocritics, particularly ecofeminists like Patrick Murphy and Greta Gaard, go further by suggesting that all forms of oppression—whether between ethnic groups, between men and women, or between culture and nature—have common roots and that a movement toward a nonhierarchical value system is essential to the survival of both planet and species (see Murphy and Gaard 1–13).

[3] In her 1849 novel *Shirley*, Charlotte Brontë represents Milton's Eve (quite possibly read in an edition illustrated by Medina) in exactly this way, when the heroine breaks out in an inspired feminist critique: "Milton's Eve! Milton's Eve! . . . Milton tried to see the first woman; but . . . he saw her not. . . . It was his cook that he saw; or it was Mrs Gill, as I have seen her, making custards, in the heat of summer, in the cool dairy, with rose-trees and nasturtiums about the latticed window, preparing a cold collation for the rectors,—preserves and 'dulcet creams'—puzzled 'what choice to choose for delicacy best; what order so contrived as not to mix tastes, not well-joined, inelegant: but bring taste after taste, upheld with kindliest change'" (269–70).

[4] For more on these images, see Furman-Adams and Tufte, "With Other Eyes" 159–72.

[5] Images by Petrina can be seen in Paradise Lost *and* Paradise Regained (New York: Limited, 1936), at the William Andrews Clark Library, University of California, Los Angeles; images by Groom can been seen in *Paradise Lost* (London: Golden Cockerel, 1937), also at the William Andrews Clark Library.

[6] For an idea of this discussion, see Furman-Adams and Tufte, "With Other Eyes" 151–59.

[7] For a fine analogue that may have served as a source for Groom, see Rembrandt's typical rendering of *The Supper at Emmaus* (1648; now in the Louvre).

[8] For more on Groom's use of the Song of Songs, see Furman-Adams and Tufte, "With Other Eyes" 168–71.

[9] For more on this misogynic tradition, see Furman and Tufte 89–99.

[10] Blake downplays Eve's oral voraciousness in his 1808 version of the scene, but, in both the 1807 and 1808 illustrations, our first mother is represented as a full and equal participant in her own fall.

Imitating Milton in the Classroom

Sean Keilen

I have been experimenting with an approach to teaching *Paradise Lost* that is so obsolete it would seem like a radical innovation to reintroduce it now. And that approach is imitation.[1] Working under the imperatives of critical thinking, the theory that has dominated the pedagogy of composition courses in the United States for the last forty years, literature professors typically ask their students to write arguments about Milton rather than to write like him.[2] This approach to teaching and learning constructs a barrier between scholarly and creative writing that the presence of creative writers in many English departments reinforces rather than breaches. It has also led to a professionalization of the English major and an erosion of the distinction between graduate and undergraduate programs. The consequences of these developments are debatable, but I think that one thing is becoming clear. By requiring our students to write arguments about literature, and nothing but arguments, we are depriving them and ourselves of the benefits of different ways of understanding the books that we love. Imitation, in my classroom, is a form of close writing that promotes and reinforces close reading and critical thought.

By asking my students to imitate Milton, I place as much value on their engagement with *Paradise Lost* as I do on the information about the poem that they acquire by more conventional means (course lectures, photocopied excerpts from older works of art, scholarly commentaries and monographs, biographies of Milton and histories of his period, and other reference works). I also encourage them, in the process of trying to think and write like Milton, to approach their own writing as a craft. As part of this endeavor, I urge my students to grapple with the idea that the classical tradition is much more than a canon of texts, particularly for Milton, who argues that "he who would not be frustrate of his hope to write well . . . ought himself to be a true poem, that is, a composition and pattern of the best and honorablest things" (*Apology* 890). This tradition is also a repertoire of possibilities for perception, representation, and action. In this sense, it is a resource for the formation of the self, a spiritual exercise of the kind that Milton describes when he frames his experiences as a young reader as episodes in a story about the development as an ethical person and poet. "[E]ven those books which to many others have been the fuel of wantonness and loose living," he writes, "proved to me so many incitements . . . to the love and steadfast observation of . . . virtue" (891).

I want to cultivate a dialogue between my students and the text—a dialogue that calls on them to exercise judgment in ways that take stock of the historical conditions of Milton's education—and so I immerse them in the techniques of reading and writing that were typical of the curriculum in the humanist grammar school (Milton went to Saint Paul's [see Clark]). The goal of this curriculum was to train boys to read, speak, and write Latin fluently, and consequently it devoted a great deal of time to translation from Latin literature into English and back into Latin again—an exercise that has no application in the English-only environment of today's Milton courses. Yet several other techniques that the humanists adapted from ancient *progymnasmata* (literally, "preexercises") are well-suited to the project of bringing students to understand what *Paradise Lost* means in relation to the classical tradition by inviting them to experience how it felt to write it. In my courses, I prefer to use three of these techniques: *ecphrasis, syncrisis,* and *ethopoeia*.[3] *Ecphrasis* is vivid description, the bringing of a person, place, or thing before the reader's eyes as though it were present. *Syncrisis* is an exercise in drawing comparisons and contrasts between subjects of equal or unequal qualities. *Ethopoeia* is a dramatic impersonation of the character (ethos) of a historical or fictional person.[4]

I assign as many as three of each of these exercises during the course, and my students, using *Paradise Lost* as raw material, apply to its language, rhythms, and plot the very techniques that Milton used when composing it. The descriptions of Satan's body in 1.192–210 and of Eden in 4.205–87 serve as models for the *ecphrases* that I ask my students to write first in prose and later in iambic pentameter.[5] In trying to represent Satan and Eden as Milton might have done, they learn something about the knowledge that Milton had at his disposal and about his extraordinary ability to distill that information, drawn from many different kinds of sources, into the representation of a single character, place, or episode. While they study Milton's lexicon and attempt to increase their vocabularies to be able to imitate the poem convincingly, they also learn about the rhythms, metaphors, similes, and Latinate syntax that go into even the most elementary descriptions in *Paradise Lost*. Ordinarily, I ask my students to submit a brief commentary with their imitative compositions, explaining what choices they have made and why. These commentaries give me another chance to evaluate how closely they are reading *Paradise Lost* and what meaning they attribute to Milton's choices.

The more accustomed my students become to imitation as a way of thinking and writing about Milton's poem and its sources, the more they admire its achievements and are forgiving of its shortcomings. The experience of practicing imitation also seems to clarify for them that similarity and difference have important ethical implications for Milton, in addition to formal ones. The "Universe, and all created things" are the work of an artist-God in *Paradise Lost* (7.227), and, in describing God in these terms, Milton frames an audacious analogy between the cosmos and the poem that describes it and between God and the poet. Contradictory imperatives issue from these analogies: first, a temptation to believe that whenever two things appear to be the same (the creation of the world and creation generally, God and human beings), they are the same; second, an exhortation to see through such resemblances and distinguish good from evil and true from false. The exercise of *syncrisis*, provided that it remains faithful to the poem's text, is an effective way for students to test their comprehension and form opinions about controversial topics such as Milton's allegiances as a poet (Is he a godly or satanic figure?), the status of Adam and Eve (Before the fall, are they equally or unequally free?), the relationship of different orders of being to each other (Should we conclude that angels are better than human beings or vice versa? Should we conclude that devils are worse?), and the relative merits of pagan and Christian ideas about heroism, piety, virtue, and the good life.

Ethopoeia is the most challenging exercise that I ask my students to perform, since it requires them not only to imagine the way that Milton would think and write but also to form a judgment about the way that a particular character in *Paradise Lost* would think, feel, and act in a given situation and then demonstrate that judgment in verse. Sometimes I ask them to impersonate Mammon in the context of the rebuttal against starting a war with heaven that he might have made had Satan given him a chance to do so (2.389). Other good topics for *ethopoeia* include the following: What is Adam thinking while he names the animals (8.349–55) or waits for Eve to return for lunch on the day that they fall from grace (9.838)? What does Eve think when she sees her reflection in the pool (4.453–65) or looks back at Eden after the angel has led them through the gate (12.641–44)? Whether they take the form of monologues or dialogues, the impersonations are an opportunity to raise questions about mode and voice in *Paradise Lost* and to encourage my students to notice that the epic is not merely a narrative poem, told by one voice, but also a kind of play, full of articulate characters, connecting Milton to the dramatic tradition in which he was steeped, although he did not follow Shakespeare's path to the stage.

A final assignment asks my students to write a minimum of forty or fifty lines of blank verse, using all these techniques together in a passage that could be fitted into a lacuna in Milton's poem. They might choose to expand the debate among Satan's followers in book 2 or the argument between Gabriel and Satan in book 4, to imagine what Eve was thinking during her brief absence from Raphael's visit (8.40), or to embellish Adam's remorse about the vision of human history that Michael gives him after the fall. From my perspective, it is important that the students choose the moment that they will write. The choices are revealing in that they bring to my attention those places in *Paradise Lost* that my students are struggling to interpret and understand, the places where they find a fault line running through the poem that they must investigate and fathom with their own writing. Frequently, the final assignments give me a better sense of what the entire poem has come to mean for them than anything they have said in class discussion throughout the term. When I return the final assignments, I also give students an anthology of the verses that they have written, arranged according to the order that their passages would appear in Milton's poem.

I would like to conclude by acknowledging that even those Miltonists who are open to teaching *Paradise Lost* along the lines that I have described may have practical concerns about the way that such a course would work. For one, how ought we assign grades to imitative writing? The topic of evaluation is bound to create anxiety for a profession that has eschewed the appraisal of works of art as one of its core functions (value judgments of this kind are moot when literature is dissolved into the broad category of discourse) and devoted a great deal of energy to ignoring the unavoidable subjectivity of our judgments about argumentative essays (the things that make an essay persuasive for one reader make it specious for another). When I first began to ask my students to be imitators, I shared these concerns, but I quickly discovered that it was a mistake to worry. Asking students to imitate *Paradise Lost*, and to think of their own writing as craft, makes the encounter with this work of art and its sources more like the study of a foreign language than it ordinarily is. It will be evident that some students have read and listened to the text more closely than others, made better connections across its length and breadth, and also plumbed the depths of its allusions to the classical tradition more energetically—in effect, become more fluent in its peculiar language. Some compositions will be more skillful than others in their demonstration of Milton's sounds, rhythms, and ancient-modern syntax. Finally, a few students will simply put more effort into the work than others, read more books that Milton read, and write more lines. All these factors make it easier to assign just grades. Anecdotally I would report that students who earn grades lower than B seem to understand why those grades are appropriate for their work and do not dispute them. Students also collect their final assignments from the box outside my office in greater numbers than they ever did when I asked them to write conventional term papers. That is one of the best reasons that I can give for teaching *Paradise Lost* and the classical tradition in this way—that is, by asking my students to study Milton's tradition by becoming part of it themselves. They value their work enough to want to keep it and to keep it going.

NOTES

[1] On the benefits of making imitation a cornerstone of contemporary writing pedagogy, see Corbett.

[2] For an assessment of critical thinking pedagogy, see Prince.

[3] A modern translation of the ancient texts on which the humanists drew may be found in *Progymnasmata: Greek Textbooks of Prose Composition and Rhetoric*, translated by Kennedy. See also *Progymnasmata of Aphthonius*, translated by Nadeau. Rainolde's *Foundacion of Rhetorike* (1563) is the first English version of Aphthonius, although Nadeau describes it as "a very free adaptation" of Lorich's Latin adaptation of Agricola's earlier Latin translation of the Greek text (264). For a brief synopsis of Rainolde's text, see the description on *Silva Rhetoricae*, by Burton.

[4] Regarding these and other *progymnasmata*, see *Silva Rhetoricae*; *Renaissance Figures of Speech*; Mack.

[5] All references to *Paradise Lost* are to Hughes's edition in his *Complete Poems and Major Prose*.

Teaching *Paradise Lost* through Adaptation; or, Books Promiscuously Read

Lauren Shohet

When I ask myself how I would like my classes to influence students ten or twenty years down the road, my answers include keeping the works we once read together active in their minds. We always hope that students revisit the primary texts around which we build our courses (not to mention our careers and sensibilities); it is also important to cultivate fit readers of texts that derive from the books that linger on former students' shelves: to produce readers who notice and participate in the continuing conversations that come about when canonical texts like *Paradise Lost* are invoked in new artworks, Hollywood movies, television episodes, political dialogue, or even advertisements. The continuing adaptability of canonical texts, in a variety of popular and elite cultural registers, is arguably part of what keeps them vibrant. Moreover, insofar as adaptations of canonical texts embed interpretive arguments about their sources, fostering the development of audiences engaged with these textual progeny recruits nonprofessional readers into our discussions.

Recognizing allusion makes adaptations come alive. Adaptation studies can also offer rich benefits for readers more invested in the source texts than in the appropriations. Attending to echoes of a text like *Paradise Lost* in ensuing traditions can make students better readers of sources: even simply cataloging points of contact demands careful reading and rereading of the source to identify the elements the adaptation retains or omits. Extending the task into remarking what the adaptation transforms and what it leaves intact—and accounting for the effects of its choices and perhaps their reasons (formal, political, theological, or otherwise)—can further develop students' engagement with the original. When, for example, in C. S. Lewis's *The Magician's Nephew* Polly never enters the garden where Digory is tempted ("Digory himself understood that the others wouldn't and couldn't come in with him. He went forward to the gates alone" [171]), students can debate whether this constitutes a rejection or an intensification of *Paradise Lost*'s position on Eve's (in)sufficiency to stand. Does Polly's exclusion suggest that Eve's postscriptural and post-Miltonic femininity always already suffers from the diminished agency that is a consequence of the fall that already occurred in the source texts, making her ineligible for further trial? Or does Polly's physical absence from the garden in *Magician's Nephew* implicitly draw attention to the silent Eve's virtual exclusion from Adam's conversations with angels in analogous scenes of *Paradise Lost*? Or does Polly's exclusion limn the narrative consequence of shifting genres from theodicean epic to children's fantasy fiction? If the last, how firmly do students wish to claim that genre delimits content? And does students' consideration of whether genre reshapes argument in *The Magician's Nephew* inflect their response to (or patience with)

Dryden's *State of Innocence* as operatic libretto? These questions suggest how studying adaptation and remediation can generate overarching considerations of form, interpretation, and critical practice. Adaptations of varying extensiveness, fidelity, and perhaps even quality can form the basis for students' analyses of *Paradise Lost*, of texts that adapt it, and of metaquestions arising from intertextual studies to mutually complicate and enrich one another.

Adaptation, Allusion, and Historical Distance

Reminding students that *Paradise Lost* is itself an adaptation (of Scripture, of epic, of romance) attests to the potential seriousness of adaptation studies and offers opportunities for questions of adaptation to effectively dovetail with other approaches detailed in the present volume. Cross-reading the poem's self-conscious discussion of its status as adaptation with related early-modern ventures offers one angle of analysis. We can, for instance, compare *Paradise Lost's* invocation of the "Heav'nly Muse, that on the secret top / Of *Oreb*, or of *Sinai* didst inspire / That Shepherd, who first taught the chosen Seed" (1.6–8),[1] its "argument / . . . more Heroic than the wrath / Of stern *Achilles*" (9.13–15), or its investment in first inhabiting, then surpassing, its own tradition when it undertakes "Things unattempted yet" (1.16) with Lucy Hutchinson's resolve in *Order and Disorder*, her seventeenth-century adaptation of Genesis, to remain "fixed on what is true / And only certain, kept upon record / In the Creator's own revealed Word" (1.176–78) or with her caution that Eden will forever remain uncapturable by "th'apelike art of man" with its "Licentious pens or pencils" (3.145, 146; see also Norbrook, "*Order*"). Considering the ways that the narrator of *Paradise Lost* manages problems of adaptive retelling in relation to other possible strategies reveals both distinctive and typical elements in the Miltonic response. Examining problems like the construction of female frailty as issues also addressed by other writers adapting Genesis—such as Hutchinson, Aemilia Lanyer's apology for Eve, or visual texts such as Jan Sadeler's engravings of the creation (see McColley, *Gust*)—reveals readable choices in Miltonic texts where twenty-first-century students might otherwise see only limitations.[2]

Or we can explore *Paradise Lost's* allusions in company with later texts' citations of the poem. This approach can work well with short texts or glancing engagements, making it appropriate for courses without time to study longer adaptations. Students can consider uses of Milton's Eve in constructions of female curiosity in the lyric "Telling Them Apart," by the contemporary poet Lisa Sewell ("The girl is the one who does not recognize / her own face in the glass until too late, / until long after the voice—call it God, / call it Freud—has pointed to that other shape [*less fair, / less winning soft*] and instructed her desire" [1–5]) and in *The Simpsons* episode "Bible Stories" (Groening). The Sewell poem muses on mirrors, language, desire, and identity through lenses of psychoanalysis, theology, and feminist theory. *The Simpsons* episode stages related issues in a popular register. These Bible stories are indeed Milton stories, including a revision of Adam's lament about the inadequacy of animal companionship as Homer Simpson's complaint that "something's missing" as he frolics with beasts after his wife's departure; an echo of Adam's analysis that the Father needs no mate because "Thou in thyself art perfet" (8.415) in Homer's paean to God, "You're so great, I can't believe you don't have a girlfriend"; and a hilariously abbreviated staging of book 10's postlapsarian ruptures in marital, devotional, and meteorological harmony. Interested, like Milton's Eve and Sewell's girl, in discourse and knowledge, an idle Marge Simpson asks God for "some general-interest reading"; God provides a *People* magazine. Is *People* adequate? Does Marge want more? For that matter, on what grounds can we distinguish lesser from different modes of knowledge? This last question can lead back to comparing Adam's objective but fragmented "Limb by Limb" self-perusal (8.267–68) with Eve's mediated contemplation of her face in the pool (4.456–65). Looping through questions to responses to ensuing questions as we study adaptations can remind students that recognizing an allusion invites, rather than constitutes, a reading.

Intention, Quality, Cogency

When the 1997 Taylor Hackford film *The Devil's Advocate* names its Satan figure John Milton (played by Al Pacino), this box-office movie raises questions about the seriousness of the film's allusion. The appellation could cannily locate Milton among the devil's party, or it could facilely invoke a literary icon for cultural capital. Appreciative students argue that the film's engagements of *Paradise Lost* are not only protracted (a very partial list includes Satan lurking at Eve's ear, bridges and highways instantiated at the fall, architecture recalling Satan's flight above earth, and a family drama of Satan, Sin, and Death) but also insightful. For instance, the film's wedded pair first glimpse their new dwelling over the shoulder of a welcoming neighbor, who later is revealed as a demon, framed by a wallpaper vine. Hackford-as-shrewd-Miltonist partisans claim the bow-backed window seat where Mary Ann (Charlize Theron) declares her love for Kevin (Keanu Reeves) as Adam and Eve's "inmost bower" (4.438), a connection they extend to reading Mary Ann's decorating the apartment with "undulating acanthus leaf" wallpaper and "arbor green" paint as iterations of Eve's aesthetic horticulture. Other students demur. Even some who grant that Mary Ann's blond curls—made conspicuous when Milton urges her to cut them and reassume her natural color—recall Eve's "wanton ringlets" (4.306) argue that the film unconvincingly invokes and then cheaply abandons the image, as the shorn Mary Ann becomes dull, dispirited, sterile, and ultimately suicidal. How, they ask, does marshaling Satan against eroticism make sense?

I have come to think that *The Devil's Advocate* offers a tenable and interesting position on Eve's ringlets: insofar as the film's demons consistently diminish pleasure—Milton's makeover suggestions make Mary Ann less beautiful; the neighbor-demon counsels against the pleasing verdant paint Mary Ann prefers; Kevin's long hours at Milton's demonically staffed law firm separate the wedded pair—*The Devil's Advocate* suggests that "wanton" pleasures are indeed Edenic and God-granted, only Satan "bid[ding] abstain" (4.748). Manifestations of Mary Ann's alienation, in this reading, echo the structure of Eve's despairing monologue in 10.967–1006. Such extended readings may not spontaneously blossom in the classroom, but they can be catalyzed by asking students to—for instance—compare the counsel offered Mary Ann in the film with the narrative, Satanic, and angelic instruction of Eve in *Paradise Lost* or to compare the sequence of Mary Ann's depredations with the progression of Eve's proposals from sorrow to celibacy to suicide. If protracted analysis of popular entertainment provokes the response that a good reader, not the adaptation, is doing the work, so much the better: we can ask students to reflect on the methodological investments that underlie their positions on this problem. How do they identify overreading? What, if anything, is wrong with it? How far does *Paradise Lost* control its own interpretation? Adaptation studies can make a familiar Miltonic crux pop in the classroom—in this example offering opportunities to engage William Blake (*Milton*) or Stanley Fish (*Surprised by Sin*) on the poet's control of readerly and even authorial sympathy or to ask whether and why related arguments in the idioms of art and criticism should be treated differently.

Adaptation as Thought Experiment

Considering adaptive responses to such details of the source allows one kind of work: discerning and perhaps evaluating interpretations encoded in fictional forms. Another set of projects focuses on illuminating large-scale questions by examining an adaptation's alteration of one element while preserving others. For instance, by retaining specific textual elements while ranging far outside the generic profile of *Paradise Lost*, Mary Shelley's *Frankenstein* provides a locus classicus for protracted examination of adaptation as thought experiment. When Shelley's male Creature reenacts Eve's mirror scene, he raises questions of identity, misrecognition, alterity, and beauty:

> I had admired the perfect forms of my cottagers—their grace, beauty, and delicate complexions: but how was I terrified, when I viewed myself in a transparent pool! At first I started back, unable to believe that it was indeed I who was reflected in the mirror; and when I became fully convinced that I was in reality the monster that I am, I was filled with the bitterest sensations of despondence and mortification.   (109)

Shelley's regendering of her gazer, as well as the precise contrast between Eve's response and the Creature's, invites analysis of contrasts between Shelley's "monstrousness," "terror," "despondence," and "mortification," which exactly correspond to Milton's "sympathy," "love," "fair[ness]," "soft[ness]," and "ami-abl[e] mild[ness]" (4.465–79). This allows students to think about the work that beauty does in and for *Paradise Lost* as well as the work that horror does in *Frankenstein*. What value and what danger accrues to the beauty that makes Eve "pin[e] with vain desire" (4.466), that makes Adam's "Authority and Reason on her wait" (8.554), and that leaves Satan "Stupidly good, of enmity disarm'd" (9.465)? Shelley's Creature knows, even before "starting back," that the watery image is of himself, whereas Eve does not; beyond this, the Creature shrewdly recognizes the distinctions among image, self, and reality ("I was *reflected in* the mirror," then "became fully convinced that I was in reality the monster that I am" [emphasis added]) that, as Christine Froula details ("When Eve"), are tac-itly imposed on an unwitting Eve when "a voice" informs her, "What there thou seest fair Creature *is* thyself" (4.468; emphasis added). Is Eve's beauty linked to her ignorance? How does beauty work, Neoplatonically, to edify? When, by contrast, does Milton's "too heav'nly form" obfuscate (10.872)? One can take *Frankenstein* as a thought experiment that asks, What if Milton's Eve had not been beautiful? We can also take Victor's reneging on his promise to recom-pense the Creature's Adamic solitude as a thought experiment that asks, What might have happened had Milton's God indeed thought it good for man to be alone? When adaptations throw light on the road not taken in a source text, they can yield insight into a source's choices.

Helping Students Generate the Questions and Hear the Conversations

One of the richest extended adaptations, to my mind, is Philip Pullman's fantasy fiction trilogy His Dark Materials. These novels' engagements of *Paradise Lost* are both nuanced and accessible. Categories students can investigate include accounting for the human condition, testing the limits of human potential, dis-cerning truth in a confusing cosmos, building just political systems, negotiating individual identity and communal participation, locating human beings within ecosystems, defining love and friendship, reconciling science and faith, and ex-ploring the ethical dimensions of art. Once students choose (or are assigned) an issue shared by the epic and the trilogy, they can analyze what differences the distinctions between the two texts make. The trilogy's recasting of salva-tion offers one example of a problem that requires students to read carefully across both works to access the texts' full propositions. Pullman's Lyra and Will renegotiate the terms of death, for a new dispensation in which every ghost earns its own release from the underworld, in pointed distinction to Christian, especially Reformist, salvation. In Pullman, ghosts' coin for passage is narrative: release into joyous universal consciousness requires every individual's "truth about what they've seen and touched and heard and loved and known in the world" (*Amber Spyglass* 317); the universe depends on the consciousness re-leased back into the world with each spirit's ascent. Everlasting life is denied the oblivious: "if people live their whole lives and they've got nothing to tell about it when they've finished, then they'll never leave the world of the dead" (492–93). Asking students to compare the economies and ecologies of immortality in Pullman and Milton leads them into readings of major issues of both the trilogy and the traditions it addresses.

The series His Dark Materials is also useful for its thematizing of adaptation. As students can discover by collecting scenes of reading, listening, or investigation, the novels offer many figures for ways that new artworks enter into the repertoire. Drawing out these moments helps students see how their interpretive labor maintains the tradition they are studying. The trilogy's readjudication of exile takes up specifically Miltonic invitations to fallen reading. Whereas the Christian tradition requires that Adam and Eve forsake Eden while allowing them to remain together, Pullman's lovers learn that they cannot long survive outside their separate worlds of origin; in the new dispensation, only one door can remain open between worlds, and to leave that door available for the infinitude of souls to pass forth from the underworld Will and Lyra must sacrifice their mutual immanence. In *Paradise Lost*, Adam laments loss of presence, mourning that exile from the garden will prevent him from recounting to his sons that God "under *this* Tree / Stood visible, among *these* Pines his voice / I heard, here with him at *this* Fountain talk'd" (11.320–22; emphasis added). As students can find (if necessary, one can send them searching for pines and fountains in the novels), Lyra and Will both mourn and mitigate their loss in closely parallel terms. Lyra "led [Will] past a pool with a fountain under a wide-spreading tree, and then struck off . . . toward a huge many-trunked pine" (*Amber Spyglass* 507). At "a wooden seat under a spreading, low-branched tree," they agree that in their separate worlds, at the summer solstice, each will "sit on this exact same bench" and "pretend we were close again—because we *would* be close, if you sat *here* and I sat just *here* in my world" (508). This imaginative proximity encapsulates readership—the relationship of source texts to adaptations, or the relationship readers create with characters—and shows Lyra (whom I have argued elsewhere to figure narrative art; see Shohet) modeling the kind of transformative reading in which the newly fallen Adam needs instruction, so that he may read the signs, tracks, and analogies that the archangel Michael promises God will provide to compensate his new aloofness:

> God is *as* here, and will be found alike
> Present, and of his presence many a sign
> Still following thee, still compassing the round
> With goodness and paternal love, his Face
> Express, and of his steps the track Divine.
>   (11.350–54; emphasis added)

His Dark Materials emphasizes the labor of reading as both painstaking and joyous, and it makes shifts in modes of reading a primary register of the difference between innocence and experience. Lyra has been guided throughout her journey by an "alethiometer," or "truth-measure," that she reads during child-hood with extraordinary, instinctive competence ("without even having to think about it . . . [feeling] her mind settle into the right meanings" [*Golden Compass* 204]). Fallen, Lyra must relearn to read the alethiometer as adults do, by pains-takingly cross-referencing the instrument's thirty-six multivalent symbols with "the books . . . in Bodley's Library," where "the scholarship to study them is alive and well" (*Amber Spyglass* 513). As the angel Xaphania tells her, "You [once] read it by grace . . . you can regain it by work" (491). This recapitulates the experience of many students invested in fantasy-fiction exegeses: they fear that critically analyzing the books they love will spoil their pleasure. This positions them to evaluate Xaphania's promise to Lyra that reading "by work"—"carrying a pile of books everywhere"—"will be even better . . . deeper and fuller than grace that comes freely" (491). Adaptation studies asks students to carry around that pile of books and see what fruit that labor bears.

Pragmatic Choices

Which texts do we load into that pile? I find worthwhile whatever adaptive texts can sponsor chiastic insight: mutual illumination of the source, the adaptation, and the operations of (re)reading, (re)writing, and (re)forming. Teachers' rela-tive commitment to these three areas of analysis, as well as the amount of time available for intertextual excursions, will shape choices of adaptations. I have used texts of different length, complexity, and fidelity in a variety of courses that read *Paradise Lost* in toto (classes on Milton, epic, genre theory, and even a class on adaptation). My undergraduate Milton class has read the first five books of Hutchinson's *Order and Disorder*; my undergraduate adaptation class reads all of *Paradise Lost*, *His Dark Materials*, and Vergil's *Aeneid* as well as excerpts of Ovid's *Metamorphoses*. Briefer options include both short adaptive texts and extracts from longer texts, particularly when these take up precise figures or problems of the poem. Here, juxtaposing passages can show students how to align creative and analytic discourses in ways that let commentary emerge. The apartment-as-garden scene from *The Devil's Advocate*, for example, can be ex-tracted for pairing with Miltonic passages, potentially even in classes that read only apposite portions of *Paradise Lost* (surveys of British literature or multidis-ciplinary early-modern-studies seminars).

Aligning specific passages from multiple sources can sponsor fruitful class discussions and also serve as a model for more extended work students might undertake outside class, in papers or in future work. The problem of election that could vex courses from Milton to histories of Christianity to surveys, for instance, comes up in extractable passages of both *Paradise Lost* and adaptive texts. Evaluating the narrative, psychological, and theological (dis)satisfactions of the Miltonic Father's "Some I have chosen of peculiar grace / Elect above the rest" (3.183–84) in relation to, say, Lewis's election of "chosen beasts" who will have full verbal self-consciousness (*Magician's Nephew* 124) can illuminate both techniques and frustrations of Miltonic theodicy. Adding in John Calvin's version of election (bk. 3, ch. 21) can extend the discussion to looking at how *Paradise Lost* adapts sources. Extracting apposite passages on particular problems can also draw in expansive texts too long for full treatment. In Alan Moore and Dave Gibbons's graphic novel *Watchmen*, for instance, one can cross-read the superhero Dr. Manhattan's view of the earth from Mars, his debate over whether to visit the earth to mitigate human catastrophe, and his transcendence of linear temporality (104–08) with the dialogue of Milton's Father and Son gazing on earth from heaven in *Paradise Lost* (3.56–414). Analyzing local moments also efficiently prompts layered analysis of allusions among texts: one can produce requisite passages to explore citations of *Paradise Lost* in the 1978 John Landis film *Animal House*—which depicts a fraternity house as Miltonic Pandemonium—in relation to *Paradise Lost*'s citations of the *Iliad*'s ships (*Iliad* 2.484, in *Paradise Lost* 1.376) or the palaces in Ovid's *Metamorphoses* (*Metamorphoses* 1.171–72 and 4.762–64, in *Paradise Lost* 1.710–17; see E. Brown; Hughes's footnote to *Paradise Lost* 1.1710–17).[3]

Brief adaptive moments also can be framed to give students practice in drawing together passages from across the epic, while still offering text for crossreading—a good first step even in courses that eventually ask students to find their own adaptive cruxes. Students might draw evidence from *Paradise Lost* for arguments about modes of knowledge, authority, gender, and language to consider in relation to Homer Simpson's misnaming the animals. In this episode, when Marge asks Homer, "What do you call the ground-hog?" he replies, "ground-monster," and I regret to report that he names the unicorn Gary. To help students see what Miltonic issues *The Simpsons* scene engages, one could provide students with, say, the poem's remark that animals "receive / From [Adam] thir names" (8.343–44) and his ensuing insightful nominations ("I nam'd them . . . and understood / Thir Nature" [8.352–53]) before asking students how the two texts differ when considered in one another's company and when considered individually. One might also ask why Homer is assigned his task, particularly when Marge already knows a better name for the groundhog—or is the postlapsarian name merely more familiar, not better? Beyond Homer's and Adam's shared male privilege, does Homer's fallen state contrast to Adam's wisdom (elevating it by contrast) or burlesque it (suggesting a continuity from "our first Father" [4.495] to Homer)? If this gap between divine dispensation and right nomination in *The Simpsons* allows the text to comment on its authority figure, might one ask similar questions about Eve's claim that she sees "*another* Sky" in the pool (4.459; emphasis added), when the narrator has not divulged that Eve ever looked up at the first sky that could teach her the name? On a less sophisticated plane, why is naming a unicorn Gary funny? For beginning literature students, these questions can reveal much about style, discourse, and generic expectation.

Adaptation studies of different scopes can sponsor a range of classroom and writing activities. Asking students to bring in an example of ambient Milton can increase their sensitivity to cultural uses of Milton even beyond teachers' spheres of awareness. Classes can also explore discrete engagements centered on a single problematic; divided into small groups, each with a different non-Miltonic passage (either chosen by the students or assigned to them), students can prepare remarks about the passage and a discussion question for the full class that pairs their assigned adaptive passage with apposite material in *Paradise Lost*. The assignment that recently has concluded my undergraduate Milton course exemplifies my hopes for adaptation studies' potential to both broaden and deepen student engagement: it demands protracted engagement with complex texts, substantial independent effort, effective collaboration, and payoff for analyzing Milton. I had been frustrated by the cumbersomeness of working non-Miltonic texts into a Milton syllabus: so many of the most provocative candidates proved prohibitively time-intensive for students to read and discuss as a class. Thus I have developed a culminating assignment, announced at the beginning of the course, that asks students to choose among a handful of extended, important adaptations or source texts (recent options have included His Dark Materials, Blake's *Milton*, the *Aeneid*, *Watchmen*, and *Frankenstein*), which they read outside class. I then turn several class sessions over to breakout work on those texts, alternating between independent and small-group analysis. Students prepare for the first session by crafting discussion questions for groups of four to six classmates working on the same adaptation. Within their groups, students spend a class session discussing these initial questions. Immediately after this conversation, students prepare and exchange questions to address in their journals, with each student choosing two for journal response. This in turn generates two more discussion questions from each student for the next class meeting, and the cycle is repeated. Thereafter, groups prepare a brief (ten-minute) presentation to the class, as well as a discussion question on *Paradise Lost* that arises from their work. I explain that the presentations should convey the least one needs to know about the adaptation to understand the force of the question about *Paradise Lost* that it catalyzed for the group: the full class should be left with a sense of the terms of the adaptation's engagement and why it provoked the question it did. The segment concludes with the group leading a class discussion of their question. (Students have the option of drawing the adaptation into their final papers as well.) The ensuing discussions are often surprisingly insightful, and I am particularly interested in how many students tell me that they read adaptations presented by other groups after the course is over. The fit audience appears to become less few.

NOTES

[1] All citations of Miltonic texts are to Hughes's *Complete Poems and Major Prose*.

[2] Wittreich gives many teachable examples, now easily accessible on *Early English Books Online* for classroom use (*Feminist Milton*).

[3] Featured in many adaptations, underworld scenes make a convenient locus for comparative work on issues of disorder and order, relationship of political and other discourses, how distance from creators sponsors innovation versus derivation, and heroism or antagonism of the dispossessed. In the adaptations discussed here, see esp. Moore and Gibbons's *Watchmen* (for Pandemonium, see ch. 8, p. 18); in *The Devil's Advocate*, Moyez's subterranean "pagan" altar; in Lewis, *The Silver Chair*, chs. 10–12; in Pullman's His Dark Materials, *Amber Spyglass*, chs. 21, 23, and 26 (for Pandemonium, see 316).

Teaching *Paradise Lost*
through the New Milton Criticism

Peter C. Herman

At the beginning of *How Milton Works*, Stanley Fish asserts that "conflict, ambivalence, and open-endedness—the watchwords of a criticism that would make Milton into the Romantic liberal some of his readers want him to be—are not constitutive features of the poetry but products of a systematic misreading of it" (14). The notion that Milton and incertitude constitute mutually exclusive categories has a very long history in Milton criticism, running from Andrew Marvell ("Thou hast not missed one thought that could be fit, / And all that was improper dost omit" [48–49]) through Fish and beyond (see Herman, *Destabilizing* 1–24).[1] Russell M. Hillier, for example, in a 2009 article in *Milton Quarterly*, explicitly refutes the notion that Milton's epic in any way complicates its binary oppositions:

> Although such a dualism is somewhat unfashionable critically, to my mind the poetry instead bears out a far less ambiguous or ambivalent relationship between, on the one hand, the virtue of Milton's God, his Son, and his angels, and, on the other, the Machiavellian *virtù* of fraud and force displayed by Satan and his minions; rather, the poem seems to insist upon a more defined polarity between the virtue of Milton's God and the *virtù* of his Satan than Kahn subscribes to. (22)

The notion that there might be a dialogue between Milton's endorsement of classical values in, say, the "Doric lay" at the end of "Lycidas" (line 189) and the "Doric pillars" and the "Dorian mood / Of flutes and soft Recorders" to which the devils march in *Paradise Lost* (1.714, 1.550–51) merits only dismissal, not serious consideration. For critics such as Marvell, Fish, and Hillier, while their projects differ considerably, there is nonetheless a common denominator: "there are no moral ambiguities" in Milton's world and, consequently, no linguistic or metaphorical ambiguities (Fish, *How Milton Works* 53).

Recently, however, this position has come under significant pressure. A new movement has arisen, named by Joseph A. Wittreich as the new Milton criticism,[2] and this critical approach argues that "conflict, ambivalence, and openendedness" are indeed the constitutive features of *Paradise Lost*. As Wittreich puts it in his call for a new approach to studying and teaching *Paradise Lost*: "instead of confronting opposing points of view in order to silence one of them, [Milton studies] might be empowered and emboldened by the competing interpretations to produce finer honings of its own (not always nuanced) readings" ("'He Was Ever'" 36). Here I briefly show how one can adapt this approach to the classroom by focusing on two particularly salient examples of how Milton goes out of his way to create incertitude and how this incertitude can act as a powerful entrée into both Milton's epic and the protocols governing most Milton criticism.

First, I turn to Milton's comparison of Satan to a whale. After the equally ambivalent association of Satan with Briareos (Herman, *Destabilizing* 27–30), the epic narrator compares the fallen angel's size with

> that sea-beast
> Leviathan, which God of all his works
> Created hugest that swim th'ocean stream:
> Him haply slumb'ring on the Norway foam
> The pilot of some small night-foundered skiff,
> Deeming some island, oft, as seamen tell,
> With fixèd anchor in his scaly rind
> Moors by his side under the lee, while night
> Invests the Sea, and wishèd Morn delays.
>   (1.200–08)

The teaching point is to have students realize that what Milton wrote and what the notes to various editions say he wrote are clean, different things, a lesson that sharpens students' sense of both Milton's text and the protocols of Milton criticism. The key is in the ending. In *Paradise Lost*, Milton concludes the simile without telling us what happened: we leave the pilot anchored to the whale: "while night / Invests the sea, and wishèd Morn delays" (1.207–08), and I highlight these two lines when teaching this passage. Milton's contemporary editors, however, alter the ending, and to make the point, I put each of the following annotations in a *PowerPoint* slide and ask students to compare what the editor says happened with Milton's text:

> "The story of the deceived sailor and the illusory island was a commonplace (see, e.g., *Orlando Furioso* 6.37–41) often applied to Satan."
>   (Lewalski [Blackwell] 17)

> "Of all the biblical allusions to the mysterious sea-monster Leviathan, the closest is Isaiah's prophecy that the Lord 'shall punish Leviathan, the piercing serpent, even Leviathan, that crooked serpent; and he shall slay the dragon that is in the sea' (xxvii. 1). The tale of the mariners who mistake the leviathan for an island is widespread."   (Hughes 216)

> "As the type of deceptive monster, 'leviathan' became synonymous with Satan, and the story of mariners anchoring on his back only to be swept under to their death was as popular as the similar Will-o'-the-Wisp or ignis fatuus story. Ariosto pictures a similar beast in the *Orlando Furioso* 6.37, a whale so large its back seems to be an island."   (Flannagan 360n80)

"Tales of enormous sea creatures and of mariners who mistook them for islands were common, as were moral applications of such stories."

(Kerrigan, Rumrich, and Fallon 301)

"The sailors in the skiff are overcome by darkness. They fasten anchor to what they suppose to be an island but is in fact a whale. The whale dives, dragging them down with it — a symbol of the devil."   (Teskey 9)

"*Leviathan* [is] a whale, but the name was also associated with Satan.... The story of the illusory island was a commonplace often applied to Satan. . . . Boiardo and Ariosto tell how the paladin Astolfo mistook a whale for an island and was carried off (*Orl. Inm.* II xiv 3, *Orl. Fur.* VI.37–43)."

(Leonard 716)

"The monster of Job xli, identified in Isaiah's prophecy of judgment as 'the crooked serpet' (*Is.* Xxvii I), but also sometimes thought of as a whale. The anecdote of the illusory island is from the *Physiologus*, where the moral drawn is that the devil is similarly deceitful. . . . [The simile] illustrates the delusiveness of Satan and the danger of trusting his false appearance of greatness in the early books of the poem."   (Fowler 56)

Students quickly realize that each of the editors, either implicitly (Lewalski, Hughes, Flannagan, and Kerrigan, Rumrich, and Fallon) or explicitly (Teskey, Leonard, Fowler) assume that the "deceptive monster" of a whale dives and the mariners are drowned. Otherwise, there would be no "moral application," as Kerrigan, Rumrich, and Fallon put it, no application to Satan. All but one editor assert that the whale symbolizes Satan.

Milton's editors will often refer the reader to the literary history of this story, and the notes afford an opportunity, as Thomas Luxon suggests in his essay in this volume, to model our research methods "for everyone right there in the class." Fowler, Hughes, and Leonard direct students to a 1925 *Modern Language Notes* article by James Pitman arguing that the source for Milton's image is "the ubiquitous *Physiologus*" (439), an Old English collection of moralized beast fables (A. Cook). Using my university's "smart classroom" technology, I project the article (available on *JSTOR*) on the board and then have the class read it alongside the source (available through Project Gutenberg). We discover that after the sailors land on the whale, build a fire, and begin to "Enjoy the gentle weather, suddenly / Under the salty waves [the whale] plunges down / Straight to the bottom deep he drags his prey" (15). One can do the same exercise with the references to Ariosto and Boiardo.

By placing side by side the offered source and the annotations with Milton's poem, students quickly realize that assuming the whale drags the sailors down to a watery grave does not comport with the actual ending of this simile. Students also realize that none of the editors draws attention to how Milton departs from his sources by leaving the ending unresolved. (And with luck, students also realize the utility of chasing down footnotes.) Class discussion then revolves around the following questions: Why does Milton not supply an ending for this story? Since the story of the whale mistaken for an island was commonplace, what are the effects of departing from expectation? How does not knowing what happens to the Norwegian pilot affect our understanding of Satan? What does the whale's failure to exhibit any hostile or evil intent in *Paradise Lost* do to our understanding of Satan? Turning to the contemporary editions, the class discusses why there is such unanimity about something that is not in Milton's text. Why, I ask, do editors supply the ending Milton denies? Why do the editors who direct students to various sources suppress Milton's key departure from these texts? How does adding the ending alter our understanding of the passage? What seems to be at stake in such editorial practice? The upshot of this discussion is usually that students begin to understand that editors have an interpretive agenda and that, while notes can be supremely useful (directing the reader to the analogues, for instance), they also need to be read nearly as carefully as one reads Milton's verse. Then, circling back to Milton, I ask if any other moments in Milton's verse might prepare the reader for what Milton does in this simile, and students will usually recall the unresolved dynamic between "L'Allegro" and "Il Penseroso," the weird shift to indirect speech at the conclusion of "Lycidas," and Milton's deep frustration with England in *The Ready and Easy Way*.

While at times Milton will create incertitude by leaving things hanging, at other times he does so by giving us multiple versions of the same event with no sure way of deciding which version, if any, is the right one. The best example of this sort of incertitude is the two versions of Adam and Eve's first meeting (see also Sauer's essay in this volume). Since we find Eve's version in 4.481–90 and Adam's in 8.481–520, I usually wait until we get to Adam's narrative before reminding the class that Eve has previously gone over this material, and then I ask the class to compare the two versions. Usually, my students quickly understand that Adam and Eve give contradictory versions of key events. Eve says that initially she was less than enthused by Adam's appearance:

> fair indeed and tall,
> Under a Platan, yet methought less fair,
> Less winning soft, less amiably mild,
> Than that smooth wat'ry image; back I turned.   (4.477–80)

Adam thinks that Eve's turning away reflects her desire to be "wooed, and not unsought be won" (8.503). Adam then addresses God, thanking him for Eve:

> but fairest this
> Of all thy gifts, nor enviest. I now see
> Bone of my bone, flesh of my flesh, my self
> Before me.   (8.493–96)

Eve, however, reports that Adam does not address God, but her: "Thou follow-ing cried'st aloud, 'Return faire Eve, / Whom fli'st thou? Whom thou fli'st, of him thou art, / His flesh, his bone" (4.481–83). Moreover, the tone in which Adam addresses Eve is completely different, according to the speaker. Adam says that he addresses Eve with "pleaded reason" (8.510); Eve says that Adam barks a series of questions (quoted above) that ends with a claim of ownership:

> to give thee being I lent
> Out of my side to thee, nearest my heart
> Substantial life, to have thee by my side
> Henceforth an individual solace dear;
> Part of my soul I seek thee, and thee claim
> My other half.   (4.483–88)

Finally, while both agree that their first meeting ends in sex, their narrative of how they got there differs. According to Adam, Eve "approved" his "pleaded reason" (8.509, 510), and thus "To the nuptial bow'r / I led her blushing like the morn" (8.510–11); but in Eve's telling, after Adam claims her "My other half" his "gentle hand / Seized mine" (4.488–89), and as I have noted elsewhere, Mil-ton never uses "seize" for anything positive (Herman, *Destabilizing* 54).

After the class anatomizes the similarities and differences between the two speeches (and it is probably a good idea to keep a running tally), class discus-sion centers on the thematic resonances of having contradictory accounts of the same event with no evident way of deciding between them. First, I ask the class if they can figure out what actually happened. Is one speaker more reliable than the other? If so, why? Does the fact that Adam is speaking to Raphael and that Eve is speaking to Adam shape their narratives? Does Adam edit his version of events to make him look more attractive, given his desire to please Raphael? Does Eve's version suggest some of the reasons for her fall? Why does Milton give us two different versions of the same event? And are there any other parts of *Paradise Lost* in which different narrators give differing accounts of the same events?[3]

Rather than banish incertitude from the classroom, as Fish and others would have us do, I suggest making the new Milton criticism the center of our peda-gogy. This approach encourages students to read Milton's text very closely, at-tending to what precisely the words mean rather than what we would like them to mean. In addition, this approach encourages students to attend to the nar-rative patterns within *Paradise Lost* as a whole, to connect passages in books that are often quite far apart. Finally, by allowing incertitude to explain *Para-dise Lost* rather than explaining the incertitude away, the new Milton criticism allows *Paradise Lost* to become more accessible, and thus a more profound literary experience, for our students. Milton is not expounding truth from on high but exploring how truth seems to dissolve into separate, mutually exclusive narratives that defy closure.

NOTES

[1] All references to Marvell and to Milton are to Kerrigan, Rumrich, and Fallon's Modern Library edition, *The Complete Poetry and Essential Prose of John Milton*. While I use Lewalski's Blackwell edition of *Paradise Lost* for scholarship, I use the Modern Library edition of the epic poem in class, since its modernizations make reading Milton much easier for my students.

[2] Wittreich coined this term in "'He Ever Was'" 36. For a full genealogy of the new Milton criticism, see Herman, "Paradigms" 14–18.

[3] Raphael and Adam give different versions of mankind's creation (7.519–32; 8.338–45); the Muse and Raphael give different accounts of the Son's elevation (3.313–52; 5.606–17); and God's version of the past, present, and future in 3.80–99 departs from what the Muse tells us throughout *Paradise Lost*. God's assertion, for instance, that "man will hark'n to his glozing lyes" masks the fact that Adam and Eve fall for very different reasons (3.93).

Dieting in Paradise: Angelic Eating, Metaphysics, and Poetry in *Paradise Lost*

William Kolbrener

Food matters—for university students, and also for Milton. When I open the discussion of book 5 with the gambits "Do you believe in angels?" and "Do the angels of your imagination eat?," I know these questions will elicit interest. Students are likely to provide the terms for our class discussion, and someone inevitably mentions that angels, as spiritual beings, should have no need for physical sustenance. Which leads to the question, Why do Milton's angels eat?

Even as Adam sees Raphael—of "glorious shape" (5.309)—descending from the heavens as the book opens, Adam, in imitation (or in anticipation?) of the hospitable patriarch Abraham (Genesis 18.6), instructs Eve to begin preparations for their angelic guest: "go with speed, / And what thy stores contain bring forth" (5.313–14).[1] Eve turns to her Edenic kitchen "on hospitable thoughts intent" (5.332), while Adam engages in "discourse" with Raphael (5.395), preparing the way for the Miltonic joke—"no fear lest dinner cool" (5.396)—followed by an invitation to the angelic visitor:

> Heav'nly stranger, please to taste
> These bounties, which our Nourisher, from whom
> All perfect good, unmeasured out descends,
> To us for food and for delight hath caused
> The earth to yield: unsavory food, perhaps,
> To spiritual natures; only this I know,
> That one celestial father gives to all.   (5.397–403)

That Adam seems to hedge his bets—wondering whether earthly delights are perhaps "unsavory food" to "spiritual natures"—suggests that the poet is not "merely nodding" (as Longinus said of Homer) or trying, in his portrayal of idiosyncratic angelic habits, to elicit the interest of possibly nodding readers. To the contrary, the poet comments self-consciously on the episode: the angels are not hidden in some special-effects "mist" (5.435), the epic narrator interjects, as is "the common gloss of theologians" (5.435–36). The angels of Milton's Eden actually eat.

To further raise the stakes surrounding angelic eating, I turn to Richard Bentley, the great (and *chutzpadik*) eighteenth-century editor of Milton (see also the essays by Welch and Leonard in this volume). Bentley found much wanting in *Paradise Lost*. In his 1732 edition of the poem—paralleling Nahum Tate's version of *King Lear* for the eighteenth century, complete with happy ending—Bentley attributes parts of the poem that do not accord with his conception of the epic to Milton's incompetent daughter, his meddling editor, or, more likely in Bentley's estimation, a *"bad Printer."* To the proposition that angels eat, Bentley declares: "if the devils wanted feeding," the poet made "poor provision for them in hell" (Milton, *Milton's* Paradise Lost: *A New Edition* 162). Why is Bentley so exercised by the prospect of angels eating? Is Bentley's comment just a snide jab at the poet for leaving out the details of angelic—here satanic—sustenance, or does his displeasure with Milton's gustatory angels tell us about a gap between his eighteenth-century sensibility and Milton's? That Milton takes pains to distinguish his angels as beings who eat, and that Bentley shows such discomfort, allows us to restate the question, What's up with Milton's angels, who as it turns out not only eat but also do other things associated with the human body? Indeed, students may be interested to know—or point out themselves, if they have read ahead—that angels engage in other physical and distinctively human activities: if there's time, I turn to Adam's blush-inducing question to Raphael in book 8 and the latter's response, the Miltonic soft-core description of angelic pleasures (8.615–29).

That angelic eating may provide a way into what matters in *Paradise Lost* requires a couple of detours. That is, understanding Milton's conception of the relationship between spirit and matter requires context. A brief discussion of earlier Catholic conceptions of body and soul, as well as the relationship between spirit and matter forwarded by Milton's philosophical contemporaries, helps elaborate his idiosyncratic vision of that relationship. By briefly reviewing the Augustinian distinction between soul and body and the rejection of the physical entailed in embracing such a perspective, and by elaborating the contours of the strict Cartesian (as well as Hobbesian) philosophical distinction between spirit and matter, I prepare the way for seeing angels' eating as more than a poetic throwaway.[2] Given this twin set of framing contexts, students are likely to begin to see that Milton's angels transgress precedent theological and contemporary philosophical categories. That is, if earlier Catholic and contemporary (as well as later eighteenth century) philosophical traditions insist on the rigid distinction between categories, then students may already sense that Milton's blurring of such categories—evidenced in angels partaking of the physical pleasures of food and sex—has implications for the epic as a whole. After the brief excursus in intellectual history, I explore the connections between food and cosmology and speculate about how that connection might lead to a better understanding of Milton's conception of poetry.

I further focus the discussion by examining the context in which angelic eating appears. Raphael, in the midst of his Edenic repast, responds to Adam's anxious invitation and his question about the suitability of food to spiritual beings. Students are almost always struck by how the simple question about dinner leads the angel to a metaphysical discourse on the cosmos, the origin and progressive destinies of all created beings:

> All things proceed, and up to him return,
> If not depraved from good, created all

Such to perfection, one first matter all,
Endued with various forms, various degrees
Of substance, and in things that live, of life;
But more refined, more spiritous, and pure,
As nearer to him placed or nearer tending
Each in their several active spheres assigned,
Till body up to spirit work, in bounds
Proportioned to each kind.   (5.470–79)

I start by asking the class about the conception of creation implicit in the passage and the Miltonic affirmation that all is derived from "one first matter all." After understanding Milton's distance from the ex nihilo conception of creation—here the vagaries of theological argument can seem significant to undergraduates—we focus on the poet's depiction of the upward movement of a unified creation in which "all things proceed and up to him return." Given the previous elaboration of historical contexts, we find Milton clearly differentiating himself from theological and philosophical contemporaries. Miltonic emphasis on "continuity," to borrow a term from *Areopagitica* (958), permits students to understand that angelic eating is not merely a Miltonic one-off, an anomaly, but a representative instance in Milton's cosmos where there is a continuity between spirit and matter (*Areopagitica* 936).

At this point in the lesson, I usually ask a student to help us visualize the Miltonic cosmos by drawing a picture on the board of the tree that Raphael describes to elaborate his vision of the cosmos:

So from the root
Springs lighter the green stalk, from thence the leaves
More airy, last the bright consummate flow'r
Spirits odorous breathes: flow'rs and their fruit
Man's nourishment, by gradual scale sublimed
To vital spirits aspire, to animal,
To intellectual, give both life and sense,
Fancy and understanding, whence the soul
Reason receives, and reason is her being,
Discursive, or Intuitive; discourse
Is oftest yours, the latter most is ours,
Differing but in degree, of kind the same.   (5.479–90)

The exercise provides comic relief in pressing students' artistic talents and imaginations to draw the "odorous breathes" of Milton's spirituous flowers. Looking carefully at the passage, students follow Milton's creation as it is "by gradual scale sublimed" from the physicality of "the green stalk" to the less substantial "leaves" to the "consummate flower" and then, as the picture attenuates into spirit, the "odorous breathes" (where the volunteer artist either falters or becomes creative) onward to the spirits and the faculties of men and angels. After this practical attempt at visualizing Milton's cosmos, students usually refine their earlier observations: angels in *Paradise Lost* eat because Milton imagined the relationship between spirit and matter as fluid, allowing for the ascent from the material to the spiritual.

Students are—by this time—likely to be alive to the force of eighteenth-century critical rejections of parts of Milton's poem. Bentley does not like the Miltonic merging of spirit and matter not only for violating poetic decorum but also for undermining Enlightenment assumptions—inherited from René Descartes, refined by Isaac Newton—about the necessary incompatibility between spirit and matter. It is useful to add that Samuel Johnson, who shares Bentley's Enlightenment suppositions, had similar objections, and offered similar protests: for him, Milton's supposed confusion of spirit and matter impoverished his poetry. The poet, Johnson claimed, "perplexed his poetry with his philosophy" as his "infernal and celestial powers are sometimes pure spirit, and sometimes animated body" (qtd. in Shawcross, *Milton: The Critical Heritage* 305–06). For Johnson, Milton could not keep things straight—"Doesn't Milton know," Johnson asks implicitly, "that spirit and matter are separate?" From here, I ask my students whether their conceptions about spirit, matter, and angels are more Johnsonian or Miltonic. Johnson's and Bentley's perspectives can be shown to be not merely quaint misreadings but Enlightenment rejections of the terms of Milton's poetry. Angelic eating provides the pedagogical opportunity for understanding Milton's sensibility and his distance from the Enlightenment sensibility.

But what, if anything, I ask next, does Milton's arcane metaphysics have to do with his conceptions of poetry? Or, more pointedly, is there really a connection among food, cosmology, and poetry? To explore these questions, I remind students of Raphael's answer to Adam's hesitant invitation to join them at their "heaped" Edenic table (5.391). The food bestowed upon man, the angel replies, is suitable even for "purest Spirits," since both men and angels "contain"

> Within them every lower faculty
> Of sense, whereby they hear, see, smell, touch, taste,
> Tasting concoct, digest, assimilate,
> And corporeal to incorporeal turn.   (5.410–13)

Milton emphasizes the similarity between men and angels—evidencing physicality and the "faculty of sense." Where the creation, represented in Milton's conceit of the tree, moves upward from matter to spirit, those of higher degree, employing their sensual faculties, render through the processes of digestion the material spiritual and from "corporeal to incorporeal turn." The student who has read book 5 carefully may point out similarities between angelic digestion and Raphael's description of the processes and problems of theodicy, as the angel wonders anxiously:

                    for how shall I relate
To human sense th'invisible exploits
Of warring Spirits . . .
· · · · · · · · · · · · · · · · · · · ·
                        . . . how last unfold
The secrets of another World, perhaps
Not lawful to reveal?   (5.564–70)

Although Raphael hesitates at the challenges of theodicy, rendering these "secrets of another World," he continues:

                            yet for thy good
This is dispens't, and what surmounts the reach
Of human sense, I shall delineate so,
By likening spiritual to corporal forms.   (5.570–73)

Where angelic digestion moves from corporeal to incorporeal, Raphael imagines the task of relating "invisible exploits" as comparable to "likening spiritual to corporeal forms." Though Raphael faces the prospect of describing the "secrets of another world," much like the poet of *Paradise Lost*, the corporality of language and the material images employed are on a continuum with those spiritual secrets that the angel—and the poet—feels compelled to reveal. Indeed the poet, like Raphael, uses the physical to manifest the spiritual: the continuum between those spheres allows "invisible exploits" to be revealed through the physicality of the poetic image. Here, then, angelic eating opens up a reading of cosmology—one of similarity, likeness, and continuity—that further opens up an understanding of Miltonic theodicy. Revealing the secrets of another world is dependent on the poem's vision of cosmic unity where spirit and matter are connected.

But if there is an emphasis on likeness and the continuity between spiritual and physical, why is the poet so anxious about the prospects of theodicy? That Milton does express such anxiety (one can look, as well, at the invocations to books 3 and 7) allows students to be sensitive to the Miltonic assertion of likeness as well as difference in the creation in book 5. In the inversion of angelic digestion, Raphael transforms spiritual to physical, while angelic digestion, when able to "transubstantiate" through "concoctive heat," moves from the physical to spiritual realms (5.438, 437). But even Raphael wonders about the likeness that underlies theodicy: "*what if* Earth / Be but the shadow of Heaven, and things therein / Each to the other like, more than on Earth is thought (5.574–76; emphasis added). I ask students to consider Raphael's conditional phrasing and how it may help us understand the poet's understanding of his task. The continuity between spirit and matter—on which epic theodicy is based—brings us back to Raphael's simile (5.470–79), where, on second reading, we look for Miltonic assertions of not only similarities but differences, of not only "continuity" but the "contiguity" paired with it in *Areopagitica* and *Paradise Lost*. For, according to Raphael, the eventual return to "perfection" and "one first matter all" is figured as a process, where there is a hierarchy or "proportion" of "various forms" and "various degrees." The comparatives "more refined," "more spiritous," "nearer to him," and "nearer tending," as well as the temporal adverb "Till," reveal that the unity of spirit and matter is always, for Milton, represented as a direction, not an end.

When book 5 is read together with the following book, students will see that sometimes that end is not achieved. I turn to the satanic process of inventing gunpowder in book 6 as a way of showing a parallel satanic "art" that, although working according to similar principles, fails to refine into spirit:

> in a moment up they turnd
> Wide the Celestial soil, and saw beneath
> Th' originals of Nature in their crude
> Conception; sulfurous and nitrous foam
> They found, they mingled, and with subtle art,
> Concocted and adusted they reduced
> To blackest grain, and into store conveyed.   (6.509–15)

While angels transform physical to spiritual, the corresponding satanic "art" of concocting leads from the physical to the further physical, as the crude "originals of nature" are "adusted" and "reduced." Concocting—the angelic cooking that leads to spirit—can lead downward as well, not from corporeal to incorporeal, but from corporeal to more corporeal.

But not only the satanic host gets it wrong. Milton compares angelic eating with the process employed by the "empiric alchemist" who "Can turn, or *holds it possible to turn* / Metals of drossiest Ore to perfet gold" (5.440, 5.441–42; emphasis added). What, I ask, does Milton's comparison of angelic transubstantiation of the physical with the doubtful science of the alchemist—who holds it only "*possible* to turn" basest metals to gold—entail for understanding Milton's conception of the poet? of his ideal reader? Just as the angel's process of finding likenesses is qualified by Raphael's "what if," so Milton wonders about the efficacy of readerly digestion in his metaphor of the empiric alchemist (concocting, digesting, and assimilating, one can point out to students, are also alchemical processes). In this reading, Milton again confounds our assumptions, especially those of literary critics who claim that Milton's cosmos is built exclusively on similarity or difference. For though Milton's cosmos of continuity allows for theodicy, Miltonic assertion of degree and difference in the cosmos makes both the reading and the writing of poetry difficult and anxious tasks.

Raphael, despite his anxieties about revealing "the secrets of another world," still persists in the activity of "likening spiritual to corporeal forms"; so for Milton, poetry, with the dangers that attend both its writing and its reading, is the way he chooses to "justify the ways of God to men" (1.26). I turn finally to

Milton's *Of Education* to show that the conception of the corporeal image in the epic is informed by his arguments about poetry in the earlier tract. Poetry, Milton writes, is "precedent" to philosophy—including the writings of Plato, Aristotle, and Cicero—for it is "simple, sensuous, and passionate" (977). Cartesians reject poetry on these very grounds, but for Milton poetry has priority because of its connection to the physical. The assertion in the early prose tract of the passionate sensuality of poetry anticipates the epic poet's unapologetic insistence that angels eat and the derivative belief that holds as "Food of the mind" the "sweet intercourse / Of looks and smiles" between Adam and Eve in paradise, "for smiles from reason flow" (9.238–39). No Cartesian dichotomies here as reason, smiles, and food flow into one another. The sensuous and passionate are not—as they would be from a Catholic theological or Enlightenment philosophical perspective—lowly and impoverished but, for Milton, necessary for reaching the "highth" of his "great argument" (1.24). With some coaxing, students may understand, like the Edenic couple, that "knowledge is as food" (7.126), and, as eating angels attest, the ascent to the spiritual includes a very physical process of "tasting" that can from "corporeal to incorporeal turn."

NOTES

¹ All citations from Milton are from *The Complete Poetry and Essential Prose of John Milton*, edited by Kerrigan, Rumrich, and Fallon, which I find the most accessible edition for undergraduates.

² A great introduction to Milton's philosophical context is S. Fallon's *Milton among the Philosophers*.

Ecocritical Milton

Jeffrey Theis

Considering Milton from an Ecocritical Perspective

A well-noted irony is that Milton, a blind poet, created in *Paradise Lost* some of
the most visually and spatially complex environments known to literature. Too
often, however, the undergraduate classroom focuses solely on the epic's characters and seemingly ignores the fact that what these characters think and how
they respond to the poem's primary issues derives from how they inhabit and
define various environments. Over the past several years, ecocritical approaches
to early modern writing have become a fruitful lens for literary analysis, and
Paradise Lost responds particularly well to this line of study. Considering
Milton's great epic from an ecocritical perspective—an interdisciplinary approach focusing on human constructions of and interactions with the natural
world—not only refreshes and renews the teacher but also helps students make
connections between seemingly disparate issues and themes in Milton's text.
Milton's representations of physical environments create a kind of connective
tissue that shapes one's local and global interpretations of the epic.

In my classroom, student debate is most heated over the possible tension between free will and God's foreknowledge that Adam and Eve will misuse their
ability to choose. But debate is also impassioned regarding how the kinds of
knowledge—forbidden, permissible, experiential, and intellectual—relate to
the spatialized limits God imposes on Adam and Eve's quest for knowledge. "Be
lowly wise," says Raphael to Adam as he redirects Adam's quest for astronomical
knowledge to knowledge of the terrestrial world (8.173).[1] When Satan learns of
the prohibition to eat of the Tree of Knowledge, he says, "knowledge forbidden?/
Suspicious, reasonless. Why should their Lord / Envy them that?" (4.515–17).
Both quotations tend to elicit quite strong and negative reactions from students,
but if we consider Raphael's "lowly" not as a pejorative but merely as spatial, and
perhaps also humble, then we begin to see that Milton wants his characters and
his readers to pay acute attention to local environments, for that is where characters most immediately engage and learn from one another and their world.

Hell, heaven, Eden, and even chaos have complexly rich physical environments in which Milton materializes his theology and his views on politics and
gender: each of these places juxtaposes provocatively with one another. For example, the description of hell's environment as a confusion of elements (where
"the dusky air / That felt unusual weight" and "dry land / . . . if it were land that
ever burned / With solid, as the lake with liquid fire" [1.226–27, 227–29]) and
the fallen angels' disgusted reaction to their physical bodies and surroundings
(e.g., the fallen angels' attempt to organize hell's elements by building Pandemonium) not only materialize their punishment but also tell us about their
ambivalent relation to matter. The environment and inhabitants of hell, then,
bring into sharp relief Milton's representation of Eden as a profuse, sometimes

perplexing environment that is "wild above rule or art" (5.297). This comparison meaningfully complicates and then illuminates for students why a task as seemingly mundane as gardening is so important to Adam and Eve. Whereas with Pandemonium the fallen angels build a hyperstylized monument to themselves that attempts to transcend their immediate environment, the gardening tasks in Eden perpetually put Adam and Eve in direct engagement with their surroundings. Moreover, such a comparison of environments helps students chart Eve's ambivalent relationship to the natural world (her georgic and culinary labors along with her poetry derive from her interactions with the natural world, and she finds paradise's fecundity a threat in book 9).

The war in heaven also has a decidedly ecological component. In book 6, the rebels invent and use canons, the loyal angels counterattack by throwing mountains, and the Son's first act before vanquishing Satan is ecological restoration:

> At his command the uprooted hills retired
> Each to his place, they heard his voice and went
> Obsequious, Heav'n his wonted face renewed,
> And with fresh flow'rets hill and valley smiled.
> This saw his hapless foes but stood obdured.   (6.781–85)

The violence inflicted on heaven's landscape also juxtaposes with Adam and Eve's transgression, when "Earth felt the wound, and Nature from her seat / Sighing through all her works gave signs of woe, / That all was lost" (9.782–84) at the moments when Eve and then Adam eat the forbidden fruit. Both in heaven and on earth nature is not merely a mirror for created beings' transgressions; rather, each transgression responds with hostility to a material environment organized by God. Finally, the complex debates about the status of chaos and its realm—is it good, evil, neutral?—that challenge readers can become less daunting if students think about chaos from the perspective of materiality and creation.

An ecocritical approach need not focus on large-scale environments; analysis of specific plants can also help students engage Milton's ideas. The Tree of Knowledge, for example, can be analyzed through many pedagogical and theoretical approaches, but it can also be considered in the light of Raphael's plant analogy in book 5. Raphael uses the plant as an analogy for how the physical can be transformed into the spiritual. While he is initially speaking of how he can eat earthly food, he soon links plants and ingestion to the transformation of human beings into higher spirits (5.469–505). The "interdicted" tree (5.52) and Raphael's plant offer two contrasting models of knowledge and transformation—one quick and easy, the other slow and multistaged. An ecocritical approach would highlight that Raphael's plant is indistinct—it could be any plant—whereas the prohibited tree is singular and set apart. The slow process of growth endemic to Raphael's model shares affinities with the patience required of the careful gardener, but the prohibited tree presents a nondialectical, utilitarian exchange in which human beings only take the fruit. Students can consider what kinds of knowledge are available to created beings and how different kinds of knowledge fit into the environment, in particular, and into God's hierarchical world, in general.

While I subscribe to the growing view that Milton is a proto-environmentalist, I also believe that an ecocritical approach need not, nor should, take an oversimplistic view that nature in *Paradise Lost* is to be seen through a spoliation/ conservation binary. An ecocritical approach helps students see Eden and the earth as complex systems that challenge human beings even as they sustain them. Students come to find that Milton's natural world demands a dialectical relationship between humanity and creation. Eden is not pastoral ease; rather, it is physical and intellectual nourishment for Adam and Eve. But that nourishment comes through the physical and interpretive work of engaging nature, figuring out one's place within it, and understanding how a sometimes threatening, sometimes beneficent environment manifests God's connection to his creation.

The primary reason to teach *Paradise Lost* with an ecocritical lens is that Milton's theology and philosophy are decidedly ecological, but it is also worth remembering that most students of the twenty-first century are apt to be receptive to this side of Milton. In an era of climate change and debates over humanity's place within and impact on the natural world, students have grown up in educational systems and a culture that gives priority to an environmental view of the world. Thus while some students might be put off by Milton's complex allusions and his penchant to remind readers of his own formidable learning, they can be pulled in by the epic's ecological debates that are often prescient.

Putting Theory into Practice

The pedagogical techniques to achieve an ecocritical reading of *Paradise Lost* are dependent on how much of the course a teacher devotes to the epic. Milton's descriptions of various places in the poem are beautifully profound, but they can also be challenging for teachers to bring alive to their students. Getting teachers and students to sustain focus on these passages should be one pedagogical goal. If covering the entire epic, teachers can create a reading journal component wherein students respond to environments in *Paradise Lost* as they encounter them. In this journal, students not only describe the environments of hell, chaos, Eden, and heaven but also think about the ways characters interact with each place (e.g., through movement, architecture, gardening, warfare). Teachers can be as directive or hands-off as they feel is appropriate. One can, for example, invite students to respond to a set of prompts like the following:

1. Describe this location.
2. How do characters engage or not engage their immediate surroundings?
3. Do characters have or create buildings in their local environments? If yes, describe them and how they fit into the environment.

This approach provides students the framework within which to develop interpretation based on close reading of the text. They also will have material that they can go back to if they write a formal paper later in the term.

To facilitate an online discussion, teachers might use specific questions, such as the following:

> Why might it be important to see Adam and Eve gardening so much in Eden before the fall, and how might their gardening address God's injunction to "till and keep" nature as well as God's later punishment of labor by the sweat of one's brow?
>
> Do Adam and Eve garden in the original Genesis story?
>
> Is Eve's engagement with the garden similar to or different from Adam's?
>
> Does the architecture of Pandemonium relate in any way to hell's environment?
>
> Which environment seems better to you, heaven or Eden?
>
> Why might the Son make a point of restoring heaven's environment before he vanquishes the rebel angels?

Either the journal or the online discussion questions (or both) can help students learn that Milton develops key topics, such as his brand of theology, gender roles, hierarchy, and obedience versus autonomy, in a way that places a typical character-driven focus within a rich spatial context. Milton uses the interaction between characters and environments to shape and develop these topics so that different environments serve as foils for one another.

The visual arts are also an excellent means to help students develop an eco-critical reading of Milton. Wendy Furman-Adams's essay in this volume offers a sustained guide to merging literary and art history analyses of the epic, and I recommend that teachers adapt their pedagogical techniques to a critique of nature in *Paradise Lost*. I suggest focusing on a specific environment in the epic and providing at least two contrasting images to help students see that different artists make interpretive choices. One might compare, for example, John Martin's *Raphael Instructing Adam and Eve* with Gustave Doré's *Raphael Visits Adam and Eve*. Students might begin by analyzing what the two artists emphasize in their illustrations. The teacher can delve into garden or landscape painting history or keep things simple and focus on the images at hand and the primary text. Other exercises might have students compare the many depictions of Eve's temptation in book 9 or consider whether nature is wild or tame and how characters fit into the Edenic setting. Students might then look to specific passages in *Paradise Lost* to consider whether the visual interpretations correspond to the students' interpretations of the scene. Such images can help readers examine the iconographic tradition of Eden and determine whether or how Milton's view on nature is innovative or traditional. This approach often helps students who are visual learners, but all students can enter into a discussion regarding what aspects of Milton's representation of Eden each artist focused on. Thus students are brought back to the text as they think about how artists seize on certain words and images to frame their representation of the natural world. This highly focused assignment can be successful even if one is only reading excerpts in a survey class. But if one uses this technique in a course on Milton or seventeenth-century British literature, one might consider including other early modern visual images of paradise and Adam and Eve.[2] If students read sections on Eden in book 4, for example, one can situate Milton in his historical context by bringing in sixteenth- and seventeenth-century representations of Adam and Eve in paradise, or one can analyze visual and poetic representations of gardening (e.g., in georgic manuals and in Andrew Marvell's "The Garden").

An advanced class on Milton might also add secondary criticism to the above suggestions. Scheduling the criticism later in the reading of the epic helps counter a tendency of students to blindly accept the scholar's argument since they will already have been forging their own interpretations—especially if they have been writing journal entries on *Paradise Lost*'s multiple environments. It can be particularly effective to include a secondary reading when students read book 9. At this stage in their reading, students have traversed hell, heaven, and Eden in detail; they have seen how disobedience to God registers as destruction in heaven and a materially unsettled hell. By book 9 an ecocritical piece can help students explore why the penultimate scene of the tragedy starts with concern over gardening labor, and it helps readers juxtapose knowledge of God through nature with the knowledge promised through the prohibited tree. Finally, students can consider why Milton chooses to register the outcome of Eve's and then Adam's eating the fruit first in ecological terms (9.782–84).

Diane McColley's "Milton and Ecology," in *A Companion to Milton*, is relatively low on jargon and would be especially useful in a course reading many of Milton's works. Ecocritical articles on specific parts of *Paradise Lost* offer students the chance to dig metaphorically deeply into a particular episode or topic.[3]

An ecocritical reading of *Paradise Lost*, then, provides a way to revisit traditional debates and issues while also leading to new insights on those issues. Character-based readings of the epic, focused on the dramatic and personality-driven qualities of *Paradise Lost*, tend to isolate and foreshorten Milton's creative achievements. Certainly Eden is called a "woody theater" (4.141), and the entire epic carries traces of Milton's initial plan to write of man's fall as a play—a genre that could favor actors over a static scenic backdrop of nature. In choosing the genre of epic, however, Milton creates richly imagined environments in which the material world and the issues and opportunities human beings encounter are inseparable. Knowing Milton's natural world helps students appreciate the nature-based wisdom Adam and Eve lost with their first disobedience.

NOTES

[1] All references to *Paradise Lost* are to the 2008 Modern Library edition, edited by Kerrigan, Rumrich, and Fallon. I chose this edition primarily because the notes are clear, detailed, and accessible for undergraduates, and the price of the paperback *Paradise Lost* is affordable.

[2] See Furman-Adams and Tufte, "'Earth Felt the Wound,'" for some striking images as well as a compelling model of how art history conjoins with an ecocritical approach. See McColley, *A Gust for Paradise*, for a good selection of contemporary biblical images. McColley also situates Milton within early modern environmental writing in *Poetry and Ecology*.

[3] On Milton's animals, see Edwards's series "Milton's Reformed Animals"; on Eve, see Hiltner, *Milton and Ecology*. Theis, "The Environmental Ethics of *Paradise Lost*," juxtaposes the different environments and characters' engagements with those environments; Theis, "Milton's Principles of Architecture," considers how built spaces respond to their immediate environment; and Theis, *Writing the Forest in Early Modern England*, examines Milton's forest environments.

Paradise Lost in the
British Literature Survey Course

Boyd Berry

There is a common assumption, both among students and among members of English departments, that the poetry of John Milton is very difficult or that teachers of it must be very learned. Some of us (for I am one) resist that view, and my effort here entails some resistance. For the most part I eschew considerations of background, although I have, elsewhere, pursued them at some length. ("Background" is what a Miltonist has that others in his department lack.) Rather, I wish to emphasize the acts of Adam and Eve speaking—as acting speakers—first, because like us and like our students, they are human and fallible, and, second, because they are male and female human beings.

This essay, in contrast to many of the essays in this volume, considers the teaching of a British literature survey course—that is, a course in which the reading of non-Miltonic texts would necessarily entail abbreviating Milton's writings, including *Paradise Lost*. Bending to the constraints presented by the curriculum and the administration, I was able to present *Paradise Lost* in a rewarding way not much practiced today by Miltonists, who seem often to want to consider the poem almost as canonical, literally, as some read the Bible, as truth manifest. Following a now ancient sort of structural analysis of *Paradise Lost* (i.e., studies of *architechtonike*), I decided to choose between what provisionally I referred to as the story about Satan and the story about human beings. I figured that the latter would have been quite important (to put it mildly) to the evangelical Milton. But focusing on the story about the human beings would necessarily exclude much of the "good stuff" in *Paradise Lost*, particularly all the conversations in books 5–8 as well as Satan's speeches. I felt that exclusion was a loss, since conversing in the poem accounted for a substantial portion of the good stuff (Satan does not converse, for one thing, and when characters talk to themselves, they open themselves to sin). Still, focusing on other parts seemed to provide a good place to talk with the students about the satisfaction that the fall of book 9 provides and about how we read the first eight books anticipating silently that dirty fall, a characterization that students—and perhaps some of their teachers—often reject.

The result was that, as a basis for discussion, I provided students with books 3, 4, 9, and 10, along with a plot summary of the omitted books. I called attention to the symmetry of my selections—two books from the beginning and two books from the end, or two books from the first six and two books from the last six; I had in mind Joseph Summers's point that in redistributing ten books into twelve, Milton had created a new "pattern at the center," focused on the Son rather than on Abdiel (112). Furthermore, my selections avoided the problem I had had with other selections, such as those in the Norton anthology. They lacked, to my eye, a sense of completedness; more simply, they lacked an action. Books 3–4 and 9–10 primarily focus on the activities of Adam and Eve, while also raising larger issues. Book 9 focuses on the fall, one of the most notable actions Adam and Eve take, as well as on the argument they get into before the fall about where to work. While some students may prefer reading the doings of Satan, cultivating their taste for the nasty, Adam and Eve are actually much closer to the situation of the students, in that they are attracted to the voice of Satan, they have to figure out the very odd world that the fiction proposes or implies (i.e., no possibility of news), and they have to make choices. These human-centered books imply or evoke for the students larger themes in the whole.

Book 3 can be seen as outlining the situation of Adam and Eve in the broadest sense, since here we encounter God as he bends down his eye to view his creation and creatures. Further, Adam and Eve have choices to make, which is to say they must act—or, more strenuously, commit an act—something absolutely essential to what I take to be a story about free will. Indeed, the Father directly denies that "Predestination" operates (3.114).[1] Students, and many critics, argue that the passage suggests God's desire to evade responsibility for the fall, and so I would guess that students are attracted to the idea that all is doomed from the start, that the reference to predestination is not seriously meant. They feel their choices are severely curtailed by the fictional world of the tale.

Book 4 provides us with our first glimpse of the couple, active and loving (e.g., they pray in praise of the deity, in a lovely psalm). Adam and Eve not only speak but also interact in non-Petrarchan language (minimally, the lady gets to talk equally with the male voice). Earlier in such a course, we have read male sonneteers and noticed how they silence females. *Paradise Lost* is often thought to be heavily male-dominant, understandably, so this consideration may come as something of a surprise.

Book 9 not only presents the much expected bad action but also prefixes to it an argument that it is difficult not to term angry—that is, "fallen." Eve says she wants to work alone to get more done, from a solidly capitalistic point of view, and Adam resists her thoughts in increasingly excited language. Some of the logic advanced in this argument does not seem entirely sensible, unsurprisingly. Eve asks, for example:

> If this be our condition, thus to dwell
> In narrow circuit strait'n'd by a Foe,
> . . . .
> How are we happy . . . ?   (9.322–26)

She implicitly challenges God's arrangement of their world, which is at least partly why Adam quickly reacts. In addition, when Adam argues he's only interested in preventing "the attempt itself" (9.295), he does not argue, as Milton had in *Areopagitica*, that persons should aggressively confront their tempters. Neither does Adam argue for cloistering, with its Roman overtones, although that is what he seems to want to provide.

Bad actions of this sort persist in book 10, as one might expect, given the fall in book 9. Adam, talking no longer to Eve but "to himself" (10.845), goes off to talk himself into despair, which he does successfully. Eventually he admits that he is responsible for his plight, which shows improvement since evading responsibility is central to the story, but when Eve seeks to talk with him, he snaps, "Out of my sight, thou Serpent" (10.867), showing absence of love and blocking our ability to hear what Eve has to say.

A kind of sorting out of their relationship occupies the remainder of book 10. If the dispute at the opening of book 9 provides an example of how to talk in a fallen manner, the very end of book 10 offers examples of talking in quite a different register, a prayerful one that is dominant again at the end of book 12. Following the drift of Adam and Eve's talk in this transition is not simple. Yet once Adam and Eve start talking to each other in book 10, they first retell the prohibition, and then Adam mentions prayer; he recalls the forgiving tone that the Son adopted when sentencing them, "When angry most he seem'd and most severe" (10.1095). God's language was not as angry, Adam recalls. This exchange is a fine example, incidentally, of the importance of conversations and their tone.

Finally, these selections allow students to notice modulations in tone that seem to me often overlooked, such as the change from unfallen in book 4 to fallen in book 9 or when Adam and Eve pray with one voice and one mind at the end of book 10. One can counsel students to listen to the talkers and suggest they label each speech by its speaker. Indeed, I partly arrived at my selection by looking for revisions, or changes of tone that effectively depart from the thrust of earlier speeches. Eve's voice alters clearly in book 9, for instance, giving clues, if students can hear the modifications, to the values implied by *Paradise Lost*'s story.

At the outset, I pointed out that my remarks are, within this volume, outliers, and one hesitates to propose that *Paradise Lost* has a happy ending. True, much

Christian writing proposes both an unhappy ending and a happy one, and such a reading can arise if one focuses on Adam and Eve in these selections. My trust is that students will continue to point to unhappiness in the poem, providing plenty of opportunities for discussion, and that one need not acquiesce. Anti-God talk is often attractive, for a host of reasons, when trying to read this poem, and there is basis for that sort of talk. To me, however, it seems useful to focus on actions that human beings take as well as other possibilities.

NOTE

[1] All references to *Paradise Lost* are to Hughes's edition of the epic in *Complete Poems and Major Prose*.

Teaching *Paradise Lost*
in a Western Civilization Course

Randall Ingram

In many ways *Paradise Lost* would seem to be the kind of core text or great book suitable for programs in humanities or Western civilization: it explicitly addresses other important texts; it takes up some of the traditional themes of these programs, such as the problem of evil and the relation between the sexes; and yet it also reflects the highly specific concerns of a particular artist working at a particular moment. These factors help make teaching *Paradise Lost* in a Western civilization course rewarding. In my case, when I began teaching *Paradise Lost* in The Western Tradition, at Davidson College in 2002, I found that this widened perspective enriched my teaching of the poem in my usual English courses, including a survey of early British literature and a course on Milton. At the same time, although *Paradise Lost* seems to fit into The Western Tradition neatly, Milton's epic raises questions about the purpose and design of such courses.

The Humanities Program at Davidson includes a four-semester, team-taught, interdisciplinary survey of "the Western tradition" from *Gilgamesh* to the Beatles. By the time students reach the seventeenth century, in the third semester of the program, they have studied Homer, Genesis and excerpts from the Hebrew scriptures, Plato, Vergil, Mark and excerpts from the Pauline epistles, Augustine, Dante, Luther, Shakespeare, and more. If nineteen-year-olds can be fit readers of Milton's poem, these students would seem to be, if not better equipped, then differently equipped from the English majors I usually teach. Despite the appeal of teaching *Paradise Lost* to this community of readers, I had to learn to present Milton less in the terms of the local history that informs my scholarship and more in the sweeping terms of human nature. Human nature, my graduate training had taught me, was a doubly coercive term that universalizes a specific subject position as human and essentializes culture as nature. By contrast, the Humanities Program at Davidson College began in 1962 with a confidence announced in its first syllabus for Humanities 11–12: "the human condition is basically the same in every age" ("Humanities 11–12" iv). Over the years, as the staff has changed, so have assumptions and writing about the program, which now advertises on its Web site that students will study "competing views of human nature, including skepticism about the existence of 'human nature'" ("Western Tradition"). With this formulation, the current generation of professors promises a neutral overview of "competing views" and leaves room to wiggle out of "human nature" altogether. Yet even to teach in a program that promotes an examination of human nature required me to approach my teaching of *Paradise Lost* differently. Nothing in my training and scholarship, my years of teaching a survey of early British literature and a course on Milton, had provided me with a pithy, lecture-ready answer to what once might have been a commonplace question: what view(s) of humanity does *Paradise Lost* offer?

Plenary lectures introduce texts and topics in the Western tradition, and my lecture responds to the question by casting the fall as a profoundly complex, capacious explanation for human behavior. A hurried reading can leave students with a remote idea of the fall as a textual crux in Genesis or as a theological issue in Augustine or Luther, but not as a powerful argument with claims about their own apparently secular actions in the twenty-first century. To help illuminate these claims, the lecture begins with a rather showy moment of standing silently at the podium, followed by a meditation on beginnings:

> We should pause to consider this moment, certainly the most promis-ing part of the lecture. I have not yet misspoken; your mind has not yet drifted. So let's savor. . . . We should savor because we know that it won't last; I'll misspeak; your mind will wander, probably many times. If you experience lectures as I do, including brilliant lectures like this one, you'll drift off, then catch yourself, drift off, then catch yourself, drift off and then catch yourself—each time, perhaps, vowing to pay better attention. This, in part, is what fallen-ness means.

Students sometimes understand only the human impulse to evil in Reforma-tion theology, but the lecture argues that this impulse is only part of the story. I direct students' attention to Satan's soliloquy on Mount Niphates in book 4, particularly that speech's pattern of self-correction. Over and over Satan offers an inaccurate, self-justifying claim, then qualifies, interrogates, or retracts it to show a startlingly accurate understanding of his situation:

> O, had his powerful destiny ordained
> Me some inferior angel, I had stood
> Then happy; no unbounded hope had raised
> Ambition. Yet why not? Some other Power
> As great might have aspired, and me though mean
> Drawn to his part; but other powers as great
> Fell not, but stand unshaken, from within
> Or from without, to all temptations armed.   (4.58–65)[1]

Even Satan seems to have moments of clear self-assessment and good intentions, but those moments pass. For him, as for the drifting attention in an audience, the fall involves an ongoing cycle of resolution and relapse. This example can complicate students' ideas about fallen identity, a matter central to a semester that includes texts such as Luther's *On Christian Liberty* and Marlowe's *Doctor Faustus*. The pattern offered by Satan's and my audience's self-corrections can deepen traditional debates about the nature of human motivations.

My lecture also encourages students to consider how far this notion of the fall might inform what students sometimes come to think of as human nature. I ask students to consider whether the common excitement about beginnings can be understood as an unexpected consequence of the fall. "If you get excited by the first page of a book," I say, "or the opening credits of a film or even the first few minutes of a lecture, if you feel especially alive when you have new shoes or a new boyfriend or a new girlfriend, you might recognize this excitement as a glimpse of an original innocence, a moment of promise unclouded by disappointment." I hope with these examples to counter students' tendency to dismiss the prelapsarian condition—that is, that Adam and Eve are boring characters who live only in ignorance—and to convey an image of paradise less as a mythical place than as an intensely delightful and dimly recognizable inner state, always fleeting after the fall.

The students of The Western Tradition are especially receptive to this line of exploration because during the week before my lecture they read this excerpt from Pascal's *Pensées*: "without this mystery [of the fall], the most incomprehensible of all, we are incomprehensible to ourselves. The knot of our condition receives its turns and convolutions in this abyss, so that man is more inconceivable without this mystery than this mystery is inconceivable to man" (69). With the clock ticking on the class period, I simplify Pascal's elegant passage to four words: "We need this story." We (the precedent of Pascal's first-person pronouns helping to constitute an "us," at least briefly) can use the fall to help explain actions that might otherwise be inexplicable, even to ourselves. Moreover, as Miltonists have variously demonstrated, *Paradise Lost* has the remarkable ability to reveal readers' implication in the fall. Following Pascal and Milton, then, I ask students to reflect on their own baffling behavior, why they might eat or drink what they know they should not, how they might set excellent resolutions ("I will pay attention to every minute of this lecture"), only to fail, reresolve, and begin the cycle again. This pattern approximates the pattern of Satan's speech on Mount Niphates and the struggles of Adam and Eve through much of books 10–12. Although Satan is a unique case, he, Adam, and Eve exemplify a rich concept of fallen identity; they can discern the best courses yet cannot stay on them. The sophomores of The Western Tradition can be surprised to recognize this tension in their own actions and, indeed, in the actions of human institutions more broadly. Of course, this view of the fall is highly traditional, with parallels in far more primary texts than Pascal's *Pensées*. But even the highly capable, predominately Christian students of The Western Tradition often begin *Paradise Lost* with little appreciation of the explanatory power or relevance of this view. Nor, for that matter, had I taken the time to tease out meanings of the fall in my English courses. But teaching in a program that involves an examination of human nature has helped me render more immediately the richness of the fall as an etiological myth, to the benefit of my teaching of *Paradise Lost* in other contexts.

Several class periods of discussions follow the opening lecture, and while many of the same topics engage students in The Western Tradition as in other introductory courses, my students tend to link *Paradise Lost* to other texts from the program. Like their professors, these students define *texts* inclusively, so that they are quick to compare Milton's representation of Adam's and Eve's eating to that of Dürer, Michelangelo, and others. Some of the liveliest discussions, however, involve epistemology. By the time that students read *Paradise Lost*, they have read excerpts from Descartes's *Discourse on Method* and some of Bacon's aphorisms from the *Novum Organum*. They have also attended a lecture on early modern philosophy and have ready definitions of rationalism and empiricism. The lecturing philosopher cautions students against forcing intricate arguments into the pat categories of rationalist and empiricist. Armed with these cautions, students are nevertheless eager to map the characters and situations of *Paradise Lost* between the two poles. For example, students question whether prelapsarian creatures in Milton's epic tend to be rationalists, their unfallen reason allowing them to reach conclusions with limited sensory data. Having read Bacon, classes are especially interested in discussing the role of experimentation in paradise, and these conversations can get heated. Students inclined to see paradise as a repressive regime argue that the instruction of Adam and Eve is designed to preclude experimentation and to stifle their desire to try things for themselves, a desire that seems to be an element even of prelapsarian human nature. Others point out that Bacon and seventeenth-century writers figured experimentation as a necessary, if far from ideal, counterbalance to the weaknesses of fallen reason; Adam and Eve do not have reason to experiment. This classroom debate duplicates in simplified form some of the debates among Miltonists. For instance, those students who contend that Adam and Eve have no need for empirical evidence might find a parallel in Stanley Fish's controversial claim that, throughout Milton's writings, "the only evidence that one can consult is the evidence within" (*How Milton* 121). For the purposes of The Western Tradition, however, I am less interested in how students respond to the criticism on Milton than in how discussions of Milton's epic seem always to involve critical, simultaneous examination of *Paradise Lost* and of other texts from the course.

In fact, discussions extend from *Paradise Lost* and other texts to questions about Western civilization courses generally. Because of their preparation in earlier semesters, my students identify many of Milton's references and allusions. In a single passage students might recognize material from several semesters; having been assigned essays on the messages encoded in Achilles's shield in the *Iliad* during the previous year and having read Galileo during the previous week, these students pay special attention to Satan's shield, which is compared with "the moon, whose orb / Through optic glass the Tuscan artist views / At evening from the top of Fesole" (1.287–89). At such moments, *Paradise Lost* can seem a reward for months of careful reading and an affirmation that students have been initiated into a club of fit readers.

Milton, though, sometimes seems to have considered his predecessors clubbable in an altogether more violent sense; his aggressive rewriting of past texts disrupts illusions of serene social cohesion. In passages such as the catalog of devils in book 1, students find some of the familiar figures and narratives of previous semesters assembled, transformed, and mocked. An epic written by a brilliantly idiosyncratic student of the Western tradition, *Paradise Lost* helps students conceive of that tradition not as a stable body of knowledge, to be memorized and accurately repeated, but as a field of contention—in brief, something worth fighting over. That bracing valuation makes *Paradise Lost* an essential text in the crowded syllabus of a Western civilization course.

NOTE

[1] All references are to the Modern Library edition of the poem, edited by Kerrigan, Rumrich, and Fallon, in their *Complete Poetry and Essential Prose*. I assign and cite this edition for several reasons: the modernized spelling and well-prepared texts suit my audience of undergraduates; the selections from the prose are sufficient for my courses; the apparatus is excellent, my favorite surprise being a footnote on "adamantine" that refers to the X-Men character Wolverine's skeleton of "adamantium" as a measure of hardness; and although the volume is a big cinderblock, the materials are nice—it features good paper, a clear font, and so on.

The John Milton Reading Room:
Teaching *Paradise Lost* with an Online Edition

Thomas H. Luxon

I started building *The John Milton Reading Room* in 1997. I have used its Web-based edition of *Paradise Lost* (and the rest of Milton's verse and selections of his prose) in Milton courses at Dartmouth College for a decade, and every time I use it for teaching, fresh examples of its effectiveness emerge.[1]

Both Samuel Barrow and Andrew Marvell, who wrote commendatory verses for the second edition of *Paradise Lost* published in 1674, exclaimed over what the poem includes; Marvell's list is shorter than Barrow's, so I will quote it here:

> When I beheld the Poet blind, yet bold,
> In slender Book his vast Design unfold,
> Messiah Crown'd, Gods Reconcil'd Decree,
> Rebelling Angels, the Forbidden Tree,
> Heav'n, Hell, Earth, Chaos, All.   (1–5)

Milton tried to weave everything he knew, and every question that fascinated him, into a short Bible story, the first Bible story, about first things. He took a simple, even elliptical, narrative that usually takes up no more than four printed pages and invested it with all "the best and sagest things" he knew about theology, history, cosmology, philosophy, and natural history for, as he put it in *The Reason of Church Government*, the instruction of "mine own Citizens throughout this Iland in the mother dialect" ([Wolfe et al.] 811–12). One result of this effort is that Milton's epic is encyclopedic: a wealth of knowledge arranged not alphabetically or topically or chronologically but by an originary story, *bereshit* — "in the beginning."

Students, even before they encounter Milton's challenge to their moral fitness as readers, feel disqualified by the barrage of erudition Milton mounts, especially in the first seven books of the poem. Before I built an online edition, I would bring a small library to class — a Bible, my Ovid, some Homer — but this preparation simply shifted attention from Milton's learning to my (often partial) learning, all of which had the effect of making students feel so hopelessly unlearned that some resolved to abandon Milton altogether or to put off reading him until they had finished a doctorate.

Teaching *Paradise Lost* with a Web-based edition addresses this problem head-on by making the ever-growing resources of the Web immediately available to students. The huge range of reference resources now available on the Web can be linked directly from the *Milton Reading Room* annotations: *Encyclopædia Britannica*, the *OED*, the *MLA Bibliography*, the *WebMuseum*, *Early*

English Books Online, and much, much more. Research in the service of reading, a practice Milton's epic demands more than most poems do, can be tied directly into the presentation of the text. We need no longer allow our research methods and practices to remain a mystery to our students; we can model them for everyone right there in class. Scholarly tools and resources that once lived in single copies in the reference room can now be part of every class.

The rest of this brief essay relates anecdotes of some of the successes my students have had using and helping build *The John Milton Reading Room*. I am privileged to be able to offer two different Milton courses at Dartmouth, a general introduction to Milton's poetry and prose and a capstone course for English majors. Since 2000 I have refrained from ordering a Milton collection for either course; instead I rely almost entirely on the *Milton Reading Room* for assigned readings of the poetry and selected prose. I also put on reserve Don M. Wolfe's edition *Complete Prose Works*, for Yale University Press. Wherever possible, the annotations in the *Milton Reading Room* encourage students to follow links to other Web-based resources. When studying book 8 of *Paradise Lost*, for example, students encounter Adam's request for a partner "fit to participate / All rational delight" (8.390–91). The *Milton Reading Room* annotation invites them to have a look at the part of the *Doctrine and Discipline of Divorce*, where Milton defines "rational" as opposed to carnal "burning" and claims that such was Paul's true meaning in 1 Corinthians 7.9, "It is better to marry than to burn." One touch opens the relevant portion of the *Doctrine* in a new window. In class we can set the texts side by side for comparative study. But the annotation offers them an even deeper exploration, with a link to Paul's first letter to the Corinthians and yet another to the *Blue Letter Bible*'s version of Strong's concordance (and Greek lexicon) so they can work out an interpretation of Paul's statement and compare it with Milton's ("Concordance"). Finally, a link to page 31 of the anonymous Presbyterian *Answer to a Book Entituled,* The Doctrine and Discipline of Divorce (courtesy of *Early English Books Online*) helps them see just how unorthodox Milton's reading of Paul appeared to the mainstream readers of his day. All these texts and resources can be opened simultaneously for study and discussion in the classroom and for further exploration anywhere students have an Internet connection. Instead of snowing students with references to things they have never read, the *Milton Reading Room*'s annotations take them to the relevant texts and allow them to read enough to begin drawing conclusions and forging research plans.

One of my seminar students recently took advantage of the *Milton Reading Room*'s search capability in his study of the four invocations in *Paradise Lost* (at the beginnings of books 1, 3, 7, and 9). (Book 9's, as my student pointed out, is more accurately a proem than an invocation, since the narrator refers to his muse's "nightly visitation" as "unimplor'd" [9.22].) During class discussion, he called everyone's attention to four words that appear prominently in all four invocations: "adventurous," "wander," "attempt," and "bold." Dividing the task among eight students with laptops, we were able, in just a few minutes, to search the entire poem for those words in various forms and spellings. The list of quotations we compiled prompted and informed a stimulating discussion of the various moral valences associated with these words. When the narrator calls this poem "my adventrous Song" (1.13), he uses a word that has very negative connotations in twelve of the fifteen times it occurs. Eve, Satan, and the fallen angels are those usually described as "adventrous" throughout the poem.

In book 3, the narrator-poet asks us to imagine that the "heav'nly Muse" taught him to "venture down" to hell and now helps him revisit the world of light "with bolder wing" (3.19, 19, 13). The word "bold," we discovered in almost no time, appears twenty-nine times in the poem, and in all but four cases it indicates moral culpability: Satan and the serpent are bold in words and deed; Adam calls Eve's transgression a "Bold deed" (9.921); and the Father declares that Adam must be driven out from Paradise, "Least therefore his now bolder hand / Reach also of the Tree of Life, and eat, / And live for ever" (11.93–95). These findings invite us to consider the poet's epic project in a less flattering light than we usually do. His attempt is bold and his adventure involves wandering (3.27). The poet's heroism can appear lacking in patience, one of the hitherto "Unsung" heroic virtues Milton means to celebrate (9.33).

This kind of work and the discussion it prompts is made possible by using an online, searchable text. But I would like to highlight one more advantage to using the *Milton Reading Room* for instruction—its section titled "Research Links." This collection of links provides students with an array of important resources for the study of Milton's work, resources always one step away from the page they are reading. The online tool for searching the *MLA Bibliography* is especially useful, since it makes it possible for us to move seamlessly from our discussion of the poem to a search for records of the ongoing professional discussions of the poem. With the help of a librarian, I can train my students to use this resource (and others) to help them understand some of that ongoing conversation and even find a place in it for their ideas and observations. The *Milton Reading Room* helps me alleviate some of their anxiety over Milton's learnedness and translate it into an opportunity for them to advance in learning with "bolder wing."

NOTE

[1] Unless otherwise indicated, all references to Marvell's "On *Paradise Lost*" (included in the frontmatter to *Paradise Lost*) and to Milton's works are to Luxon's Web edition *The John Milton Reading Room* (www.dartmouth.edu/~milton); the online, annotated edition was developed specifically for teaching courses on Milton.

Paradise Lost as an Oral Epic

Hugh Richmond

Teaching is mostly oral performance, requiring dynamism, pacing, diversity, and progression. Much literature was written for oral performance or may gain from it, including not just drama but also lyrics and narratives, as the successful staging of many a novel confirms. Specifically, many early epics were composed for recitation, from Homer's *Iliad* to the *Chanson de Roland*. Our experience at the University of California, Berkeley, is that performance by theater professionals, faculty members, or students greatly increases the impact and intelligibility of assigned texts such as Shakespeare's plays and Milton's *Comus* and *Paradise Lost*. Little or nothing in the way of costumes or props is required, but memorization is absolutely essential: reading aloud from the printed page rarely achieves textual mastery. The performers' cadence, tone, and physical presence in such presentations enormously clarify their scripts' meaning and implications for other students, as well as ensuring a deeper understanding by the performers, who are credited chiefly for communicating their understanding of their scripts through intelligible phrasing and emphasis, not for display of professional performance skills. A little advice and notes at a single brief rehearsal before each presentation are very advantageous and may be offered by the instructor or any interested assistant. This advice is usually limited to correction of self-evident and elementary lapses in phrasing, posture, or audibility. To encourage students to volunteer to perform, I count their performance as a substitute for some minor class exercise such as a quiz or midterm or, more constructively, offer them the option of writing an analytic essay on what they learned from performing before the class. Public speaking ought to be a part of all education, and my students have always expressed great appreciation of a modest opportunity to develop their oral skills.

I was led to this oral experience of Milton's poetry by oral presentations of such brief poems as his sonnets, ranging in tone and style from the indignant imperiousness of "Avenge, O Lord, thy slaughter'd Saints"; the colloquial wryness of his defense of his *Tertrachordon*; the epicurean delights of his dinner invitation to Lawrence; and the pathos of his lament for his wife, "Methought I saw my late espoused Saint." These choices make good preliminary exercises for dramatic recitations, as do the personal overtones of his prose pamphlets, such as the appalling implications about his first marriage in *The Doctrine and Discipline of Divorce* (bk. 1, ch. 3). Among the best brief excerpts for recitation from his longer works are Satan's speeches in praise of Rome and Athens in *Paradise Regained*. These speeches present remarkably vivid surveys of the two cities as seen from a high vantage point, like modern television travelogues, heightened by the irony of the guide's identity. From excerpts, my students aspired to the more ambitious project of staging complete short works such as *Comus*, which was transposed to a graduation celebration by my undergraduates and video recorded. The accompanying music was also recorded for us by professional musicians. Since its composition, *Comus* has often been revived by professionals and amateurs because of its modest production requirements, enforced by its origins at Ludlow Castle as an enterprise for the family of the earl of Bridgewater. It proves far more amusing and vivid when performed than when read on the printed page and was partly designed by Milton for nonprofessional performers from the Bridgewater family.

This kind of performance approach to *Paradise Lost* has been recognized by John G. Demaray in *Milton's Theatrical Epic: The Invention and Design of* Paradise Lost. The blind Milton must have recited *Paradise Lost* for it to be written down by a scribe. Indeed, it was first conceived as a play, as surviving drafts of plot and speeches confirm. The text of *Paradise Lost* responds powerfully to vocal interpretation in ways that reverse conventional judgments by critics limited to silent reading of it. The option to perform a part of *Paradise Lost* led to a startling presentation of selections about Satan's intrusion into Eden by a group of my Filipino students who transposed the location to their homeland. The performance opened with an Edenic setting in their native islands, and the students acted out their own Tagalog translation of Milton's text for the idyllic prelapsarian Adam and Eve, accompanied by indigenous native manners and costumes. But then an English-speaking Satan arrived disguised as a Calvinist missionary, bringing a corrupting knowledge of sin, expressed at this point through parts of Milton's original English text. The progression from native innocence to sophisticated corruption was painfully vivid. I regretted not having made a video recording of this unique classroom experience. Such recordings can be valuable for use in subsequent classes as models or interpretative illustrations.

Other options for this performance approach to study of *Paradise Lost* offer great critical gains in understanding many of the poem's dramatic scenes: the speeches by Satan and his cohorts in their debate in hell; the contrasting family dialogues between God and the Son; the choric interjections by Milton as a human reincarnation of the psychology behind many such intense passages; and above all the dramatic progression of a marital relationship displayed in the dialogues between Adam and Eve. The couple's dialogues prove to have elements of psychological subtlety and even high comedy—which may remind us that the poem is a work contemporary with Restoration drama.

The unexpected ease of memorization of such scenes by students confirms the vividness and plausibility of Milton's style, insights, and characterizations. Although at first it may seem challenging for students to memorize and sustain speeches that (even when edited down) run to fifty lines of blank verse of sophisticated rhetoric, as in the debates of the devils, I have found, to my surprise, that my students had no such problem, for the devils' speeches proved so structured by natural progressions of feeling that the multiple clauses had a psychological continuity that made memorization easy. This factor led to our discovery of the devils' identities as coherent mental structures, if not with the complexities and discontinuities that make human psychologies so much harder to master. Each of Milton's devils is a study in mental aberration or neurosis or, as Milton might call it, the morality play Vice. Every diabolic characterization is a diagnosis of the initiation, progression, and outcome of a mental disease, each linked to its causal antecedent and consequent outcome. Thus Satan's resentment of his dependency and subordination leads to resistance, subterfuge, conspiracy, violence, intransigence, nihilism, and self-destruction, all reflected in the positions advocated by his followers. Students readily grasp these Miltonic insights after performing the speech of each devil as a study in neurotic sensibility, not as a mere rhetorical performance.

Satan suggests the overriding ego of a dislocated personality in his first speech, which has the obsessive determination of a resentful failure incapable of coming to terms with its own inadequacy (1.84–121).[1] The performing student can recognize the progression in the mental condition in this speech, from ruefulness to inflexible anger, which asserts a potency invalidated by the contextual circumstances. The insidious rationalizations of Beelzebub's response (1.128–49) illustrate the diplomatic sophistries invited by failure, which we made more overt by casting this devil as a fawning female. This flexible accommodation to failure leads in turn to the suicidal macho aggression in the speech by Moloch (2.51–105), whom we typecast as an aggressive football lineman.

Such argumentative progressions gave the debate in hell accessibility and sequence helpful to memorization. Thus the virile brutality of Moloch is followed by another potentially feminine casting if we make Belial's speech (2.119–225) one of passive accommodation in the face of superior physical force. Initially students can rationalize the latent motivation in each speech as an actor, not as a literary critic. Mammon's option (2.229–83) reflects a further choice in the face of loss—that of the practical businessman out to turn a bad situation into local profit. The wily Beelzebub resolves the conflict of options by advocating safely local action, however insignificant, as a sop to frustration: activity will offset fear, as Satan then confirms. Thus the debate is a perfectly unified psychomachy relevant and fully intelligible to modern psychology. In our consolidated script this debate produced a manageable scene of some 250 lines that required each student participant to memorize and understand about 50 lines, providing each with training in public speaking without protracted effort.

The relation of the diabolic neuroses to living human reality ultimately requires consolidation in a full human personality, hence the emergence of the author as the incarnation of all these attitudes, after the debates in hell (3.1–55). This passage offers further dramatic insight, because Milton's political defeat and blindness reduce him to a personal analogue of Satan's hell, full of darkness and despair. But, unlike Satan and his cohorts, Milton presents himself as more than despairing and works his way up to a positive glimpse of heaven. This realistic progression gives immediacy and meaning to the text, if a student can be persuaded to dramatize Milton's personality as a match to the narrative progression of the epic from hell to heaven, analogous to subjective passages in the prose writings, such as the marital problems latent in *The Doctrine and Discipline of Divorce*.

The debate in heaven in 3.80–322, like the debate in hell in book 2, invites a dramatic psychologizing. God the Father has been compared with Milton's rather dogmatic father, and, if this divine analogue is realistically presented by live performers, God is far more paternally concerned with the fate of his son than grimly determined to be repressive of delinquency or devising a theological resolution of the problem of evil. It is salutary in meeting the misreadings of Percy Bysshe Shelley and William Empson if students can be invited to explore this heavenly debate as an epitome of familial attitudes, tensions, and outcomes.

Yet the full social enactment of all these attitudes comes at the climax of the epic in the realistic progression of the psychologies of Adam and Eve into fully aware and mature human beings, sharing the positive attitudes of heaven after running through a similar progression of negative attitudes to those in the debates in hell. A series of vignettes can be performed by students to demonstrate this progression. The idyllic cadences of the couple's early dialogues are modified when Eve decides that she should be allowed independence of Adam's supervision (9.205–383), and then she is further attracted by the option of superiority offered by Satan, leading to a debate with herself about whether to confine the advantage to herself (9.473–834). Eve decides that option is too risky, leaving Adam free of potential penalty, in a speech that is a comic masterpiece of solipsism. She then seduces him into acceptance of any penalties by sharing her choice, inviting a testimony of devotion by Adam that is an ironic contrast to their initial mutual loyalty, since it requires him more or less to accept a suicide compact (9.856–1032). After their disobedience has been discovered, a brutal Adam shockingly reproaches her and the couple quarrels bitterly, only for a repentant Eve to seek reconciliation (9.967–1187). Thereafter Adam dissuades her from her suicidal inclinations, so that mutual affection and marital resiliency are restored (10.888–1096).

This archetypal series of exchanges delineates the first marital quarrel of any newly married husband and wife, in lively scenes approaching the character of John Dryden's roughly contemporary comedy *Marriage à la Mode*. The nuances of feeling involved invite dramatic performance but do not require excessive histrionic skills. Most undergraduates have probably observed or experienced something like this kind of emotional cycle, so the range of emotion is well within the reach of their verbal powers. With the addition of a few speeches by Raphael and the Son, this sequence can be compacted into a core playlet that elucidates the whole epic, because the emotions of Adam and Eve realistically incarnate the full range of experience allegorized by the fallen angels, from Satan's ambitions and the options presented in the debate in hell to the subsequent celestial ones in which the angels resolve the crisis.

These sequences in heaven, hell, and Eden are vividly dramatic and mutually illuminating if played together with Milton's soliloquies, added as analogous modern experiences of the progression from error to resolution. Extracting and abbreviating the direct speech of all these characters in the epic produces a compact neoclassical drama needing about two hours to perform, but each of the four progressions can also stand on its own. Single speeches in each progression can be treated dramatically—such as Eve's soliloquy meditating on whether to involve Adam in her transgression or her contrasting plea for reconciliation with him—but it may be preferable to establish contrasting pairs of speeches, attitudes, or personalities, to evoke the intrinsic dramatic tension of the whole epic.[2]

NOTES

[1] All references to *Paradise Lost* are to my *John Milton's Drama of* Paradise Lost, a two-hour script of the poem designed for a performance class, edited down to include only a selection of direct speeches. In my experience, these passages cannot easily be excerpted spontaneously from any complete standard text.

[2] Brief examples of the performance approaches described here can be found in the video documentary *Milton by Himself*, distributed by Films for the Humanities. Our two-hour script based on the dialogue in *Paradise Lost* provides a consecutive sequence of all scenes that can be acted (Richmond, *John Milton's Drama*). Although the script presents a coherent play, it includes appropriate individual speeches for oral performance and self-sufficient scenes that can be staged with minimal or no cost. The text's introduction is a descriptive essay about how such staging works in practice. Full videos of our productions of *Comus* and *Paradise Lost* are available on the Web at *Milton Revealed*, a project of the Townsend Humanities Lab.

Premeditated Verse:
Marathon Readings of Milton's Epic

Angelica Duran

Having students read poetry aloud is a venerable pedagogical practice that aids them in hearing, producing, and thereby understanding the subtle poetic strategies that are sometimes difficult to apprehend from visual or silent reading. The dividends of dedicating class time to reading sonnets aloud far outweigh their one-minute reading time. But what about works like John Milton's 10,565-line *Paradise Lost*, which can take anywhere from nine and a half to thirteen hours to read aloud? Such readings are appropriately called *marathon readings*. While many were exposed to marathon readings of *Paradise Lost* for the first time in 2008, among the flurry of celebrations commemorating the four-hundred-year anniversary of Milton's birth, marathon readings are mainstays at some colleges and universities and to a lesser degree secondary schools, held in anglophone institutions in Australia, Canada, New Zealand, the United States, and Milton's native United Kingdom, but also in Belgium, Norway, and other locales.

Marathon readings of *Paradise Lost* take on a variety of forms that correspond to instructors' available time, resources, and student base (Howard), as I discovered from following up with fellow Miltonists who mentioned either on the Milton-l list or at conferences that they had organized such readings. The readings are founded on equally varied pedagogical aims: highlighting the auditory and intellectual architecture unique to long poetic works; engaging in student, campus, and community extension and service; experiencing and promoting an important specialized form of oral communication; and enjoying the pleasure of the oral text. The following description of the aims and forms of marathon readings of *Paradise Lost* may convince instructors to coordinate their own marathon readings: just one time, perhaps intermittently, or even annually or biannually.

Pedagogical Purpose

Among the instructors I consulted, the primary purposes for undertaking marathon readings in academic settings are monitoring students, providing oral and listening skills, and enhancing community engagement. Louis Schwartz (University of Richmond) is refreshingly honest about why he uses marathon readings every time he teaches the undergraduate Milton course (biannually): "simply to get everyone to read the whole thing through at least once." Getting to the heart of why instructors want students to read the entire poem, Ross Leasure (Salisbury University) appropriately effuses that marathon readings provide the opportunity for all involved to get a "greater appreciation of the breath-taking scope of Milton's theodicy," something that cannot be accomplished in interrupted, individual, or silent readings of the text. Margaret Dean (Eastern Kentucky University) notes that either by design or through Milton's combination of pithy aesthetics and epic conventions, the twelve-book epic takes a day to read aloud. Marathon readings render null instructors' rationale to eliminate long readings from their syllabus because students will not read them anyway or will be too bored. I have noticed richer class discussions and much greater competence on final exams in the semesters in which I have coordinated marathon readings of *Paradise Lost* than in those in which I have not.

Some students are resistant to marathon readings. Others, however, are intrigued by the novelty, and still others are relieved to learn and apply a different set of skills to literature. Student evaluations often cite marathon readings as a favorite part of the course. One method to win over student support used by Dean, who has conducted marathon readings of *Paradise Lost* biannually since 1997, is to have students vote on whether they will hold one, rendering compulsion into willing agency in ways that redound on one of the main themes of *Paradise Lost*. She recalls one student evaluation in a class in which the vote was 17 to 1 in favor of conducting the marathon reading: "I was the student who voted against it: and I was wrong." Indeed, sometimes a byproduct of holding marathon readings annually or biannually is that they serve as recruitment tools. Dean has heard "that some students enroll in the course because they heard or participated in a reading." Gregory Lowe describes the general attitude from his students at Collins Hill High School that such a reading "looks better in the rearview mirror." Committed teachers recognize that this attitude is a common one for some of the most instructive methods. One common benefit worth mentioning here is that marathon readings of *Paradise Lost* often create an immediate and deep sense of esprit de corps among class members and between otherwise unaffiliated communities that come together for such events.

Setting up marathon readings that include readers outside the class demonstrates to students that Milton's epic is a beloved text that continues to foster individuals' creativity. As Beverley Sherry records of the annual competitive marathon readings of *Paradise Lost* at the University of Otago:

> The teams had rehearsed together and rejoiced in such names as "The Homeridae" (members of the Classics Department who read Book 1), "Alliance Diabolique" for Book 2, the "Free Spirits" for Book 3, "Hell's Belles" (4th-year English Honors students) for Book 4, "The Supremes" for Book 6 (a most enthusiastic group drawn from local care agencies). As some relaxation, three books (7, 11, 12) were read unrehearsed by all comers.   ("*Paradise Lost*" 128)

In the first marathon reading of *Paradise Lost* I conducted, I simply invited different classes and groups to be responsible for different books and was astounded by the talent and energy displayed. The sonorous delivery of book 2 by faculty members and graduate students in visual and performing arts generated an animated classroom discussion about the obvious benefits of the great amount of scansion that the actors regularly do to hone their craft. The husband-and-wife team assigned to read Adam and Eve in book 4 became teary-eyed—much to their obvious surprise—when "Eve" read the "Sweet is the breath of morn" passage (4.641–58). The Renaissance English professors Charles Ross and Paul White stole the show in book 5 by the way their Satan and Abdiel's bantering mimicked their own (collegial) relationship. We all sat wide-eyed as the students from Ann Astell's English 264: The Bible as Literature performed book 8, all in costume (borrowed from local churches), with makeshift scaffolds holding bedsheets depicting the seven days of creation and brief interludes of guitar music composed just for the event by one of the students.

The books in which readers simply sat and read in one-hundred-line intervals were also vital parts of the ebb and flow of the marathon reading. Milton's poetry read aloud provides enough emotional force. Stella Revard (Southern Illinois University) recalls her reaction at her first marathon reading, held the year of her retirement:

> All was fine until I got to the very end [of *Paradise Lost*] and then I choked up and could hardly finish. The students attributed it to my sadness at retirement. But I said, "No it's not that; it's the poem." For the first time I felt the whole weight of the poem had come down upon me in an overwhelming way. An effect perhaps that only a marathon would produce.
>
> ("Marathons")

Practical Considerations

Coordinating a marathon reading of *Paradise Lost* is the most difficult the first time. But it does not have to be difficult per se. Mario DiCesare (Binghamton University, State University of New York) conducts marathon readings only for his students, gathered at his home with potluck food to sustain the happy group. In contrast, the reading conducted at Stanford University in 2008 had over a hundred participants and required ample funding for its advertisement, program, hospitality items, props, and food. Some instructors are very hands-on, while others assign students to coordinate the event so that students can acquire organizational skills on top of poetic ones. Here I touch on just a few of the most important practical items to consider in designing your own.

The Text   At the core of any marathon reading of *Paradise Lost* are the poem and its oral delivery. When readings are limited to a class, teachers should remind students to bring their copy of the course text. When readings include other individuals, classes, or groups, coordinators should remind participants to bring their copies and should have extras on hand. The most successful marathon readings generally require some training on oral recitation of poetry. Coordinators save speakers embarrassment and the audience discomfort by ensuring that at least student readers prepare by scanning their assigned text, reading it aloud, or bringing in a list of difficult words to pronounce; no one wants to encounter "Serapis," "Asmadai," or "Gorgonian" unawares (1.720, 6.365, 10.297).[1] Coordinators should decide whether readers will read in one-hundred-line intervals, individuals will be assigned parts, or a combination of these methods, with, say, community members reading book 1 at one-hundred-line intervals, then students reading the parts of the Narrator, Satan, Beelzebub, Moloch, Belial, Mammon, Sin, Death, and Chaos in book 2. Instructors who regularly assign students short pieces of poetry to memorize may want to consider assigning the first fifteen to twenty-six lines of the invocations to books 1, 3, 7, and 9 to groups of students: the choric feat makes for a strong opening and is well-appreciated by audiences. Where readers are invited to sign up at the last minute, it is important to have enough extra copies of the poem on hand, and to mark those copies at appropriate stopping points, to avoid the distracting practice of waving down readers to stop reading when their turn is done.

The Location   Either before or during the course of the semester or quarter, coordinators should ensure that they have secured a space for the nine and a half to thirteen hours for the marathon reading—eleven to twelve hours seems to be the favorite amount of time for a comfortable reading pace. If the marathon reading is for the class, the usual venue is the department lounge or the coordinator's home. The campus union and library and local coffee shop and public library are also options, if the class would welcome curious listeners. If the marathon reading is public, the venue should be centrally located. Meeting places with lovely natural vistas, on or off campus, are also options. These settings require a longer lead time for booking but are worth the effort. Campus art galleries can provide a space where visual art complements verbal art and where participants can work collaboratively for the mutual benefit of two disciplines.

Advertisement   Advertising in school and local newspapers, on e-mail distribution lists, and elsewhere should be done early, with a reminder in the days immediately preceding the event. If the whole class is coordinating the event, then a group can volunteer to design advertisements, fliers, programs, and T-shirts. If the instructor is the coordinator, the design can still be assigned to individual students or groups of students, to tap into students' talents and to save time.

Food   The length of time for marathon reading of *Paradise Lost* demands that some attention be given to physical sustenance. For small groups, potluck items are always nice, perhaps with extra credit given for wittily naming the food items with reference to *Paradise Lost*: "nectarous draught" anyone (5.306)? For a large-scale marathon reading, participating members and groups can be solicited for provision or funding of food. Campus caterers and local restaurants are often willing to give discounts or even donate food for such a high-brow affair, especially when their contributions are noted on advertisements.

Those All-Important Miscellaneous Details   Every instructor will come up with unique ideas for details that teach and delight, even down to the best date to hold a marathon reading. Dates to consider include 29 September, Michaelmas, to remind participants of the performance date of Milton's *A Mask Presented at Ludlow Castle*; 9 or 10 November, to commemorate Milton's death, or 9 December, his birthday; or even 16 or 23 April, the dates associated with William Shakespeare's birth and death, to make due gestures to that other great British Renaissance writer. Costumes and props can add to marathon readings, whether they are subtle additions, such as having the multiple Satans wear a rubber snake wrapped around their forearm, or full-scale, with costumes culled from local and campus theater and church groups or from students' and instructors' personal collections. Some organizers have even created T-shirts to commemorate participation, somewhat akin to the T-shirts distributed at running marathons or other endurance events. In 2005, John Ulrich printed commemorative T-shirts emblazoned with "Got Milton?" The trick for instructors is always to keep their aims in mind, their sanity intact, and enough personal reserves to remain willing to organize future marathon readings.

Some Final Thoughts

Here I have attempted to justify the value of marathon readings of *Paradise Lost* by focusing on the benefits to students. Integrated in benefits to students are those to instructors. I end with citing the early biography by Milton's nephew and one-time student Edward Phillips. After listing just some of the impressive reading list of "Authors both of the Latin and Greek" that Milton taught a few students in his home, Phillips observes that "[t]hus by teaching he in some measure increased his own knowledge" (60). Many instructors would readily assent to Phillips's observation about the mutual benefits of teaching to students and teachers. I agree, too, specifically in relation to marathon readings of *Paradise Lost*. It was at the end of my first marathon reading that I heard, really heard for the first time, the narrator's—or is it Satan's?—often referenced line "He for God only, she for God in him" echoed aurally in Eve's final lines to Adam, "In me is no delay; with thee to go" (4.299, 12.615). No concordance or traditional (silent) research had led me to note the aural echo of the hierarchical representation of Adam and Eve's relationship in Eve's (also fraught) articulation of her willful, loving union with Adam. Nothing since then has duplicated the power of my sudden apprehension of how relationality is worked into the sound as well as the content, with the similarity of the caesuras and long *e* sounds and the differences in the meter (more tentative in the second, and rightly so), eight books apart. I can only hope that this chapter has encouraged instructors to set up the circumstances for unexpected, delightful apprehensions of Milton's poetry through marathon readings of *Paradise Lost*, for their students, perhaps for their communities, and certainly for themselves.

NOTE

[1] All references to *Paradise Lost* are to Leonard's 2000 Penguin edition. I let students use any edition of Milton's complete poems as long as it has line numbers. I order the Penguin edition because it is erudite and reasonably priced; in addition, its use of endnotes enables students to read the poetry and discover what they do and do not know before referring to the notes.

NOTES ON CONTRIBUTORS

Boyd Berry is retired from the English department at Virginia Commonwealth University. He is the author of *Process of Speech: Puritan Religious Writing and* Paradise Lost. His articles on early modern women writers have appeared in *Renaissance Papers*, *Medieval and Renaissance Drama in England*, and *Aemilia Lanyer: Gender, Genre, and the Canon*.

Michael Bryson is associate professor of English at California State University, Northridge. He is the author of *The Tyranny of Heaven: Milton's Rejection of God as King* and, most recently, *The Atheist Milton*, as well as a number of articles on Milton and the Bible in such venues as *Milton Studies*, *Milton Quarterly*, and *Religion and Literature*.

Angelica Duran is associate professor of English and comparative literature and erstwhile director of religious studies at Purdue University. Her publications focus on Milton, with a special interest on the teaching in and of early modern English literature, as reflected in her volume of collected essays for use in college courses, *A Concise Companion to Milton*.

Thomas Fulton is associate professor of English at Rutgers University, New Brunswick. He teaches graduate and undergraduate courses in sixteenth-century literature, Shakespeare and dramatic history, Milton, and the history of the book. He has published several articles on these topics and is the author of *Historical Milton: Manuscript, Print, and Political Culture in Revolutionary England*.

Wendy Furman-Adams is professor of English at Whittier College. Her essays on the illustrators of Milton's works have appeared in numerous journals and anthologies, including *Approaches to Teaching Milton's Shorter Poetry and Prose*, *Milton in Context*, and *The Milton Encyclopedia*. She is coeditor of *Renaissance Rereadings: Intertext and Context* and *Riven Unities: Authority and Experience, Self and Other in Milton's Poetry*.

Achsah Guibbory is Ann Whitney Olin Professor of English at Barnard College. Her most recent book is *Christian Identity, Jews, and Israel in Seventeenth-Century England*, which won the Milton Society of America's John T. Shawcross Award; her other books include *Ceremony and Community from Herbert to Milton*, *The Map of Time*, and the *Cambridge Companion to John Donne*.

Peter C. Herman is the author of *Royal Poetrie: Monarchic Verse and the Political Imaginary of Early Modern England*, *A Short History of Early Modern England*, and *Destabilizing Milton:* Paradise Lost *and the Poetics of Incertitude*. He edited *Approaches to Teaching Milton's Shorter Poetry and Prose* and coedited, with Elizabeth Sauer, *The New Milton Criticism*. He teaches at San Diego State University.

Randall Ingram is professor of English and director of the Humanities Program at Davidson College. He has published essays in journals such as *Milton Studies*, *SEL*, and *Journal of Medieval and Early Modern Studies*, as well as in collections such as *Milton in Context*, *Books and Readers in Early Modern England*, and *Approaches to Teaching English Renaissance Drama*.

Sean Keilen is the author of *Vulgar Eloquence: On the Renaissance Invention of English Literature* and an editor of *The Forms of Renaissance Thought: New Essays on Literature and Culture* and *Shakespeare: The Critical Complex*. A former fellow of the Guggenheim Foundation and the National Humanities Center, he teaches in the Literature Department at the University of California, Santa Cruz.

William Kolbrener is professor of English Literature at Bar Ilan University. He is author of *Milton's Warring Angels: A Study of Miltonic Engagements* and *Open Minded Torah: Of Irony, Fundamentalism and Love* and coeditor, with Michal Michelson, of *Mary Astell: Reason, Gender, Faith*. He introduces Milton's prose to an Israeli audience with the forthcoming Hebrew translation of *Areopagitica* for the Leviathan Series of the Shalem Center.

John Leonard teaches at the University of Western Ontario. He is the winner of two James Holly Hanford Awards as well as the University of Western Ontario's Edward G. Pleva Award for excellence in teaching. He is editor of the Penguin editions of Milton's *Complete Poems, Paradise Lost*, and *Selected Poems*. His most recent book is *Faithful Labourers*, a reception history of *Paradise Lost*.

David Loewenstein is Helen C. White Professor of English and the Humanities at the University of Wisconsin, Madison, and an Honored Scholar of the Milton Society of America. His books include *Representing Revolution in Milton and His Contemporaries: Religion, Politics, and Polemics in Radical Puritanism*. He has coedited *The Complete Works of Gerrard Winstanley* and is editing *Paradise Lost* for *The Complete Works of John Milton*.

Thomas H. Luxon is the Cheheyl Professor and Director of the Dartmouth Center for the Advancement of Learning and professor of English at Dartmouth College. His most recent book is *Single Imperfection: Milton, Marriage, and Friendship*, and he is the general editor of the online edition *The John Milton Reading Room*.

Catherine Gimelli Martin is professor of English at the University of Memphis. She is author of *The Ruins of Allegory:* Paradise Lost *and the Metamorphosis of Epic Convention* and *Milton among the Puritans: The Case for Historical Revisionism* and editor of *Milton and Gender* and *Francis Bacon and the Refiguring of Modern Thought*. With Hassan Melehy, she is coediting "French and English Connections in the Renaissance."

Feisal G. Mohamed is a professor in the English department and in the Unit for Criticism and Interpretive Theory at the University of Illinois, Urbana, as well as a member of the Executive Committee of the Milton Society of America. With Mary Nyquist, he has coedited the collection *Milton and Questions of History: Essays by Canadians Past and Present*. His most recent book is *Milton and the Post-secular Present: Ethics, Politics, Terrorism*.

Richard Rambuss is a professor of English at Brown University. He is the author of *Closet Devotions* and *Spenser's Secret Career* and is working on "Mardi Gras Milton: English Renaissance Literature and the Culture of New Orleans Carnival Krewes."

Hugh Richmond heads the Shakespeare program at the University of California, Berkeley. His live and video productions include *Comus, Paradise Lost*, and the documentary *Milton by Himself*. He is author of *The Christian Revolutionary: John Milton, Puritans and Libertines, Renaissance Landscapes, Shakespeare's Theatre: A Dictionary of His Stage Context*, and the Web sites *Shakespeare's Staging* and *Milton Revealed*.

Elizabeth Sauer is professor of English at Brock University and a Canada Council Killam Research Fellow. She is the author of *Paper-Contestations and Textual Communities in England* and *Barbarous Dissonance and Images of Voice in Milton's Epics* and the editor or coeditor of *Reading the Nation, Milton and Toleration, Milton and the Climates of Reading, Reading Early Modern Women,* and *Books and Readers in Early Modern England.*

Regina Schwartz is professor of literature, religion, and law at Northwestern University. She is the author of *Remembering and Repeating: On Milton's Theology and Poetics* (winner of the Milton Society of America's James Holly Hanford's Book Award), *The Curse of Cain: The Violent Legacy of Monotheism* (nominated for a Pulitzer Prize), and *When God Left the World: Sacramentality at the Dawn of Secularism.*

Gregory M. Colón Semenza is associate professor of English at the University of Connecticut, Storrs. He is the author of *Sport, Politics, and Literature in the English Renaissance; Graduate Study for the Twenty-First Century: How to Build an Academic Career in the Humanities; The English Renaissance in Popular Culture: An Age for All Time;* and, with Laura L. Knoppers, *Milton in Popular Culture.* He is working on "Fictional Milton" and "The History of British Literature on Film, 1895–2010."

John T. Shawcross, author of many books on Milton, including *The Development of Milton's Thought: Law, Government, and Religion,* and editor of *The Complete Poetry of John Milton,* was professor emeritus at the University of Kentucky.

Lauren Shohet, Luckow Family Professor of English at Villanova University, is the author of *Reading Masques: The English Masque and Public Culture in the Seventeenth Century.* She is the recipient of fellowships from the National Endowment for the Humanities, the Folger Shakespeare Library, the German Academic Exchange Service, and the Huntington Library, and her essays on Milton have appeared in numerous journals and collections.

Abraham Stoll is the author of *Milton and Monotheism* and the general editor of Hackett's five-volume edition of Spenser's *The Faerie Queene.* He is associate professor at the University of San Diego.

Jeffrey Theis is associate professor of English at Salem State University. He is the author of *Writing the Forest in Early Modern England: A Sylvan Pastoral Nation.* His essays have appeared in *Milton Studies, English Literary Renaissance, Texas Studies in Literature and Language,* and *Profession.*

Julia M. Walker is professor of English at the State University of New York, Geneseo. She publishes on Donne, Spenser, Christine de Pisan, and Milton.

Anthony Welch is associate professor of English at the University of Tennessee, Knoxville. He is the author of *The Renaissance Epic and the Oral Past* and has published essays on Milton, Davenant, Dryden, and Tate in such journals as *Milton Studies, Modern Philology, English Literary Renaissance,* and *Cambridge Opera Journal.*

Jessica Wolfe is associate professor of English and comparative literature at the University of North Carolina, Chapel Hill. She is the author of *Humanism, Machinery, and Renaissance Literature,* as well as articles on Shakespeare, Spenser, George Chapman, and Erasmus, and is completing a study of the reception of Homer in the Renaissance.

SURVEY RESPONDENTS

Corrine S. Abate, *Morristown-Bear School*
Hugh Adlington, *University of Birmingham*
Thomas P. Anderson, *Mississippi State University*
Boyd Berry, *Virginia Commonwealth University*
Carol Blessing, *Point Loma Nazarene University*
Bruce Boehrer, *Florida State University*
Nancy Mohrlock Bunker, *Macon State College*
Lisa Celovsky, *Suffolk University*
Stephanie Chamberlin, *Southeast Missouri State University*
Christine Coch, *College of the Holy Cross*
Margaret Dean, *Eastern Kentucky University*
Donald Dickson, *Texas A&M University, College Station*
Jackie DiSalvo, *Baruch College and Graduate Center, City University of New York*
Angelica Duran, *Purdue University*
Thomas Fulton, *Rutgers University, New Brunswick*
Wendy Furman-Adams, *Whittier College*
Carol Gilbertson, *Luther College*
Chanita Goodblatt, *Ben-Gurion University of the Negev*
Marshall Grossman, *University of Maryland, College Park*
Robin Gunther, *Huntingdon College*
Alan Hager, *State University of New York, Cortland*
Horace Jeffrey Hodges, *Kyung Hee University*
Christopher Ivic, *State University of New York, Potsdam*
Lee A. Jacobus, *University of Connecticut, Storrs*
Nigel Joseph, *University of Western Ontario*
Sean Keilen, *University of California, Santa Cruz*
Jason Kerr, *Boston College*
Salwa Khoddam, *Oklahoma City University*
Wesley Kisting, *Augusta State University*
George Klawitter, *St. Edward's University*
Ana Kothe, *University of Puerto Rico, Maraguez*
David Loewenstein, *University of Wisconsin, Madison*
Thomas H. Luxon, *Dartmouth College*
Catherine Gimelli Martin, *University of Memphis*
Katherine Maus, *University of Virginia*
Carol McManus, *California State University, Los Angeles*
Timothy C. Miller, *Millersville University of Pennsylvania*
Feisal G. Mohamed, *University of Illinois, Urbana*
Margaret Morlier, *Reinhardt College*
James C. Nohrnberg, *University of Virginia*
Susan Lauffer O'Hara, *Georgian Court University*
Meg Pearson, *University of West Georgia*
Richard Rambuss, *Brown University*

Hugh Richmond, *University of California, Berkeley*
Roger B. Rollin, *Clemson University*
Daniel L. Selden, *University of California, Santa Cruz*
Gregory M. Colón Semenza, *University of Connecticut, Storrs*
John T. Shawcross, *University of Kentucky*
Lynne M. Simpson, *Presbyterian College*
Gordon Teskey, *Harvard University*
Jeffrey Theis, *Salem State University*
Margaret Thickstun, *Hamilton College*
Douglas Trevor, *University of Michigan, Ann Arbor*
Martine van Elk, *California State University, Long Beach*
Anthony Welch, *University of Tennessee, Knoxville*
Joseph Wittreich, *Graduate Center, City University of New York*
Robert Wiznura, *Grant MacEwan College*
Jessica Wolfe, *University of North Carolina, Chapel Hill*
Susanne Woods, *Wheaton College*

WORKS CITED

Abrams, Meyer Howard, and Geoffrey Galt Hartman. *A Glossary of Literary Terms*. 9th ed. Boston: Wadsworth, 2009. Print.

Achinstein, Sharon. *Milton and the Revolutionary Reader*. Princeton: Princeton UP, 1994. Print.

Addison, Joseph. *Notes upon the Twelve Books of* Paradise Lost· *Collected from the* Spectator. London, 1719. *Eighteenth Century Collections Online*. Web. 8 Sept. 2009.

Aeschylus. *Prometheus Bound*. Trans. James Scully and C. John Herington. Oxford: Oxford UP, 1975. Print.

Anderson, Thomas. "'All Things Visible in Heaven, or Earth': Reading the Illustrations of the 1688 Edition of *Paradise Lost*." *Milton Quarterly* 38.3 (2004): 163–87. Print.

Animal House. Dir. Jon Landis. Universal Studios, 1978. DVD.

Answer to a Book Entituled, The Doctrine and Discipline of Divorce. London, 1644. *Early English Books Online*. Web. 10 Dec. 2009.

Aristotle. *Nicomachean Ethics*. *The Basic Works of Aristotle*. Ed. Richard McKeon. New York: Random, 1941. 935–1126. Print.

Armitage, David, Quentin Skinner, and Armand Himy, eds. *Milton and Republicanism*. Cambridge: Cambridge UP, 1995. Print.

Auerbach, Erich. "Odysseus's Scar." *Mimesis*. Trans. Willard Trask. Princeton: Princeton UP, 1953. 3–23. Print.

Augustine of Hippo. *On Christian Doctrine*. *Christian Classics Ethereal Library*. Christian Classics Ethereal Lib., n.d. Web. 24 Feb. 2010.

Auksi, Peter *The Christian Plain Style: The Evolution of a Christian Ideal*. Montreal: McGill-Queen's UP, 1994. Print.

Badiou, Alain. "Democracy, Politics and Philosophy." *YouTube*. YouTube, 1 May 2006. Web. 16 Oct. 2009.

Barker, Arthur E. *Milton and the Puritan Dilemma, 1641–60*. Toronto: U of Toronto P, 1942. Print.

Baxter, Richard. *Aphorismes of Justification, with Their Explication Annexed*. London: printed for Francis Tyton, 1649. *Early English Books Online*. Web. 3 Sept. 2009.

Beer, Anna. *Milton: Poet, Pamphleteer, and Patriot*. New York: Bloomsbury, 2008. Print.

Belsey, Catherine. *John Milton: Language, Gender, Power*. Oxford: Blackwell, 1988. Print.

Bennett, Joan S. *Reviving Liberty: Radical Christian Humanism in Milton's Great Poems*. Cambridge: Harvard UP, 1989. Print.

The Bible: Authorized King James Version. Ed. Robert Carrol and Stephen Prickett. Oxford: Oxford UP, 1997. Print.

Blake, William. *The Complete Poetry and Prose of William Blake*. Ed. David V. Erdman. Garden City: Anchor, 1988. Print.

———. "Milton." Blake, *Complete Poetry* 95–143.

———. *Milton*. Ed. Roger R. Easson and Kay Parkhurst Easson. New York: Random, 1978. Print.

———. "The Voice of the Devil." Blake, *Complete Poetry* 34–35.

Blessington, Francis. Paradise Lost *and the Classical Epic*. Boston: Routledge, 1979. Print.

Bouchard, Donald F. *Milton: A Structural Reading*. Montreal: McGill-Queen's UP, 1974. Print.

Bradford, Richard. *The Complete Critical Guide to John Milton*. New York: Routledge, 2001. Print.

Brontë, Charlotte. *Shirley*. 1849. Ed. Herbert Rosengarten and Margaret Smith. New York: Oxford UP, 2007. Print.

Brooks, Douglas A., ed. *Milton and the Jews*. Cambridge: Cambridge UP, 2008. Print.

Brown, Cedric C. "The Legacy of the Late Jacobean Period." Corns, *Companion* 109–23.

Brown, Eric. "Popularizing Pandemonium: Milton and the Horror Film." Knoppers and Semenza 5–98.

Bryson, Michael. *The Tyranny of Heaven: Milton's Rejection of God as King*. Newark: U of Delaware P, 2004. Print.

Burrow, Colin. *Epic Romance: Homer to Milton*. Oxford: Clarendon, 1993. Print.

Calvin, John. *Institutes of the Christian Religion*. Ed. John T. McNeill. 2 vols. Philadelphia: Westminster, 1960. Print.

Campbell, Gordon. "Milton, John (1608–1674)." *Oxford Dictionary of National Biography*. Ed. H. C. G. Matthew and Brian Harrison. Oxford: Oxford UP, 2004. *Oxford Dictionary of National Biography*. Ed. Lawrence Goldman. Oxford UP. Web. 23 Oct. 2009.

Campbell, Gordon, and Thomas N. Corns. *John Milton: Life, Work and Thought*. Oxford: Oxford UP, 2008. Print.

Carey, John. "Milton's Satan." Danielson, *Cambridge Companion* 160–74.

Carroll, Clare, and Constance Jordan, eds. *The Early Modern Period*. New York: Pearson, 2006. Print. Vol. 1B of *The Longman Anthology of British Literature*.

Certeau, Michel de. *Heterologies: Discourse on the Other*. Trans. Brian Massumi. Minneapolis: U of Minnesota P, 1986. Print. Vol. 17 of *Theory and History of Literature*.

Clark, Donald Lemen. *John Milton at St. Paul's School: A Study of Ancient Rhetoric in English Renaissance Education*. New York: Columbia UP, 1948. Print.

Coleridge, Samuel Taylor. "Milton." 1818. *Milton Criticism: Selections from Four Centuries*. Ed. James Thorpe. New York: Collier, 1950. 89–97. Print.

"Concordance for 1 Corinthians 7:9." *Blue Letter Bible*. Blue Letter Bible, n.d. Web. 10 Dec. 2009.

Cook, Albert S., ed. and trans. *The Old English Physiologus*. New Haven: Yale UP, 1921. Print. Yale Studies in English 63.

Cook, Patrick J. *Milton, Spenser and the Epic Tradition.* Aldershot: Scolar, 1996. Print.

Corbett, Edward P. J. "The Theory and Practice of Imitation in Classical Rhetoric." *College Composition and Communication* 22.3 (1971): 243–50. Print.

Corns, Thomas N., ed. *A Companion to Milton.* Oxford: Blackwell, 2001. Print.

———. *Regaining* Paradise Lost. London: Longman, 1994. Print.

Cowley, Abraham. *Davideis. Poems.* London, 1656. *Early English Books Online.* Web. 14 Nov. 2009.

Cowper, William. Latin and Italian Poems *of Milton, Translated into English Verse, and a "Fragment of an Intended Commentary on* Paradise Lost." Chichester: printed by J. Seagraufe for J. Johnson and R. H. Evans, 1808. Print.

Cromwell. Dir. Ken Hughes. Perf. Richard Harris and Alec Guiness. 1970. Sony Pictures, 2003. DVD.

Crump, Galbraith M., ed. *Approaches to Teaching Milton's* Paradise Lost. New York: MLA, 1986. Print.

———. "Introduction: Justifying Milton to the Modern Student." Crump, *Approaches* 1–8.

Curry, Walter Clyde. *Milton's Ontology, Cosmogony, and Physics.* Lexington: U of Kentucky P, 1957. Print.

Danielson, Dennis, ed. *Cambridge Companion to Milton.* 2nd ed. Cambridge: Cambridge UP, 1999. Print.

———. *Milton's Good God: A Study in Literary Theodicy.* Cambridge: Cambridge UP, 1982. Print.

Darbishire, Helen, ed. *The Early Lives of Milton.* New York: Barnes, 1932. Print.

Davenant, William. *Sir William Davenant's* Gondibert. Ed. David F. Gladish. Oxford: Clarendon, 1971. Print.

Davies, Stevie. *Images of Kingship in* Paradise Lost: *Milton's Politics and Christian Liberty.* Columbia: U of Missouri P, 1983. Print.

Dean, Margaret. Telephone interview with Angelica Duran. 26 May 2009.

Demaray, John G. *Milton's Theatrical Epic: The Invention and Design of* Paradise Lost. Cambridge: Harvard UP, 1980. Print.

The Devil's Advocate. Dir. Taylor Hackford. Warner Bros., 1997. DVD.

DiCesare, Mario. "Re: Recitations of *PL.*" Message to Angelica Duran. 1 Nov. 2008. E-mail.

Dobranski, Stephen B., and John P. Rumrich. Introduction. *Milton and Heresy.* Ed. Dobranski and Rumrich. Cambridge: Cambridge UP, 1998. 1–16. Print.

Dogma. Dir. Kevin Smith. View Askew, 1999. DVD.

Dryden, John. *The State of Innocence, and Fall of Man, an Opera Written in Heroick Verse.* London, 1678. *Early English Books Online.* Web. 24 Feb. 2010.

Duran, Angelica, ed. *A Concise Companion to Milton.* Oxford: Blackwell, 2007. Print.

DuRocher, Richard. *Milton and Ovid.* Ithaca: Cornell UP, 1985. Print.

Dzelzainis, Martin. "Republicanism." Corns, *Companion* 294–308.

Eckhart, Meister. *Meister Eckhart: A Modern Translation.* Trans. Raymond B. Blakney. New York: Harper, 1941. Print.

Edwards, Karen. *Milton and the Natural World: Science and Poetry in* Paradise Lost. Cambridge: Cambridge UP, 1999. Print.

———. "Milton's Reformed Animals: An Early Modern Bestiary." *Milton Quarterly* 39.3 (2005): 121–31; 39.4 (2005): 183–292; 40.2 (2006): 99–187; 40.4 (2006): 263–91; 41.2 (2007): 79–174; 41.4 (2007): 223–56; 42.2 (2008): 113–60. Print.

Eliot, T. S. *On Poetry and Poets*. New York: Farrar, 1957. Print.

Empson, William. "Milton and Bentley." *Some Versions of Pastoral*. New York: New Directions, 1960. 141–84. Print.

———. *Milton's God*. London: Chatto, 1961. Print.

Evans, J. Martin. *Milton's Imperial Epic:* Paradise Lost *and the Discourse of Colonialism*. Ithaca: Cornell UP, 1996. Print.

———. Paradise Lost *and the Genesis Tradition*. Oxford: Clarendon, 1968. Print.

Fallon, Robert Thomas. *Divided Empire: Milton's Political Imagery*. University Park: Penn State UP, 1996. Print.

Fallon, Stephen M. *Milton among the Philosophers: Poetry and Materialism in Seventeenth-Century England*. Ithaca: Cornell UP, 1991. Print.

———. *Milton's Peculiar Grace: Self-Representation and Authority*. Ithaca: Cornell UP, 2007. Print.

Ferry, Anne D. *Milton's Epic Voice: The Narrator in* Paradise Lost. Cambridge: Harvard UP, 1963. Print.

Filmer, Robert. *The Anarchy of a Limited or Mixed Monarchy*. 1648. Filmer, *Patriarcha* 131–70.

———. *Observations concerning the Originall of Government, upon Mr Hobs Leviathan, Mr Milton against Salmasius, H. Grotius De Jure Belli*. 1652. Filmer, *Patriarcha* 184–234.

———. *Patriarcha*. Filmer, *Patriarcha* 1–68.

———. Patriarcha *and Other Writings*. Ed. Johann P. Sommerville. Cambridge: Cambridge UP, 1991. Print.

Fish, Stanley. "Biography and Intention." *Contesting the Subject: Essays in the Postmodern Theory and Practice of Biography and Biographical Criticism*. Ed. William H. Epstein. West Lafayette: Purdue UP, 1991. 9–16. Print.

———. *How Milton Works*. Cambridge: Harvard UP, 2001. Print.

———. *Surprised by Sin: The Reader in* Paradise Lost. 2nd ed. Cambridge: Harvard UP, 1997. Print.

Flannagan, Roy. Preface. Milton, *Riverside Milton* vii–x.

Fleming, James Dougal. "Biographic Milton: Teaching the Undead Author." Herman, *Approaches* 24–28.

Fletcher, Angus. *Allegory: The Theory of a Symbolic Mode*. Ithaca: Cornell UP, 1964. Print.

Forsyth, Neil. *The Satanic Epic*. Princeton: Princeton UP, 2003. Print.

Foucault, Michel. "What Is an Author?" *Truth and Method*. Trans. Donald F. Bouchard and Sherry Simon. Ithaca: Cornell UP, 1977. 101–20. Print.

Fowler, Alistair. "Introduction: Metrical Structure." Milton, *Paradise Lost* [ed. Fowler] 1–48.

Frazer, Jenni. "Wiesel: Yes, We Really Did Put God on Trial." *The Jewish Chronicle*. The Jewish Chronicle, 19 Sept. 2008. Web. 9 Dec. 2009.

Froula, Christine. "Pechter's Specter: Milton's Bogey Writ Small; or, Why Is He Afraid of Virginia Woolf?" *Critical Inquiry* 11 (1984): 171–78. Print.

———. "When Eve Reads Milton: Undoing the Canonical Economy." *Critical Inquiry* 10 (1983): 321–47. Print.

Frye, Roland Mushat. *Milton's Imagery and the Visual Arts: Iconographic Tradition in the Epic Poems*. Princeton: Princeton UP, 1978. Print.

Fulton, Thomas. "*Areopagitica* and the Roots of Liberal Epistemology." *English Literary Renaissance* 37.1 (2004): 42–82. Print.

———. *Historical Milton: Manuscript, Print, and Political Culture in Revolutionary England*. Amherst: U of Massachusetts P, 2010. Print.

Furman, Wendy, and Virginia James Tufte. "'Pleasing Was His Shape, / And Lovely': The Serpent with Adam and Eve in Art by Milton and in Re-visions by Three Twentieth-Century Women." *Milton Studies* 37 (1999): 89–141. Print.

Furman-Adams, Wendy, and Virginia James Tufte. "Anticipating Empson: Henry Fuseli's Re-vision of Milton's God." *Milton Quarterly* 35.4 (2001): 258–74. Print.

———. "'Earth Felt the Wound': Gendered Ecological Consciousness in Illustrations of *Paradise Lost*." Hiltner, *Renaissance Ecology* 107–61.

———. "'Metaphysical Tears': Carlotta Petrina's Re-presentation of *Paradise Lost*, Book IX." *Milton Studies* 36 (1998): 86–108. Print.

———. "'With Other Eyes': Legacy and Innovation in Four Artists' Re-visions of the Dinner Party in *Paradise Lost*." *Milton Studies* 35 (1997): 134–78. Print.

Gaiman, Neil. *The Sandman: Season of Mists*. New York: DC Comics, 1994. Print. Vol. 4 of *Sandman*.

Gilbert, Sandra. "Patriarchal Poetry and Women Readers: Reflections on Milton's Bogey." *PMLA* 95.3 (1978): 368–82. Print.

Gilbert, Sandra M., and Susan Gubar. *The Madwoman in the Attic: The Woman Writer and the Nineteenth-Century Literary Imagination*. New Haven: Yale UP, 1979. Print.

The Girl with a Pearl Earring. Dir. Peter Webber. Perf. Scarlett Johansson and Colin Firth. Lion's Gate, 2004. DVD.

Goldberg, Jonathan. *The Seeds of Things: Theorizing Sexuality and Materiality in Renaissance Representations*. New York: Fordham UP, 2009. Print.

Goldgar, Bertrand A. "Imitation and Plagiarism: The Lauder Affair and Its Critical Aftermath." *Studies in the Literary Imagination* 34.1 (2001): 1–16. Print.

Greenblatt, Stephen. *Marvelous Possessions: The Wonder of the New World*. Chicago: U of Chicago P, 1991. Print.

Greene, Thomas M. *The Light in Troy: Imitation and Discovery in Renaissance Poetry*. New Haven: Yale UP, 1982. Print.

Gregerson, Linda. *The Reformation of the Subject: Spenser, Milton and the English Protestant Epic*. Cambridge: Cambridge UP, 2006. Print.

Griffin, Dustin H. *Regaining Paradise: Milton and the Eighteenth Century*. Cambridge: Cambridge UP, 1986. Print.

Groening, Matt. "Bible Stories." *The Simpsons*. Twentieth Century–Fox, 2007. DVD. Season 10 (1989), episode 18.

Grose, Christopher. *Milton's Epic Process:* Paradise Lost *and Its Miltonic Background*. New Haven: Yale UP, 1973. Print.

Grossman, Marshall. "Servile/Sterile/Style: Milton and the Question of Woman." Walker, *Milton* 148–68.

Guest, Edwin. *A History of English Rhythms*. 1838. New York: Haskell, 1968. Print.

Guibbory, Achsah. *Ceremony and Community from Herbert to Milton: Literature, Religion, and Cultural Conflict in Seventeenth-Century England*. Cambridge: Cambridge UP, 1988. Print.

———. *Christian Identity, Jews, and Israel in Seventeenth-Century England*. Oxford: Oxford UP, 2010. Print.

———. "England, Israel, and the Jews in Milton's Prose, 1649–1660." Brooks 13–34.

Guillory, John. *Cultural Capital: The Problem of Literary Canon Formation*. Chicago: U of Chicago P, 1993. Print.

———. "From the Superfluous to the Supernumerary: Reading Gender into *Paradise Lost*." *Soliciting Interpretation: Literary Theory and Seventeenth-Century English Poetry*. Ed. Elizabeth D. Harvey and Katharine Eisaman Maus. Chicago: U of Chicago P, 1990. 68–88. Print.

———. "Milton, Narcissism, Gender: On the Genealogy of Male Self-Esteem." *Critical Essays on John Milton*. Ed. Christopher Kendrick. New York: Hall, 1995. 194–233. Print.

———. *Poetic Authority: Spenser, Milton, and Literary History*. New York: Columbia UP, 1983. Print.

Hakluyt, Richard. *Principal Navigations. The Third and Last Volume of the Voyages, Navigations, Traffiques, and Discoveries of the English Nation*. London, 1600. *Reading the Nation in English Literature*. Ed. Elizabeth Sauer and Julia M. Wright. New York: Routledge, 2010. 37–43. Print.

Halley, Janet E. "Female Autonomy in Milton's Sexual Poetics." Walker, *Milton* 230–53.

———. *Split Decisions: How and Why to Take a Break from Feminism*. Princeton: Princeton UP, 2006. Print.

Hamlin, Hannibal. *Psalm Culture and Early Modern English Literature*. Cambridge: Cambridge UP, 2004. Print.

Hammond, Mason. "*Concilia Deorum* from Homer through Milton." *Studies in Philology* 30.1 (1933): 1–16. Print.

Harding, Davis P. *The Club of Hercules: Studies in the Classical Background of* Paradise Lost. Urbana: U of Illinois P, 1962. Print.

The Harper Collins Study Bible, New Revised Standard Version. Ed. Wayne A. Meeks. London: Harper, 1989. Print.

Hausknecht, Gina. "Arguing about Politics in *The Tenure of Kings and Magistrates* and Contemporary Debates." Herman, *Approaches* 218–21.

Herman, Peter C., ed. *Approaches to Teaching Milton's Shorter Poetry and Prose*. New York: MLA, 2007. Print.

———. "Composing *Paradise Lost*: Blindness and the Feminine." *Essays and Studies* 62 (2009): 129–46. Print.

———. *Destabilizing Milton:* Paradise Lost *and the Poetics of Incertitude*. New York: Palgrave, 2005. Print.

———. "Materials." Herman, *Approaches* 3–11.

———. "Milton and the Constitution, Ancient and American." Herman, *Approaches* 132–38.

———. "Paradigms Lost, Paradigms Found: The New Milton Criticism." *Literature Compass* 2 (2005): 1–26. Web. 24 Feb. 2010.

———. "Preface to the Volume." Herman, *Approaches* xi–xii.

———. *A Short History of Early Modern England: British Literature in Context*. Oxford: Wiley, 2011. Print.

Hesiod. *Hesiod, Homeric Hymns, Epic Cycle, Homerica*. Trans. Hugh G. Evelyn-White. Cambridge: Harvard UP, 1995. Print. Loeb Classical Lib. 57.

———. *Theogeny*. Hesiod, *Hesiod* 78–155.

———. *Works and Days*. Hesiod, *Hesiod* 2–65.

Heylyn, Peter. *Cosmographie. In Four Bookes. Containing the Chorographie and Historie of the Whole World*. London, 1652. *Early English Books Online*. Web. 3 Dec. 2009.

Hill, Christopher. *The English Bible and the Seventeenth-Century Revolution*. New York: Penguin, 1993. Print.

———. *Milton and the English Revolution*. London: Faber, 1997. Print.

Hillier, Russell M. "'By Force or Fraud / Weening to Prosper': Milton's Satanic and Messianic Modes of Heroism." *Milton Quarterly* 43.1 (2009): 17–38. Print.

Hiltner, Ken. *Milton and Ecology*. Cambridge: Cambridge UP, 2003. Print.

———, ed. *Renaissance Ecology: Imagining Eden in Milton's England*. Pittsburgh: Duquesne UP, 2008. Print.

History of Britain: The Complete Collection. Narr. Simon Schama. History Channel, 2008. DVD.

Hitchens, Christopher. "Christopher Hitchens—Free Speech." *YouTube*. YouTube, Nov. 2006. Web. 16 Oct. 2009.

The Holy Bible. BibleGateway. BibleGateway, n.d. Web. 10 Dec. 2009.

Homer. *The Iliad*. Trans. Robert Fagles. New York: Viking, 1990. Print.

———. *Iliad*. Trans. A. T. Murray. Rev. William F. Wyatt. Cambridge: Harvard UP, 1999. Print. Loeb Classical Lib. 170–71.

———. *The Odyssey*. Trans. A. T. Murray. Rev. George E. Dimock. Cambridge: Harvard UP, 1998. Print. Loeb Classical Lib. 104–05.

Howard, Jennifer. "St. Olaf Wrestles with Milton's Angel, and Prevails." *Chronicle of Higher Education* 21 Nov. 2008: B8. Print.

Huckabay, Calvin, and Paul J. Klemp, eds. *John Milton: An Annotated Bibliography, 1968–1988*. Pittsburgh: Duquesne UP, 1996. Print.

Hudson, Gladys W. Paradise Lost: *A Concordance*. Detroit: Gale, 1970. Print.

"Humanities 11–12: The Western Tradition to the Renaissance." Syllabus. Davidson Coll., 1962–63. Print.

Hume, Patrick. *Annotations on Milton's* Paradise Lost. London, 1695. *Early English Books Online*. Web. 8 Sept. 2009.

Hutchinson, Lucy. *Order and Disorder*. Ed. David Norbrook. Oxford: Blackwell, 2001. Print.

Ingram, William, and Kathleen Swaim, eds. *A Concordance to Milton's English Poetry*. Oxford: Clarendon, 1972. Print.

The John Milton Reading Room. Ed. Thomas H. Luxon. Dartmouth Coll., 1997. Web. 23 Oct. 2009.

Keeble, N. H. "Milton and Puritanism." Corns, *Companion* 124–40.

Kelley, Maurice. *This Great Argument: A Study of Milton's* De Doctrina Christiana *as a Gloss upon* Paradise Lost. Princeton: Princeton UP, 1941. Print.

Kerrigan, William. *The Prophetic Milton*. Charlottesville: UP of Virginia, 1974. Print.

Kerrigan, William, John Rumrich, and Stephen M. Fallon. "General Preface." Milton, *Complete Poetry and Essential Prose* xi–xv.

Knoppers, Laura Lungers. *Historicizing Milton: Spectacle, Power, and Poetry in Restoration England*. Athens: U of Georgia P, 1996. Print.

———. "Late Political Prose." Corns, *Companion* 309–25.

Knoppers, Laura Lungers, and Gregory M. Colón Semenza. *Milton in Popular Culture*. New York: Palgrave, 2006. Print.

Kolbrener, William. *Milton's Warring Angels: A Study of Critical Engagements*. Cambridge: Cambridge UP, 1997. Print.

Labriola, Albert. "Milton, John." *Dictionary of Literary Biography: Seventeenth-Century British Nondramatic Poets*. 3rd ser. Ed. M. Thomas Hester. Detroit: Gale, 1993. 153–89. Print.

Landy, Marcia. "Kinship and the Role of Women in *Paradise Lost*." *Milton Studies* 4 (1972): 3–18. Print.

Lanyer, Aemilia. *Poems of Aemilia Lanyer*. Ed. Susanne Woods. Oxford: Oxford UP, 1993. Print.

The Last Temptation of Christ. Dir. Martin Scorsese. Cineplex Odeon, 1988. DVD.

Leasure, Ross. "Milton-athon." Message to Angelica Duran. 3 Nov. 2008. E-mail.

Leavis, F. R. *Revaluation*. London: Chatto, 1936. Print.

Le Bossu, René. *Treatise of the Epick Poem*. Trans. W. J. London, 1695. Rpt. in *Le Bossu and Voltaire on the Epic*. Ed. Stuart Curran. Gainesville: Scholars' Facsims. and Rpts., 1970. Print.

Leonard, John. "*Areopagitica* and Free Speech." Herman, *Approaches* 211–17.

———. *Faithful Labourers: A Reception History of* Paradise Lost, *1667–1970*. 2 vols. Oxford: Oxford UP, 2012. Print.

———. Preface. Milton, *Complete Poems* xi–xxi.

L'Estrange, Roger. *No Blind Guides, in Answer to a Seditious Pamphlet of J. Milton's*. London, 1660. *Early English Books Online*. Web. 4 Dec. 2009.

Levine, Joseph M. *The Battle of the Books: History and Literature in the Augustan Age*. Ithaca: Cornell UP, 1991. Print.

Lewalski, Barbara K. *The Life of John Milton*. Rev. ed. Malden: Blackwell, 2003. Print.

———. "Milton on Women—Yet Once More." *Milton Studies* 6 (1974): 3–20. Print.

———. "Milton: Revaluations of Romance." *Four Essays on Romance*. Ed. Herschel Baker. Cambridge: Harvard UP, 1971. 55–70. Print.

————. *Paradise Lost and the Rhetoric of Literary Forms*. Princeton: Princeton UP, 1985. Print.

————. "Textual Introduction." Milton, *Paradise Lost* [ed. Lewalski, Blackwell] xxx–xxxvi.

Lewis, C. S. *The Magician's Nephew*. New York: Harper, 1983. Print.

————. *A Preface to* Paradise Lost. Oxford: Oxford UP, 1960. Print.

————. *The Silver Chair*. New York: Collier, 1970. Print.

Lieb, Michael. *Poetics of the Holy: A Reading of* Paradise Lost. Chapel Hill: North Carolina UP, 1981. Print.

————. *Theological Milton: Deity, Discourse, and Heresy in the Miltonic Canon*. Pittsburgh: Duquesne UP, 2006. Print.

Lilburne, John. *Just Defence*. 1653. *The Leveller Tracts, 1647–1653*. Ed. William Haller and Godfrey Davies. New York: Columbia UP, 1944. 450–64. Print.

Literary Resources. Ed. Jack Lynch. Rutgers U, n.d. Web. 23 Oct. 2009.

Locke, John. *Two Treatises of Government*. 1690. Ed. Peter Laslett. Cambridge: Cambridge UP, 1994. Print.

Loewenstein, David. *Milton:* Paradise Lost. Cambridge: Cambridge UP, 2004. Print.

————. "The Radical Religious Politics of *Paradise Lost*." Corns, *Companion* 348–62.

————. *Representing Revolution in Milton and His Contemporaries: Religion, Politics, and Polemics in Radical Puritanism*. Cambridge: Cambridge UP, 2001. Print.

Loewenstein, David, and Janel Mueller, eds. *The Cambridge History of Early Modern English Literature*. Cambridge: Cambridge UP, 2002. Print.

Logan, George, Stephen Greenblatt, Barbara K. Lewalski, and Katherine E. Mauss, eds. *The Sixteenth Century / The Early Seventeenth Century*. New York: Norton, 2006. Print. Vol. B of *Norton Anthology of English Literature*. 8th ed.

Lowe, Gregory. "Please Fill in the Blanks." Message to Angelica Duran. 10 July 2009. E-mail.

Luminarium: Anthology of English Literature. Ed. Aniina Jokinen. Jokinen, 1996–2007. Web. 23 Oct. 2009.

Machacek, Gregory. "Allusion." *PMLA* 122.2 (2007): 522–36. Print.

Mack, Peter. "Rhetoric, Ethics, and Reading in the Renaissance." *Renaissance Studies* 19.1 (2005): 1–21. Print.

Maltzahn, Nicholas von. "Acts of Kind Service: Milton and the Patriot Literature of Empire." *Milton and the Imperial Vision*. Ed. Balachandra Rajan and Elizabeth Sauer. Pittsburgh: Duquesne UP, 1999. 233–54. Print.

————. "The Whig Milton, 1667–1700." *Milton and Republicanism*. Ed. David Armitage, Armand Himy, and Quentin Skinner. Cambridge: Cambridge UP, 1998. 229–53. Print.

Marotti, Arthur F. *Religious Ideology and Cultural Fantasy: Catholic and Anti-Catholic Discourses in Early Modern England*. Notre Dame: U of Notre Dame P, 2005. Print.

Marshall, Stephen. *A Sermon Preached before the Honourable House of Commons*. 1640. *Early English Books Online*. Web. 3 May 2012.

Martin, Catherine Gimelli. "Introduction: Milton's Gendered Subjects." Martin, *Milton* 1–15.

————, ed. *Milton and Gender*. Cambridge: Cambridge UP, 2004. Print.

————. *The Ruins of Allegory:* Paradise Lost *and the Metamorphosis of Epic Convention*. Durham: Duke UP, 1998. Print.

Martindale, Charles. *John Milton and the Transformation of Ancient Epic*. London: Croom, 1986. Print.

Martz, Louis Lohr. *The Paradise Within: Studies in Vaughan, Taherne, and Milton*. New Haven: Yale UP, 1964. Print.

Marvell, Andrew. "On Mr. Milton's *Paradise Lost*." Milton, *Complete Poetry and Essential Prose* 287–89.

————. "On *Paradise Lost*." *The John Milton Reading Room*. Ed. Thomas H. Luxon. Dartmouth Coll., 1997. Web. 10 Dec. 2009.

————. *The Rehearsal Transpros'd*. *The Prose Works of Andrew Marvell*. Ed. Martin Dzelzainis and Annabel Patterson. 2 vols. New Haven: Yale UP, 2003. 1: 41–438. Print.

McColley, Diane. *A Gust for Paradise: Milton's Eden and the Visual Arts*. Urbana: U of Illinois P, 1993. Print.

————. "Milton and Ecology." Corns, *Companion* 157–73.

————. "Milton and the Sexes." Danielson, *Cambridge Companion* 175–92.

————. *Milton's Eve*. Urbana: U of Illinois P, 1983. Print.

————. *Poetry and Ecology in the Age of Milton and Marvell*. Aldershot: Ashgate, 2007. Print.

McDowell, Nicholas, and Nigel Smith, eds. *The Oxford Handbook of Milton*. Oxford: Oxford UP, 2009. Print.

————. Preface. McDowell and Smith, *Oxford Handbook* v–vi.

McGrath, Alister E. *Justitia Dei: A History of the Christian Doctrine of Justification*. 2 vols. Cambridge: Cambridge UP, 1986. Print.

Miller, Timothy C., ed. *The Critical Response to John Milton's* Paradise Lost. Westport: Greenwood, 1997. Print.

Milton, Anthony. "A Qualified Intolerance: The Limits and Ambiguities of Early Stuart Anti-Catholicism." *Catholicism and Anti-Catholicism in Early Modern English Texts*. Ed. Arthur F. Marotti. Basingstoke: Macmillan; New York: St. Martin's, 1999. 85–115. Print.

Milton, John. *Accedence Commenc't Grammar*. Milton, *Complete Prose Works* 8: 31–128.

————. *An Apology against a Pamphlet*. Milton, *Complete Prose Works* 1: 862–953.

————. *Areopagitica*. Ed. William Kerrigan, John Rumrich, and Stephen M. Fallon. Milton, *Complete Poetry and Essential Prose* 923–66.

————. *Areopagitica*. Ed. C. A. Patrides. Milton, *Selected Prose* 196–248.

————. *Areopagitica*. Ed. Don M. Wolfe et al. Milton, *Complete Prose Works* 2: 485–570.

————. *Christian Doctrine*. Milton, *Complete Prose Works* 6: xxiv–863.

————. *The Complete Poems*. Ed. John Leonard. London: Penguin, 1998. Print.

————. *Complete Poems and Major Prose*. Ed. Merritt Y. Hughes. New York: Odyssey, 1957. Print.

———. *The Complete Poetry and Essential Prose of John Milton*. Ed. William Kerrigan, John Rumrich, and Stephen M. Fallon. New York: Mod. Lib., 2007. Print.

———. *The Complete Poetry of John Milton*. Ed. John T. Shawcross. Rev. ed. New York: Anchor, 1971. Print.

———. *Complete Prose Works of John Milton*. Ed. Don M. Wolfe et al. 8 vols. New Haven: Yale UP, 1953–82. Print.

———. *De Doctrina Christiana*. Ed. Frank Allen Patterson. New York: Columbia UP, 1931. Print. Vols. 14–17 of *Works of John Milton*. 21 vols. 1931–38.

———. *De Doctrina Christiana. Selected Prose*. Ed. C. A. Patrides. Milton, *Selected Prose* 359–97.

———. *The Doctrine and Discipline of Divorce*. Ed. Thomas H. Luxon. *The John Milton Reading Room*. Ed. Luxon. Dartmouth Coll., 1997. Web. 10 Dec. 2009.

———. *The Doctrine and Discipline of Divorce*. Ed. William Kerrigan, John Rumrich, and Stephen M. Fallon. Milton, *Complete Poetry and Essential Prose* 853–921.

———. *The Doctrine and Discipline of Divorce*. Ed. Don M. Wolfe et al. Milton, *Complete Prose Works* 2: 217–356.

———. *Eikonoklastes*. Milton, *Complete Prose Works* 3: 337–601.

———. *John Milton: A Critical Edition of the Major Works*. Ed. Stephen Orgel and Jonathan Goldberg. Oxford: Oxford UP, 1990. Print. The Oxford Authors.

———. *A Mask*. Milton, *Riverside Milton* 123–71.

———. *Milton's* Paradise Lost: *A New Edition*. Ed. Richard Bentley. London, 1732. Facsim. rpt. New York: AMS, 1974. Print.

———. *Of Education*. Milton, *Complete Poetry and Essential Prose* 967–81.

———. *Of True Religion*. 1673. Milton, *Complete Prose Works* 8: 417–40.

———. *Paradise Lost*. London, 1667. *Early English Books Online*. Web. 4 Dec. 2009.

———. *Paradise Lost*. London, 1668. *Early English Books Online*. Web. 4 Dec. 2009.

———. *Paradise Lost*. London, 1674. *Early English Books Online*. Web. 4 Dec. 2009.

———. *Paradise Lost*. Ed. Clare Carroll. Carroll and Jordan 1823–2072.

———. *Paradise Lost*. Ed. Scott Elledge. 2nd ed. New York: Norton, 1993. Print.

———. *Paradise Lost*. Ed. Roy Flannagan. Milton, *Riverside Milton* 297–710.

———. *Paradise Lost*. Ed. Alastair Fowler. London: Longman, 1971. Print.

———. *Paradise Lost*. Ed. David Hawkes. New York: Barnes, 2004. Print.

———. *Paradise Lost*. Ed. Merritt Y. Hughes. Milton, *Complete Poems and Major Prose* 173–469.

———. *Paradise Lost*. Ed. David Scott Kastan. Indianapolis: Hackett, 2005. Print.

———. *Paradise Lost*. Ed. William Kerrigan, John Rumrich, and Stephen M. Fallon. New York: Mod. Lib., 2008. Print.

———. *Paradise Lost*. Ed. William Kerrigan, John Rumrich, and Stephen M. Fallon. Milton, *Complete Poetry and Essential Prose* 291–630.

———. *Paradise Lost*. Ed. John Leonard. London: Penguin, 2000. Print.

———. *Paradise Lost*. Ed. Barbara K. Lewalski. Oxford: Blackwell, 2007. Print.

———. *Paradise Lost*. Ed. Barbara K. Lewalski. Logan, Greenblatt, Lewalski, and Mauss 1830–2055.

———. *Paradise Lost*. Ed. Thomas H. Luxon. *The John Milton Reading Room*. Ed. Luxon. Dartmouth Coll., 1997. Web. 10 Dec. 2009.

———. *Paradise Lost*. Ed. Stephen Orgel and Jonathan Goldberg. New York: Oxford, 2008. Print.

———. *Paradise Lost*. Ed. Gordon Teskey. New York: Norton, 2005. Print.

———. "Paradise Lost: *A Poem Written in Ten Books*": *An Authoritative Text of the 1667 First Edition*. Ed. John T. Shawcross and Michael Lieb. Pittsburgh: Duquesne UP, 2007. Print.

———. Paradise Lost *by John Milton: Parallel Prose Edition*. Ed. Dennis Danielson. Vancouver: Regent Coll., 2008. Print.

———. "Psalm 2." Milton, *Complete Poems and Major Prose* 162.

———. *The Ready and Easy Way to Establish a Free Commonwealth*. Milton, *Complete Prose Works* 7: 405–63.

———. *The Reason of Church Government*. Ed. Scott Elledge. Milton, *Paradise Lost* [ed. Elledge] 356–61.

———. *The Reason of Church Government*. Ed. William Kerrigan, John Rumrich, and Stephen M. Fallon. Milton, *Complete Poetry and Essential Prose* 835–44.

———. *The Reason of Church Government*. Ed. Dan Wolfe et al. Milton, *Complete Prose Works* 1: 745–861.

———. *The Riverside Milton*. Ed. Roy Flannagan. Boston: Houghton, 1998. Print.

———. *Second Defense of the English People*. Milton, *Complete Poetry and Essential Prose* 1069–110.

———. *Selected Prose*. Ed. C. A. Patrides. Columbia, Missouri: U of Missouri P, 1985. Print.

———. *The Tenure of Kings and Magistrates*. 1649. Milton, *Complete Poetry and Essential Prose* 1021–56.

Milton by Himself. Prod. Hugh M. Richmond. Dir. Paul Shepard. Films for the Humanities, 1988. DVD; videocassette.

The Milton Encyclopedia. Ed. Thomas N. Corns. New Haven: Yale UP, 2012. Print.

A Milton Encyclopedia. Ed. William B. Hunter et al. 9 vols. Lewisburg: Bucknell UP, 1978–83. Print.

Miner, Earl Roy, and Jennifer Brady, eds. *Literary Transmission and Authority: Dryden and Other Writers*. Cambridge: Cambridge UP, 1993. Print.

Miner, Earl Roy, William Moeck, and Steven W. Jablonski. Paradise Lost, *1668–1968: Three Centuries of Milton Criticism*. Lewisburg: Bucknell UP, 2004. Print.

Mitchell, Stephen, trans. *The Book of Job*. Rev. ed. San Francisco: North Point, 1987. Print.

Moore, Alan, and Dave Gibbons. *Watchmen*. New York: DC Comics, 1995. Print.

Moore, Leslie E. *Beautiful Sublime: The Making of* Paradise Lost, *1701–1734*. Stanford: Stanford UP, 1990. Print.

Moore, Olin H. "The Infernal Council." *Modern Philology* 16.4 (1918): 1–25. Print.

Morton, Thomas. *New English Canaan*. London, 1637. *Early English Books Online*. Web. 4 Dec. 2009.

Mueller, Martin. "*Paradise Lost* and the *Iliad*." *Comparative Literary Studies* 6 (1989): 292–316. Print.

Mulvey, Laura. "Visual Pleasure and Narrative Cinema." *Screen* 16 (1975): 6–18. Print.

Murphy, Patrick D., and Greta Gaard. *Ecofeminist Literary Criticism: Theory, Interpretation, Pedagogy*. Urbana: U of Illinois P, 1998. Print.

Newlyn, Lucy. Paradise Lost *and the Romantic Reader*. Oxford: Clarendon, 1993. Print.

Newton, Thomas. Paradise Lost . . . *A New Edition, with Notes of Various Authors*. 2 vols. London, 1749. *Eighteenth Century Collections Online*. Web. 8 Sept. 2009.

Nietzsche, Friedrich. *The Birth of Tragedy*. The Birth of Tragedy *and* The Case of Wagner. Trans. Walter Kaufmann. New York: Vintage, 1967. 15–146. Print.

Norbrook, David. "*Order and Disorder*: The Poem and Its Contexts." Hutchinson xii–lii.

———. *Writing the English Republic: Poetry, Rhetoric and Politics, 1627–1660*. Cambridge: Cambridge UP, 2000. Print.

Nussbaum, Martha. "A Right to Marry? Same-Sex Marriage and Constitutional Law." *Dissent* summer 2009: 43–55. Print.

Nyquist, Mary. "The Genesis of Gendered Subjectivity in the Divorce Tracts in *Paradise Lost*." *Re-membering Milton*. Ed. Margaret W. Ferguson and Nyquist. New York: Methuen, 1987. 99–127. Print.

Oras, Ants. *Milton's Editors and Commentators from Patrick Hume to Henry John Todd (1695–1801): A Study in Critical Views and Methods*. London: Oxford UP, 1931. Print.

Ovid. *Heroides*. Heroides *and* Amores. Trans. Grant Showerman. Ed. G. P. Goold. 2nd rev. ed. Cambridge: Harvard UP, 1977. 10–311. Print. Loeb Classical Lib. 41.

———. *Metamorphoses*. Trans. Frank Justus Miller. Rev. G. P. Goold. 2 vols. Cambridge: Harvard UP, 1994. Print. Loeb Classical Lib. 42–43.

Pagels, Elaine. *The Origin of Satan*. New York: Vintage, 1996. Print.

Parker, Patricia. *Literary Fat Ladies: Rhetoric, Gender, Property*. London: Methuen, 1987. Print.

Parker, William Riley. *Milton: A Biography*. 1968. 2nd ed. Ed. Gordon Campbell. 2 vols. Oxford: Clarendon, 1996. Print.

Parry, Graham. *The Intellectual Context: The Seventeenth Century, 1603–1700*. London: Longman, 1989. Print.

Pascal, Blaise. *Selections from* The Thoughts. Trans. and ed. Arthur H. Beattie. Arlington Heights: Harlan, 1965. Print.

Patrides, C. A. *Milton and the Christian Tradition*. Oxford: Clarendon, 1966. Print.

Patrides, C. A., and Raymond Waddington. *The Age of Milton: Backgrounds to Seventeenth-Century Literature*. Totowa: Barnes, 1980. Print.

Patterson, Annabel M. *Nobody's Perfect: A New Whig Interpretation of History*. New Haven: Yale UP, 2002. Print.

———. "*Paradise Regained*: A Last Chance at True Romance." *Milton Studies* 17 (1983): 187–208. Print.

———. "Why Is There No Rights Talk in Milton's Poetry?" Tournu and Forsyth, *Milton* 197–200.

Pearce, Zachary. *A Review of the Text of the Twelve Books of Milton's* Paradise Lost: *In Which the Chief of Dr. Bentley's Emendations Are Consider'd*. London, 1732. *Eighteenth Century Collections Online*. Web. 8 Sept. 2009.

Pecheux, M. Christopher. "The Council Scenes in *Paradise Lost*."*Milton and Scriptural Tradition: The Bible into Poetry*. Ed. James H. Sims and Leland Ryken. Columbia: U of Missouri P, 1984. 82–103. Print.

Pechter, Edward. "When Pechter Reads Froula Pretending She's Eve Reading Milton; or, New Feminist Is but Old Priest Writ Large." *Critical Inquiry* 11 (1984): 163–70. Print.

Petrina, Carlotta. Interview with Wendy Furman-Adams, Virginia Tufte, and Eunice Howe. Brownsville, Texas. May 1992.

Phillips, Edward. "The Life of Mr. John Milton." Darbishire 49–82.

Pitman, James. "Milton and the *Physiologus*." *Modern Language Notes* 40.7 (1925): 439–40. *JSTOR*. Web. 5 Dec. 2009.

Pleasantville. Dir. Gary Ross. New Line Cinema, 1998. DVD.

Poole, William. "The Early Reception of *Paradise Lost*." *Literature Compass* 1.1 (2004): n. pag. Web. 30 Oct. 2010.

———. *Milton and the Idea of the Fall*. Cambridge: Cambridge UP, 2005. Print.

Pope, Alexander. *Poems*. Ed. John Everett Butt. New Haven: Yale UP, 1963. Print.

Porter, William M. *Reading the Classics and* Paradise Lost. Lincoln: U of Nebraska P, 1993. Print.

Potter, Lois. *A Preface to Milton*. Rev. ed. New York: Longman, 1986. Print.

Prince, Michael. "A Rescue Plan for College Composition and High-School English." *Chronicle Review* 27 July 2009: n. pag. Web. 11 Nov. 2010.

Progymnasmata: Greek Textbooks of Prose Composition and Rhetoric. Trans. George A. Kennedy. Atlanta: Soc. for Biblical Lit., 2003. Print.

Progymnasmata of Aphthonius. Trans. Ray Nadeau. *Speech Monographs* 19.4 (1952): 264–85. Print.

Pseudo-Dionysius, the Aeropagite. *The Complete Works*. Trans. Colm Luibheid. New York: Paulist, 1987. Print.

———. The Mystical Theology *and* On the Divine Names. Trans. C. E. Rolt. New York: Dover, 2004. Print.

Pullman, Philip. *The Amber Spyglass*. New York: Knopf, 2000. Print. Bk. 3 in His Dark Materials.

———. *The Golden Compass*. New York: Knopf, 1995. Print. Bk. 1 in His Dark Materials.

———. *The Subtle Knife*. New York: Knopf, 1997. Print. Bk. 2 in His Dark Materials.

Quint, David. *Epic and Empire: Politics and Generic Form from Virgil to Milton*. Princeton: Princeton UP, 1993. Print.

Radzinowicz, Mary Ann. "The Politics of *Paradise Lost.*" *Politics of Discourse: The Literature and History of Seventeenth-Century England.* Ed. Kevin Sharpe and Steven Zwicker. Berkeley: U of California P, 1987. 204–29. Print.

Rainolde, Richard. *Foundacion of Rhetorike.* London, 1536. *Early English Books Online.* Web. 23 Feb. 2012.

Rajan, Balachandra. "The Imperial Temptation." *Milton and the Climates of Reading: Essays by Balachandra Rajan.* Ed. Elizabeth Sauer. Toronto: U of Toronto P, 2006. 93–111. Print.

Rambuss, Richard. "After Male Sex." *SAQ* 106 (2007): 577–88. Print.

Raymond, Joad. "The Literature of Controversy." Corns, *Companion* 191–210.

Reiss, Timothy J. *The Meaning of Literature.* Ithaca: Cornell UP, 1992. Print.

Renaissance Figures of Speech. Ed. Sylvia Adamson, Gavin Alexander, and Katrin Ettenhuber. Cambridge: Cambridge UP, 2008. Print.

Renascence Editions. Ed. Risa Bear. U of Oregon, n.d. Web. 23 Oct. 2009.

Revard, Stella. "Marathons." Message to Angelica Duran. 5 Nov. 2008. E-mail.

———. "Milton, Homer, and the Anger of Adam." *Milton Studies* 41 (2002): 18–37. Print.

Richardson, Jonathan, and Jonathan Richardson. *Explanatory Notes and Remarks on Milton's* Paradise Lost. London, 1734. *Eighteenth Century Collections Online.* Web. 8 Sept. 2009.

Richmond, Hugh M. *John Milton's Drama of* Paradise Lost. New York: Lang, 1991. Print.

Ricks, Christopher. *Milton's Grand Style.* Oxford: Clarendon, 1963. Print.

Riggs, William. *The Christian Poet in* Paradise Lost. Berkeley: U of California P, 1972. Print.

Rivers, Isabel. *Classical and Christian Ideas in English Renaissance Poetry: A Student's Guide.* 2nd ed. New York: Routledge, 1994. Print.

Rogers, John. *The Matter of Revolution: Science, Poetry, and Politics in the Age of Milton.* Ithaca: Cornell UP, 1996. Print.

Rosenblatt, Jason P. *Torah and Law in* Paradise Lost. Princeton: Princeton UP, 1994. Print.

Ross, Malcolm. *Milton's Royalism.* Ithaca: Cornell UP, 1943. Print.

Rudrum, Alan. "Polygamy in *Paradise Lost.*" *Essays in Criticism* 20 (1970): 18–23. Print.

Rumrich, John P. *Matter of Glory. A New Preface to* Paradise Lost. Pittsburgh: U of Pittsburgh P, 1987. Print.

———. *Milton Unbound: Controversy and Reinterpretation.* Cambridge: Cambridge UP, 1996. Print.

Rushdie, Salman. *The Satanic Verses.* New York: Viking, 1989. Print.

Russell, Jeffrey Burton. *The Devil: Perceptions of Evil from Antiquity to Primitive Christianity.* Ithaca: Cornell UP, 1977. Print.

Sauer, Elizabeth. *Barbarous Dissonance and Images of Voice in Milton's Epics.* Montreal: McGill-Queen's UP, 1996. Print.

———. "The Neo-Christian Bias and Its Discontents." *Renaissance and Reformation* ns 25.4 (2001): 157–70. Print.

Schwartz, Louis. "Your Post about Recitations of *PL*." Message to Angelica Duran. 4 Nov. 2008. E-mail.

Schwartz, Regina. *Curse of Cain: The Violent Legacy of Monotheism*. Chicago: U of Chicago P, 1997. Print.

———. "Milton on the Bible: A Hermeneutic of Charity." Corns, *Companion* 37–54.

———. *Remembering and Repeating: Biblical Creation in* Paradise Lost. Chicago: U of Chicago P, 1993. Print.

Sedgwick, Eve Kosofsky. *Between Men: English Literature and Male Homosocial Desire*. New York: Columbia UP, 1985. Print.

Sewell, Lisa. *The Way Out*. Farmington: James, 2002. Print.

Seznec, Jean. *The Survival of the Pagan Gods: The Mythological Tradition and Its Place in Renaissance Humanism and Art*. Trans. Barbara Sessions. New York: Harper, 1961. Print.

Shakespeare, William. *King Lear. Riverside Shakespeare*. Ed. G. Blakemore Evans et al. Vol. 2. Boston: Houghton, 1974. 1249–305. Print.

———. *Richard II. William Shakespeare: The Complete Works*. Ed. Stephen Orgel and A. R. Braunmuller. New York: Penguin, 2002. 958–99. Print.

Shawcross, John T. *Intentionality and the New Traditionalism: Some Liminal Means to Literary Revisionism*. University Park: Pennsylvania State UP, 1991. Print.

———. *John Milton: The Self and the World*. Lexington: UP of Kentucky, 1993. Print.

———. *Milton: A Bibliography for the Years 1624–1700*. Binghamton: Medieval and Renaissance Text Studies, 1984. Print.

———. *Milton: A Bibliography for the Years 1624–1700: Addenda and Corrigenda*. Binghamton: Medieval and Renaissance Text Studies, 1990. Print.

———. *Milton and Influence: Presence in Literature, History, and Culture*. Pittsburgh: Duquesne UP, 1991. Print.

———. "Milton in Print: A Review of Some Recent Editions of *Paradise Lost*." *Milton Quarterly* 40.3 (2006): 220–34. Print.

———. *Milton, 1732–1801: The Critical Heritage*. London: Routledge, 1972. Print.

———. *Milton: The Critical Heritage*. New York: Barnes, 1970. Print.

———. "The Poet in the Poem: John Milton's Presence in *Paradise Lost*." *CEA Critic* 48-49 (1986): 32–55. Print.

———. "Textual Notes." Milton, *Complete Poetry of John Milton* 544–47.

Shawcross, John T., and Michael Lieb, eds. "*Paradise Lost: A Poem Written in Ten Books*": Essays on the 1667 First Edition. Pittsburgh: Duquesne UP, 2007. Print. Companion vol. to Milton, "Paradise Lost: A Poem Written in Ten Books": An Authoritative Text of the 1667 First Edition.

Shelley, Mary. *Frankenstein; or, The Modern Prometheus: The 1818 Text*. Ed. James Rieger. Chicago: U of Chicago P, 1982. Print.

Shelley, Percy Bysshe. "Defence of Poetry." *Shelley's Poetry and Prose*. Ed. Donald H. Reiman and Sharon B. Powers. New York: Norton, 1977. 478–508. Print.

————. *Prometheus Unbound*. London: C. and J. Ollier, 1820. Print.

Sherry, Beverley. "John Martin's Apocalyptic Illustrations to *Paradise Lost*." *Milton and the Ends of Time*. Ed. Juliet Cummins. Cambridge: Cambridge UP, 2003. 123–43. Print.

————. "*Paradise Lost* 'Made Vocal.'" *Milton Quarterly* 34.4 (2000): 128–29. Print.

Shohet, Lauren. "Reading Dark Materials." *"His Dark Materials" Illuminated*. Ed. Millicent Lenz. Detroit: Wayne State UP, 2005. 22–36. Print.

Shoulson, Jeffrey. *Milton and the Rabbis: Hebraism, Hellenism, and Christianity*. New York: Columbia UP, 2001. Print.

Shuger, Deborah K. *The Renaissance Bible: Scholarship, Sacrifice, and Subjectivity*. Berkeley: U of California P, 1994. Print.

Silva Rhetoricae: The Forest of Rhetoric. Comp. Gideon O. Burton. Brigham Young U, 26 Feb. 2007. Web. 11 Nov. 2010.

Sims, James H. *The Bible in Milton's Epics*. Gainesville: U of Florida P, 1962. Print.

Skerpan-Wheeler, Elizabeth. "Teaching Milton's Late Political Tracts in a Public, Comprehensive University." Herman, *Approaches* 121–25.

Smith, Nigel. *Is Milton Better than Shakespeare?* Cambridge: Harvard UP, 2008. Print.

————. *Literature and Revolution in England, 1640–1660*. New Haven: Yale UP, 1994. Print.

————. "*Paradise Lost* from Civil War to Restoration." *The Cambridge Companion to Writing of the English Revolution*. Ed. N. H. Keeble. Cambridge: Cambridge UP, 2001. 251–67. Print.

Spenser, Edmund. *The Faerie Queene*. Ed. A. C. Hamilton. London: Longman, 2001. Print.

Sprott, Ernest. *Milton's Art of Prosody*. Oxford: Blackwell, 1953. Print.

Steadman, John M. *Milton and the Paradoxes of Renaissance Heroism*. Baton Rouge: Louisiana State UP, 1987. Print.

————. *Milton and the Renaissance Hero*. Oxford: Clarendon, 1967. Print.

Stein, Arnold. *The Art of Presence: The Poet and* Paradise Lost. Berkeley: U of California P, 1977. Print.

Stevens, Paul. "How Milton's Nationalism Works: Globalization and the Possibilities of Positive Nationalism." *Early Modern Nationalism and Milton's England*. Ed. David Loewenstein and Stevens. Toronto: U of Toronto P, 2008. 273–301. Print.

Stewart, Jon, et al., ed. The Daily Show with Jon Stewart *Presents Earth (The Book): A Visitor's Guide to the Human Race*. New York: Grand Central, 2010. Print.

The Stuart Constitution, 1603–1688: Documents and Commentary. Ed. J. P. Kenyon. 2nd ed. Cambridge: Cambridge UP, 1986. Print.

Summers, Joseph. *The Muse's Method*. Cambridge: Harvard UP, 1962. Print.

Svendsen, Kester. *Milton and Science*. Cambridge: Harvard UP, 1956. Print.

Symonds, John Addington. *Blank Verse*. New York: Scribner's, 1895. Print.

Tasso, Torquato. *Gerusalemme Liberata / Jerusalem Delivered*. Trans. Anthony M. Esolen. Baltimore: Johns Hopkins UP, 2000. Print.

Teskey, Gordon. "From Allegory to Dialectic: Imagining Error in Spenser and Milton." *PMLA* 101.1 (1986): 9–23. Print.

Theis, Jeffrey S. "The Environmental Ethics of *Paradise Lost*: Milton's Exegesis of Genesis I–III." *Milton Studies* 34 (1997): 61–81. Print.

———. "Milton's Principles of Architecture." *English Literary Renaissance* 35 (2005): 102–22. Print.

———. *Writing the Forest in Early Modern England: A Sylvan Pastoral Nation*. Pittsburgh: Duquesne UP, 2009. Print.

Thorpe, James, ed. *Milton Criticism: Selections from Four Centuries*. New York: Rinehart, 1950. Print.

Todd, Henry John. *The Poetical Works of John Milton*. 6 vols. London, 1801. Print.

Toland, John. *The Life of John Milton*. Darbishire 83–197.

Tournu, Christophe, and Neil Forsyth. Introduction. Tournu and Forsyth, *Milton* 1–17.

———, eds. *Milton, Rights and Liberties*. Bern: Lang, 2007. Print.

Treip, Mindele. *Allegorical Poetics and the Epic*. Lexington: UP of Kentucky, 1994. Print.

Trubowitz, Rachel. "Body Politics in *Paradise Lost*." *PMLA* 121.2 (2006): 388–404. Print.

———. "'The People of Asia and with Them the Jews': Israel, Asia, and England in Milton's Writings." Brooks 151–77.

Turner, James G. *One Flesh: Paradisal Marriage and Sexual Relations in the Age of Milton*. Oxford: Clarendon, 1987. Print.

Vergil. *Aeneid*. Ed. and trans. H. R. Fairclough. 2 vols. Cambridge: Harvard UP, 1935. Print. Loeb Classical Lib. 63–64.

The Voice of the Shuttle. Ed. Alan Liu. English Dept., U of California, Santa Barbara, n.d. Web. 25 Oct. 2011.

Waldock, A. J. A. Paradise Lost *and Its Critics*. Cambridge: Cambridge UP, 1962. Print.

Walker, Julia M. *Medusa's Mirror: Spenser, Shakepseare, Milton, and the Metamorphoses of the Female Self*. Newark: U of Delaware P, 1998. Print.

———, ed. *Milton and the Idea of Woman*. Urbana: U of Illinois P, 1988. Print.

Walsh, Marcus. "Bentley Our Contemporary; or, Editors, Ancient and Modern." *The Theory and Practice of Text-Editing*. Ed. Ian Small and Walsh. Cambridge: Cambridge UP, 1991. 157–85. Print.

Webber, Joan Malory. "The Politics of Poetry: Feminism and *Paradise Lost*." *Milton Studies* 14 (1980): 3–24. Print.

"The Western Tradition." *The Humanities Program*. Davidson College, n.d. Web. 14 Aug. 2009.

Wiesel, Eli. *The Trial of God (as It Was Held on February 25, 1649 in Shamgorod)*. New York: Random, 1979. Print.

Wilcher, Robert. "The Greening of Milton Criticism." *Literature Compass*. Blog. WordPress, n.d. Web. 5 Nov. 2010.

Wilding, Michael. *Dragon's Teeth: Literature in the English Revolution*. Oxford: Clarendon, 1987. Print.

Williamson, George. "Milton the Anti-Romantic." *Modern Philology* 60.1 (1962): 13–21. Print.

Wittreich, Joseph A. Afterword. *The New Milton Criticism*. Ed. Peter C. Herman and Elizabeth Sauer. Cambridge: Cambridge UP, 2012. 231–48. Print.

———. *Feminist Milton*. Ithaca: Cornell UP, 1987. Print.

———. "'He Ever Was a Dissenter': Milton's Transgressive Maneuvers in *Paradise Lost*." *Arenas of Conflict: Milton and the Unfettered Mind*. Ed. Kristen P. McColgan and Charles W. Durham. Selinsgrove: Susquehanna UP, 1997. 21–40. Print.

———. "'Inspir'd with Contradiction': Mapping Gender Discourses in *Paradise Lost*." *Literary Milton: Text, Pretext, Context*. Ed. Diana T. Benet and Michael Lieb. Pittsburgh: Duquesne UP, 1994. 10–60. Print.

———. "Reading Milton: The Death (and Survival) of the Author." *Milton Studies* 38 (2000): 10–46. Print.

———, comp. *The Romantics on Milton: Formal Essays and Critical Asides*. Cleveland: Case Western UP, 1970. Print.

———. *Visionary Poetics: Milton's Tradition and His Legacy*. San Marino: Huntington Lib., 1979. Print.

———. *Why Milton Matters: A New Preface to His Writings*. New York: Palgrave, 2006. Print.

Wolfe, Don M. *Milton in the Puritan Revolution*. New York: Nelson, 1941. Print.

Woolf, Virginia. *The Diary*. Vol. 1. Ed. Anne Olivier Bell. San Diego: Harcourt, 1979. Print.

———. *A Room of One's Own*. New York: Harcourt, 1991. Print.

Worden, Blair. "Milton's Republicanism and the Tyranny of Heaven." *Machiavelli and Republicanism*. Ed. Gisela Block, Quentin Skinner, and Maurizio Viroli. Cambridge: Cambridge UP, 1990. 225–46. Print.

INDEX

Modern Language Association of America

Approaches to Teaching World Literature

Achebe's Things Fall Apart. Ed. Bernth Lindfors. 1991.
Arthurian Tradition. Ed. Maureen Fries and Jeanie Watson. 1992.
Atwood's The Handmaid's Tale *and Other Works*. Ed. Sharon R. Wilson,
    Thomas B. Friedman, and Shannon Hengen. 1996.
Austen's Emma. Ed. Marcia McClintock Folsom. 2004.
Austen's Pride and Prejudice. Ed. Marcia McClintock Folsom. 1993.
Balzac's Old Goriot. Ed. Michal Peled Ginsburg. 2000.
Baudelaire's Flowers of Evil. Ed. Laurence M. Porter. 2000.
Beckett's Waiting for Godot. Ed. June Schlueter and Enoch Brater. 1991.
Beowulf. Ed. Jess B. Bessinger, Jr., and Robert F. Yeager. 1984.
Blake's Songs of Innocence and of Experience. Ed. Robert F. Gleckner and
    Mark L. Greenberg. 1989.
Boccaccio's Decameron. Ed. James H. McGregor. 2000.
British Women Poets of the Romantic Period. Ed. Stephen C. Behrendt and
    Harriet Kramer Linkin. 1997.
Charlotte Brontë's Jane Eyre. Ed. Diane Long Hoeveler and Beth Lau. 1993.
Emily Brontë's Wuthering Heights. Ed. Sue Lonoff and Terri A. Hasseler. 2006.
Byron's Poetry. Ed. Frederick W. Shilstone. 1991.
Camus's The Plague. Ed. Steven G. Kellman. 1985.
Writings of Bartolomé de Las Casas. Ed. Santa Arias and Eyda M. Merediz. 2008.
Cather's My Ántonia. Ed. Susan J. Rosowski. 1989.
Cervantes' Don Quixote. Ed. Richard Bjornson. 1984.
Chaucer's Canterbury Tales. Ed. Joseph Gibaldi. 1980.
Chaucer's Troilus and Criseyde *and the Shorter Poems*. Ed. Tison Pugh and
    Angela Jane Weisl. 2006.
Chopin's The Awakening. Ed. Bernard Koloski. 1988.
Coleridge's Poetry and Prose. Ed. Richard E. Matlak. 1991.
Collodi's Pinocchio *and Its Adaptations*. Ed. Michael Sherberg. 2006.
Conrad's "Heart of Darkness" and "The Secret Sharer." Ed. Hunt Hawkins and
    Brian W. Shaffer. 2002.
Dante's Divine Comedy. Ed. Carole Slade. 1982.
Defoe's Robinson Crusoe. Ed. Maximillian E. Novak and Carl Fisher. 2005.
DeLillo's White Noise. Ed. Tim Engles and John N. Duvall. 2006.
Dickens's Bleak House. Ed. John O. Jordan and Gordon Bigelow. 2009.
Dickens's David Copperfield. Ed. Richard J. Dunn. 1984.
Dickinson's Poetry. Ed. Robin Riley Fast and Christine Mack Gordon. 1989.
Narrative of the Life of Frederick Douglass. Ed. James C. Hall. 1999.
Duras's Ourika. Ed. Mary Ellen Birkett and Christopher Rivers. 2009.
Early Modern Spanish Drama. Ed. Laura R. Bass and Margaret R. Greer. 2006.

Eliot's Middlemarch. Ed. Kathleen Blake. 1990.

Eliot's Poetry and Plays. Ed. Jewel Spears Brooker. 1988.

Shorter Elizabethan Poetry. Ed. Patrick Cheney and Anne Lake Prescott. 2000.

Ellison's Invisible Man. Ed. Susan Resneck Parr and Pancho Savery. 1989.

English Renaissance Drama. Ed. Karen Bamford and Alexander Leggatt. 2002.

Works of Louise Erdrich. Ed. Gregg Sarris, Connie A. Jacobs, and
    James R. Giles. 2004.

Dramas of Euripides. Ed. Robin Mitchell-Boyask. 2002.

Faulkner's As I Lay Dying. Ed. Patrick O'Donnell and Lynda Zwinger. 2011.

Faulkner's The Sound and the Fury. Ed. Stephen Hahn and Arthur F. Kinney. 1996.

Fitzgerald's The Great Gatsby. Ed. Jackson R. Bryer and Nancy P. VanArsdale. 2009.

Flaubert's Madame Bovary. Ed. Laurence M. Porter and Eugene F. Gray. 1995.

García Márquez's One Hundred Years of Solitude. Ed. María Elena de Valdés and
    Mario J. Valdés. 1990.

Gilman's "The Yellow Wall-Paper" and Herland. Ed. Denise D. Knight and
    Cynthia J. Davis. 2003.

Goethe's Faust. Ed. Douglas J. McMillan. 1987.

Gothic Fiction: The British and American Traditions. Ed. Diane Long Hoeveler
    and Tamar Heller. 2003.

Poetry of John Gower. Ed. R. F. Yeager and Brian W. Gastle. 2011.

Grass's The Tin Drum. Ed. Monika Shafi. 2008.

H.D.'s Poetry and Prose. Ed. Annette Debo and Lara Vetter. 2011.

Hebrew Bible as Literature in Translation. Ed. Barry N. Olshen and
    Yael S. Feldman. 1989.

Homer's Iliad *and* Odyssey. Ed. Kostas Myrsiades. 1987.

Hurston's Their Eyes Were Watching God *and Other Works.* Ed. John Lowe. 2009.

Ibsen's A Doll House. Ed. Yvonne Shafer. 1985.

Henry James's Daisy Miller *and* The Turn of the Screw. Ed. Kimberly C. Reed and
    Peter G. Beidler. 2005.

Works of Samuel Johnson. Ed. David R. Anderson and Gwin J. Kolb. 1993.

Joyce's Ulysses. Ed. Kathleen McCormick and Erwin R. Steinberg. 1993.

Works of Sor Juana Inés de la Cruz. Ed. Emilie L. Bergmann and Stacey Schlau. 2007.

Kafka's Short Fiction. Ed. Richard T. Gray. 1995.

Keats's Poetry. Ed. Walter H. Evert and Jack W. Rhodes. 1991.

Kingston's The Woman Warrior. Ed. Shirley Geok-lin Lim. 1991.

Lafayette's The Princess of Clèves. Ed. Faith E. Beasley and
    Katharine Ann Jensen. 1998.

Works of D. H. Lawrence. Ed. M. Elizabeth Sargent and Garry Watson. 2001.

Lazarillo de Tormes *and the Picaresque Tradition.* Ed. Anne J. Cruz. 2009.

Lessing's The Golden Notebook. Ed. Carey Kaplan and Ellen Cronan Rose. 1989.

Works of Naguib Mahfouz. Ed. Waïl S. Hassan and Susan Muaddi Darraj. 2011.

Mann's Death in Venice *and Other Short Fiction.* Ed. Jeffrey B. Berlin. 1992.

Marguerite de Navarre's Heptameron. Ed. Colette H. Winn. 2007.
Medieval English Drama. Ed. Richard K. Emmerson. 1990.
Melville's Moby-Dick. Ed. Martin Bickman. 1985.
Metaphysical Poets. Ed. Sidney Gottlieb. 1990.
Miller's Death of a Salesman. Ed. Matthew C. Roudané. 1995.
Milton's Paradise Lost. First edition. Ed. Galbraith M. Crump. 1986.
Milton's Paradise Lost. Second edition. Ed. Peter C. Herman. 2012.
Milton's Shorter Poetry and Prose. Ed. Peter C. Herman. 2007.
Molière's Tartuffe *and Other Plays.* Ed. James F. Gaines and
      Michael S. Koppisch. 1995.
Momaday's The Way to Rainy Mountain. Ed. Kenneth M. Roemer. 1988.
Montaigne's Essays. Ed. Patrick Henry. 1994.
Novels of Toni Morrison. Ed. Nellie Y. McKay and Kathryn Earle. 1997.
Murasaki Shikibu's The Tale of Genji. Ed. Edward Kamens. 1993.
Nabokov's Lolita. Ed. Zoran Kuzmanovich and Galya Diment. 2008.
Works of Ngũgĩ wa Thiong'o. Ed. Oliver Lovesey. 2012.
Works of Tim O'Brien. Ed. Alex Vernon and Catherine Calloway. 2010.
Works of Ovid and the Ovidian Tradition. Ed. Barbara Weiden Boyd and
      Cora Fox. 2010.
Poe's Prose and Poetry. Ed. Jeffrey Andrew Weinstock and Tony Magistrale. 2008.
Pope's Poetry. Ed. Wallace Jackson and R. Paul Yoder. 1993.
Proust's Fiction and Criticism. Ed. Elyane Dezon-Jones and
      Inge Crosman Wimmers. 2003.
Puig's Kiss of the Spider Woman. Ed. Daniel Balderston and Francine Masiello. 2007.
Pynchon's The Crying of Lot 49 *and Other Works.* Ed. Thomas H. Schaub. 2008.
Works of François Rabelais. Ed. Todd W. Reeser and Floyd Gray. 2011.
Novels of Samuel Richardson. Ed. Lisa Zunshine and Jocelyn Harris. 2006.
Rousseau's Confessions *and* Reveries of the Solitary Walker. Ed. John C. O'Neal
      and Ourida Mostefai. 2003.
Scott's Waverley Novels. Ed. Evan Gottlieb and Ian Duncan. 2009.
Shakespeare's Hamlet. Ed. Bernice W. Kliman. 2001.
Shakespeare's King Lear. Ed. Robert H. Ray. 1986.
Shakespeare's Othello. Ed. Peter Erickson and Maurice Hunt. 2005.
Shakespeare's Romeo and Juliet. Ed. Maurice Hunt. 2000.
Shakespeare's The Tempest *and Other Late Romances.* Ed. Maurice Hunt. 1992.
Shelley's Frankenstein. Ed. Stephen C. Behrendt. 1990.
Shelley's Poetry. Ed. Spencer Hall. 1990.
Sir Gawain and the Green Knight. Ed. Miriam Youngerman Miller and
      Jane Chance. 1986.
Song of Roland. Ed. William W. Kibler and Leslie Zarker Morgan. 2006.
Spenser's Faerie Queene. Ed. David Lee Miller and Alexander Dunlop. 1994.
Stendhal's The Red and the Black. Ed. Dean de la Motte and Stirling Haig. 1999.

Sterne's Tristram Shandy. Ed. Melvyn New. 1989.

The Story of the Stone (Dream of the Red Chamber). Ed. Andrew Schonebaum and Tina Lu. 2012.

Stowe's Uncle Tom's Cabin. Ed. Elizabeth Ammons and Susan Belasco. 2000.

Swift's Gulliver's Travels. Ed. Edward J. Rielly. 1988.

Teresa of Ávila and the Spanish Mystics. Ed. Alison Weber. 2009.

Thoreau's Walden *and Other Works*. Ed. Richard J. Schneider. 1996.

Tolstoy's Anna Karenina. Ed. Liza Knapp and Amy Mandelker. 2003.

Vergil's Aeneid. Ed. William S. Anderson and Lorina N. Quartarone. 2002.

Voltaire's Candide. Ed. Renée Waldinger. 1987.

Whitman's Leaves of Grass. Ed. Donald D. Kummings. 1990.

Wiesel's Night. Ed. Alan Rosen. 2007.

Works of Oscar Wilde. Ed. Philip E. Smith II. 2008.

Woolf's Mrs. Dalloway. Ed. Eileen Barrett and Ruth O. Saxton. 2009.

Woolf's To the Lighthouse. Ed. Beth Rigel Daugherty and Mary Beth Pringle. 2001.

Wordsworth's Poetry. Ed. Spencer Hall, with Jonathan Ramsey. 1986.

Wright's Native Son. Ed. James A. Miller. 1997.